Peter Fleming

BAYONETS TO LHASA

With an Introduction by Brian Shaw

BAYONETS TO LHASA

BAYONETS TO LHASA

Peter Fleming

With an Introduction by Brian Shaw

HONG KONG   OXFORD   NEW YORK
OXFORD UNIVERSITY PRESS

Oxford University Press

Oxford New York Toronto
Petaling Jaya Singapore Hong Kong Tokyo
Delhi Bombay Calcutta Madras Karachi
Nairobi Dar es Salaam Cape Town
Melbourne Auckland

and associated companies in
Beirut Berlin Ibadan Nicosia

© Nicholas Fleming 1961
Introduction © Oxford University Press 1984

First published by Rupert Hart-Davis 1961
First issued, with permission and with the addition of an
Introduction, as an Oxford in Asia paperback 1984
Reissued in Oxford Paperbacks 1986

ISBN 0 19 583862 9

OXFORD is a trade mark of Oxford University Press

Printed in Hong Kong
Published by Oxford University Press,
Warwick House, Hong Kong

Introduction

Although the late Peter Fleming was for a number of years an active journalist as well as an intrepid traveller, he was not so prolific a writer of books as his younger brother Ian (creator of the fictional hero James Bond). Only 32 years of age when the Second World War broke out, he had already reported his personal adventures in Brazil, North China and Chinese Tartary in volumes which displayed wit, impish humour, and some brashness. During the War he had his share of adventures in Norway and in Burma, for which he received the Order of the British Empire in 1945. After the War he led a quieter life, although he contributed Fourth Leaders to *The Times* and was that paper's occasional Special Correspondent. Henceforth, in writing his books, he drew on historical materials and interviews, rather than on his direct personal experience, notably in his reassessment of the Siege of Peking of 1900 and the Younghusband Mission to Lhasa of 1903–4. Following his death on 18 August 1971 while shooting grouse, his obituary in *The Times* recalled that Fleming had since 1945 for the most part played the role of 'an English country gentleman, cultured and enterprising, whose first concern was with his estate and countryside, but who remained acutely interested in what was astir in the world beyond'.

Fleming was 54 when *Bayonets to Lhasa* was published in 1961. The motives which impelled him are succinctly if a little ambiguously expressed in the Foreword: 'to arrange the pebbles [of events] into a commemorative and, I hope, a seemly cairn'. There can be no question of the seemliness of the writing in this work, where there are passages which may remind the reader of the understated eloquence of T.E. Lawrence's *The Seven Pillars of Wisdom*. And while the book

v

does contain a few minor errors of fact, these do not detract from its worth, for access to many private collections of papers (including the Royal Archives) gave Fleming the key to a more balanced view of the motives of the principals, and of the sequence of events which he describes. At the same time he modestly seeks the indulgence of the reader as he wistfully experiences the Central Asian setting of his youth once more: 'the plateaux and the mountains, the lamaseries and the salt lakes, the bitter winds, the shaggy ponies, the rough people, the rumours around the yak-dung fires'.

As a memorial to people, the volume presents three leading players: Lord Curzon, then Viceroy of India; Colonel Francis Edward Younghusband, British Commissioner to Tibet; and Colonel (later General) J.R.L. Macdonald, Commander of the Military Escort to the Commissioner. A fascinating portrait is also sketched of St. John Brodrick who, as Secretary of State for India (1903–5), contributed to the Home Government's less than enthusiastic assessment of Younghusband's achievements. The constraints and difficulties imposed on Younghusband by the unlikeable Macdonald are deftly handled and well-documented. Lord Curzon appears early on as the initiator of the Mission, and thereafter hovers in the wings as an increasingly powerless witness to the consequences. But it is Francis Younghusband himself who dominates the tale, both by his actions, and by the vigour of opinions regularly communicated in writing to his father (his principal confidant) and to others.

As a memorial to actions and ideas, the volume begins with a masterful summary of the Great Game, in which the opportunistic expansion of Russian political influence and power in Central Asia, especially from the middle of the nineteenth century, is seen as a distant but constant threat to British power and prestige in India. The authorities at Lhasa had, from 1793, with Chinese encouragement, pursued a policy of excluding foreigners from their country. While the famous Pundits had succeeded in gaining some knowledge of conditions in Tibet for the Indian Government, whose principal interest was the development of trade, and while a Sino-British agreement on Tibetan trade was signed in 1893, the country remained

INTRODUCTION

isolated and, to all but a handful of intrepid explorers, inaccessible. The Younghusband Mission of 1903-4 was conceived in part as a means to compel the Tibetans to open up to 'free trade', in part as a necessary counter to the presumed Russian influence in Lhasa from the turn of the century.

The British Home Government came to oppose the concept of a stronger British political involvement in Tibet because of the destabilizing effect this was thought likely to produce in Anglo-Russian imperial accommodations, already foreshadowed (and consummated in the 1907 Convention. The success of the Mission in reaching Lhasa and obtaining the Tibetan leaders' agreement to treaty terms, however, awakened the Chinese Government to a realization that it must act quickly and firmly if it were to forestall further British (or even Russian) movements against Tibet in the future. The Imperial Chinese Government failed in its last years in its attempts to assert the desired sovereignty over Tibet, but its successors were alerted, and bided their time. It is thus an irony that, as Alastair Lamb has written and Fleming approvingly cites, 'the most apparent result of the Younghusband Mission ... was to lay Tibet open to a reassertion of Chinese authority'. The alleged Russian dominance at Lhasa proved to be a myth, and the conclusion of the Mission's work thus marked the end (at least for the time being) of the Great Game between Britain and Russia: but it did mark the beginning of a new Great Game, that between China and the dominant power in India, which has not yet been played out. 1997 - HK → PRC

Expelled from Tibet in 1911, the representatives of the Chinese Government returned under the guise of a condolence mission following the death in 1933 of the Thirteenth Dalai Lama. Staying on uninvited after the obsequies, they soon found their presence paralleled by an equally unofficial (but invited) British Mission. In July 1949, with due dignity and pomp, the Chinese representatives were again expelled from Lhasa: the British stayed on. Hugh Richardson, Officer-in-Charge of the British Mission to Lhasa from 1936 to 1940, and again from 1946 to August 1947, changed his signboard to that of the Indian Political Mission to Lhasa after Indian in-

vii

INTRODUCTION

dependence, and remained as Officer-in-Charge until 1950. In that year the Tibetans discovered, too late, that a claimed 'independence' not based on an extension of international intercourse but on a policy of isolationism, and not based on formal recognition as a sovereign state but on *de facto* autonomy, was judged by other states to be a constitutional fiction, just as Curzon had previously characterized Imperial China's claims to suzerainty over Tibet.

Most Chinese are inclined to take the view that Tibet has always been part of China. This is not the place to rehearse the arguments of the issue. What is relevant in contemporary affairs is that, beginning in 1950 in the eastern part of Tibet (and after the events of March 1959 in the whole of Tibet), an enormity was perpetrated of which the consequences are still not clearly measured, as Lama Govinda, in the introduction to his wife's recent book *Tibet in Pictures*, states:

Tibet's was a great and ancient civilisation which flourished with unbroken vitality for more than a millennium, right up to our time, when it met with almost total destruction by the conquering hordes of a fanatical enemy who not only conquered and occupied the country, but did his best to annihilate the last traces of its culture, its religion, its art, and even its ethnographic identity. And this happened exactly at the moment when for the first time in the history of this planet, humanity was on the verge of becoming conscious of its essential oneness and its future common fate.

It is academic to discuss the motives of the destroyers. The years 1966 to 1976, in particular, are now characterized by the Chinese leadership as a period of 'ultra-Leftism' in which not only Tibetans suffered. The destruction of monasteries, the humiliation and dispersion of monks, the confiscation of religious artifacts and the wholesale contemning of the religious impulse, the conduct of the infamous *thamzing* (struggle) meetings — these and other manifestations of a true colonial attitude by Han Chinese towards Tibetans have currently been replaced by a 'policy of leniency'. This new policy dates particularly from the May 1980 inspection tour of Tibet by Hu Yaobang, General Secretary of the Chinese Communist

INTRODUCTION

Party, and has taken the form of (temporary) exemptions from a number of taxes, expansion of private plots of land, partial relaxation of the Party's opposition to the expression of religious sentiment, and the withdrawal of some Han officials from Tibet. These moves are designed primarily to improve the economic well-being of the Tibetans, and to extend somewhat the role of Tibetans in the regional government. The principal result to date seems to have been an unprecedented upsurge in the religious fervour of Tibetans, young as well as old, which may be taken as the most eloquent expression of a resurgent national identity distinct from the Han.

Tibet has proved indigestible within the Chinese polity under past policy. The focal point of Tibetan loyalty is the Fourteenth Dalai Lama, living in self-imposed exile at Dharamsala, in north-west India, since the anti-Han rebellion of March 1959. The Dalai Lama has demonstrated that his is a lively and modern mind, appreciative of contemporary realities, unlike some of his elderly advisors. In the face of continued blandishments to 'return to the motherland', he has speculated that his might be the last in the line of the incarnations of Chenresig, and that there may have occurred an erosion in the political importance of the institution of the Dalai Lama during the period of exile. He has also repeatedly insisted that the happiness of the Tibetan people is, and must be, his principal concern. He seems to accept that Tibet is now irreversibly part of China, but argues that, since the conditions of that incorporation are unsatisfactory to both parties, they should be renegotiated, although he is open-minded as to the precise details.

It remains to be seen whether the Chinese leaders are equally modern-minded and can come to accept the failure of their assimilation policy since 1949. In 1982 it was asserted that the 'nine-point principle' that had been presented as a major basis for reconciliation between Taiwan and the People's Republic was 'not applicable' to Tibet, and indeed a substantially higher level of real autonomy for Tibet than presently exists would probably produce unacceptable demands for autonomy from

INTRODUCTION

other areas (notably Xinjiang and Inner Mongolia), unacceptable, that is, without a searching re-examination of the extent, functions and domestic goals of the Chinese polity.
Despite the substantial changes that have taken place in China
since 1976, especially in the realm of the economy, there is not
as yet any indication that such a fundamental reassessment of
middle- and long-term political considerations has taken (or is
taking) place. However, the imperatives flowing from the
perceived need to reassert China's sovereignty over Hong Kong
and Taiwan, and in the process to develop a convincing institu-
tional basis (not merely an unenforceable nominal respect) for
'the rights of peoples to self-determination', may come in due
course to suggest alternative and viable formulae for a more
just accommodation between China and Tibet. (It may be
noted parenthetically that the justification for China's desired
hegemony over Tibet is fundamentally on security grounds, to
deny the territory to a potential enemy, and that this fundamental stand is substantially that of the present Vietnamese
leaders towards Cambodia; however, China's needs in this
respect are rarely cited by her leaders.)

The value of the present work lies principally in the timely
reminder that politics are made by men, and that imperial
politics, especially, depend on substantially shared assumptions and understandings between the man on the spot and the
ultimate wielders of power, if they are to succeed. As happens
when assumptions are not shared, in the case of the Mission to
Lhasa, Younghusband's actions were seen by the British
Government as a form of dangerous adventurism and insubordination, and he himself viewed the British Government's attitude as an 'abandonment' caused by both 'the jealousy borne
by the two great Powers for one another' and by 'the love of
isolation engrained in us islanders'. The twelve-day delay for
messages sent by telegraph from London to Lhasa (five days if
from Simla) did not, of course, improve the co-ordination of
policy, and made inevitable the exercise of major initiatives by
Younghusband, with the corresponding risks of repudiation.
Fleming takes Younghusband to task for his refusal to express
contrition in his defence against charges of exceeding his in-

structions: but it is his attitude, not his arguments, that Fleming takes exception to, in what is otherwise a very sympathetic portrayal. The award of Knight Commander of the Indian Empire (KCIE), rather than Knight Commander of the Star of India (KCSI), given to Younghusband at the end of 1904 was the consequence; the higher distinction was awarded only in 1917, almost apologetically, eight years after he had retired from Government service.

In his account of the Mission, published in 1910 under the title *India and Tibet*, Younghusband remarked that 'the far distant primary cause of all our attempts at intercourse with the Tibetans was an act of aggression, not on our part, not on the part of an ambitious Pro-consul, or some headstrong frontier officer, but of the Bhutanese, neighbours, and then vassals, of the Tibetans, who nearly a century and a half ago committed the first act — an act of aggression — which brought us into relationship with the Tibetans [in 1772]'. In summarizing the results of his Mission he listed the following: 'Good-will of Tibetans ... Friendship of Bhutan ... Scientific results ... Indemnity reduced by His Majesty's Government ... Period of occupation of Chumbi reduced ... Permission for Gyantse Agent to proceed to Lhasa abandoned ...'. It was with apprehension, however, that he noted the 'great forward movement in Tibet' of the Chinese Government after the Chumbi valley was evacuated by the British on 27 January 1908. The goodwill of the Tibetans served the British well while they were in power in India, and was evidenced early on by the Thirteenth Dalai Lama's choice of Darjeeling as a refuge from 1911 to 1913.

A friendship between the ruler of Bhutan and the leaders of British India, based on an understanding of mutual benefit, was perhaps the most lasting achievement to come from the Mission. Ugyen Wangchuck, who as Penlop of Tongsa had been an invaluable go-between for Younghusband and the Tibetan leaders, was granted a knighthood by the British Crown, and was accepted within Bhutan as the first hereditary king in 1907. In 1910, the British moved to pre-empt any Chinese advance southwards beyond Tibet by concluding a

INTRODUCTION

treaty with Bhutan which provided, among other things, that that Government would be guided by the advice of the British Government in their external relations. India, after independence, renewed this provision by treaty in 1949. In the wake of events in Tibet from 1959 on, Bhutan aligned itself with India and commenced a massive process of modernization to escape Tibet's fate. The Kingdom joined the United Nations in 1971 with India's sponsorship, and is today steadily enhancing its political sovereignty and capabilities for economic growth. Joint surveys are continuing with the Indian authorities to complete the demarcation of the Indo-Bhutan border (although with some difficulty on the eastern sector). Despite occasional hints after 1949 of a residual Chinese territorial interest in Bhutan, the People's Republic has, since joining the United Nations in 1971, avoided giving any formal basis for such an impression. Although low-level border probes near the ill-defined parts of the Sino-Bhutan border occurred in the past, talks have now commenced in Beijing on the formal demarcation of this border.

Fleming's study was published after the details of the Sino-Indian differences on their borders were made public, but of course before the events of October 1962 in that arena. Its publication was therefore timely. The Soviet Union has since re-entered the Great Game, through the invasion, in December 1979, of Afghanistan. Although the results cannot be clearly foreseen in this decades-long competition for a lasting political dominance in Central Asia, it seems certain that the circumstances of Tibet will play a pivotal role in the ultimate accommodations between India, China, and the USSR. The burden of Fleming's epilogue is no less true today than in 1961, and the reflective reader may feel the sting of truth in it: 'the conception underlying British policy towards Tibet was wise as well as humane — that an independent Tibet made for stability in the heartlands of Asia, and that it may not only be the Tibetans who will rue the demolition of their ramshackle autonomy'.

BRIAN SHAW

Bibliography

The following works include those published or reprinted since 1961 which have a bearing on the general subject-matter of this book. The list represents a wide range of opinion.

Dawa Norbu, *Red Star Over Tibet* (London, Collins, 1974).

Dhondub Choedon, *Life in the Red Flag People's Commune* (Dharamsala, Information Office of His Holiness the Dalai Lama, 1978).

Epstein, Israel, *Tibet Transformed* (Beijing, New World Press, 1983).

Govinda, Li Gotami, *Tibet in Pictures* (Boulder, Colo., Naropa Institute, 1982), 2 volumes.

Greenhut, Frederic A., *The Tibetan Frontiers Question* (Delhi, Chand, 1982).

Hart-Davis, Duff, *Peter Fleming: A Biography* (London, Jonathan Cape, 1974).

Kunsang Paljor, *Tibet the Undying Flame* (Dharamsala, Information Office of His Holiness the Dalai Lama, 1977).

Lamb, Alastair, *The China-India Border: The Origins of the Disputed Boundaries* (London, Oxford University Press, 1964).

——— *The McMahon Line: A Study in the Relations between India, China, and Tibet, 1904 to 1914* (London, Routledge and Kegan Paul, 1966).

——— *Asian Frontiers: Studies in a Continuing Problem* (London, Pall Mall Press, 1968).

Maxwell, Neville George Anthony, *India's China War* (London, Jonathan Cape, 1970).

BIBLIOGRAPHY

Mehra, Parshotam, *The Younghusband Expedition* (London, Asia Publishing House, 1968).

_____ *The McMahon Line and After* (Delhi, Macmillan, 1974).

_____ *Tibetan Polity, 1904–37* (Wiesbaden, Otto Harrassowitz, 1976).

_____ *The North-Eastern Frontier: A Documentary Study of the Internecine Rivalry between India, Tibet and China* (Delhi, Oxford University Press, 1979), 2 volumes.

Ngapo Ngawang Jigmei, *et al.*, *Tibet* (London, Frederick Muller, 1981).

'Peter Fleming, An Obituary', *The Times*, 20 August 1971.

Richardson, Hugh Edward, *Tibet and its History* (Oxford, Oxford University Press, 1962; revised edition 1984).

Shakabpa, W.D., *Tibet: A Political History* (New Haven, Yale University Press, 1967).

Stein, Rolf Alfred, *Tibetan Civilization* (London, Faber, 1972).

Tsering Dorje Gashi, *New Tibet* (Dharamsala, Information Office of His Holiness the Dalai Lama, 1980).

Union Research Institute, *Tibet, 1950–1967* (Hong Kong, The Institute, 1968).

Watson, Francis, *The Frontiers of China* (New York, Praeger, 1966).

White, John Claude, *Sikkim and Bhutan* (Delhi, Cultural Publishing House, 1909; reprinted 1971, 1983).

Whiting, Allen Suess, *The Chinese Calculus of Deterrence: India and Indochina* (Ann Arbor, University of Michigan Press, 1975).

Younghusband, Sir Francis Edward, *India and Tibet* (London, John Murray, 1910).

Zhou, Jin (ed.), *Tibet: No Longer Medieval* (Beijing, Foreign Languages Press, 1981).

BAYONETS TO LHASA

Younghusband

BAYONETS
TO LHASA

*The First Full Account
of the British Invasion of Tibet in 1904*

Peter Fleming

RUPERT HART-DAVIS
SOHO SQUARE LONDON
1961

To
TONY AND MARY
KESWICK

Contents

7

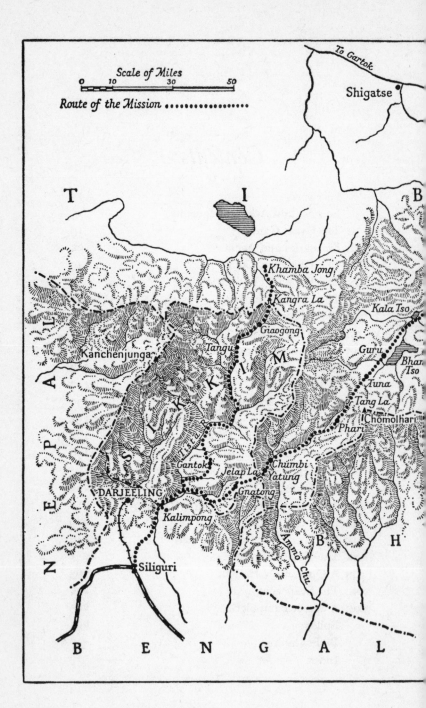

Scale of Miles

0   10   30   50

Route of the Mission ·················

To Gartok

Shigatse

T I B

Khamba Jong

Kangra La

Kala Tso

Giaogong

Kanchenjunga

Tangu

Guru

Bham Tso

S I K K I M

Tuna

Tang La

Chomolhari

Phari

Gantok

Jelap La   Chumbi

Yatung

Gnatong

DARJEELING

Kalimpong

Amo Chu

B

H

N E P A L

Siliguri

B   E   N   G   A   L

THE
BRITISH EXPEDITION
TO LHASA 1904

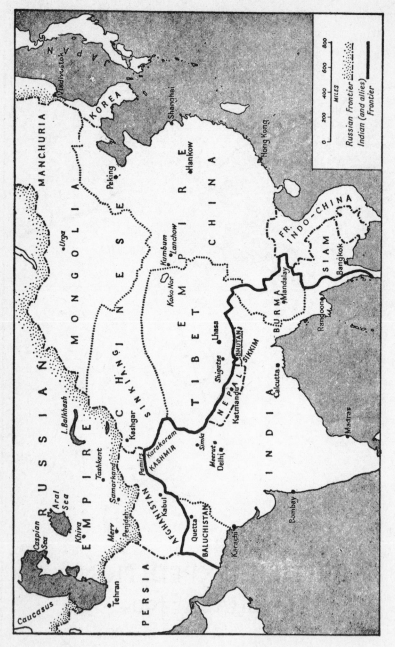

Illustrations

ILLUSTRATIONS

* These photographs, so far as can be ascertained, are here published for the first time.

MAPS

Foreword

SOME events in history seem, when we look back on them, to have been inevitable. Opinions may still differ as to whose foot dislodged the pebble that set the avalanche in motion; but we can all now plainly see that the avalanche was there, doomed sooner or later to a degringolade. The pebble may have been an accident or a caprice; but in the great scar on the hillside of our past we recognise the work of destiny.

There was nothing inevitable about the politico-military adventure described in these pages. Its main purposes were rooted in fallacy. By the time they were fulfilled they had been forgotten. Its achievements were largely disavowed and its staunch leader censured. The British incursion into Tibet was a fine feat of arms and a notable essay in diplomatic pioneering. Its outward aspect is swashbuckling, romantic and clear-cut; its inner history ambiguous and confused; its aftermath unedifying. Over it there hangs, as over some indiscretion, an air of apology and embarrassment. Of all the little wars that set the frontiers of a great Empire, the march to Lhasa is the strangest, the most striking; but as an ebullition of Imperialism it is singularly out of character.

If the hand of Fate is not conspicuous in the enterprise, its fortunes and misfortunes were strongly influenced by an agency which, though less unpredictable, was scarcely less unaccommodating: the personality of Lord Curzon. It was his mind that conceived the expedition to Tibet, his statecraft that overcame the obstacles to its launching; and many of the handicaps it carried had their origins in the prejudice which this brilliant, difficult man seldom failed to arouse against his policies and against himself.

13

FOREWORD

We do not here have the feeling of an impersonal destiny at work; nor can we descry across the valley of the past any scar upon the ravaged flanks of Central Asian history. No avalanche fell. The affair is marked only by a small, untidy scree, composed almost exclusively of pebbles. The purpose of this book is to arrange the pebbles into a commemorative and, I hope, a seemly cairn.

Nettlebed, Oxfordshire.   PETER FLEMING
    September, 1960.

Sources and Acknowledgements

SIR FRANCIS YOUNGHUSBAND, who played a central part in the events to be described, left a miscellany of private papers. In addition to material which is also available in the India Office Archives, the Younghusband Papers relating to Tibet include a series of personal letters from Lord Curzon, several from Mr (later Sir) Louis Dane, the head of the Foreign Department in the Government of India, and a number from friends or acquaintances in England, some of which throw valuable light on Younghusband's treatment after his return from Tibet. But the most illuminating documents in this collection are forty letters which Younghusband wrote to his father between October 1903 and October 1904, for in these he revealed with complete frankness his thoughts and purposes. To Sir Francis's daughter, Miss Eileen Younghusband, CBE, I owe a deep debt of gratitude for placing these papers at my disposal.

I am beholden to Her Majesty the Queen for permission to consult the Royal Archives, and to Mr Robin Mackworth-Young, the Librarian at Windsor Castle, for facilitating my researches there: to the Marquess of Salisbury, KG, PC, for letting me see Kitchener's letters to his mother: to the Baroness Ravensdale and Lady Alexandra Metcalfe, Lord Curzon's daughters, for granting me access to the private correspondence of their father and mother during the former's Viceroyalty: to the late Sir George Barnes for sending me several letters exchanged between his father (Sir Hugh Barnes, Lieutenant-Governor of Burma) and Lord Curzon: and to Lady Wilton, whose late husband, Sir Ernest Wilton, was Younghusband's adviser on Chinese affairs, for making his personal papers available.

SOURCES AND ACKNOWLEDGEMENTS

To the many kind people who have lent me letters, diaries and photographs from their own or their family's archives I would like to repeat in public the thanks I have already given them privately. Among survivors of the Mission and its Escort who have helped me with their recollections I would like in particular to thank Lt-Colonel F. M. Bailey, CIE, Lt-Colonel A. C. Hadow, Lt-Colonel J. D. Grant, VC, and Lt-Colonel the Lord Kingsale, DSO.

To nobody, however, am I more deeply indebted than to Mr Alastair Lamb, of the University of Malaya. His definitive work on Britain's relations with Tibet (*Britain and Chinese Central Asia*, Vol. I, Routledge and Kegan Paul, 1960) was not available until my book was almost finished; but the guidance which he gave me in my quest for sources was of immense value. I had no claim on his kindness, but he did not stint it.

The whole of this book was typed, and the extensive correspondence dealing with it handled, by Miss Jane Clapperton, who also helped me with the research. I cannot thank her adequately for her services, without which the work, besides taking twice as long, would have been half as congenial.

The main published official sources on the matters dealt with in these pages are three Blue Books: Cd. 1920 (*Papers Relating to Tibet* 1904) was laid before Parliament on 5 February 1904, Cd. 2054 (*Further Papers Relating to Tibet* 1904) on 2 May 1904, and Cd. 2370 (*Further Papers Relating to Tibet* 1905) on 14 February 1905. The original documents from which the Blue Books were compiled are to be found in the Public Record Office, in Nos. 1745–1756 of the series of bound volumes known as *FO 17 China*.

This somewhat unwieldy mass of raw material (which is largely, but even less compendiously, duplicated in the India Office records) contains many documents which were thought unworthy of, or unsuitable for, publication in the Blue Books; it includes, also, departmental minutes and some private or demi-official correspondence dealing with the official telegrams and despatches. It thus provides, as it were, a mirror in which

SOURCES AND ACKNOWLEDGEMENTS

Whitehall can be seen making up its face, and from it a truer, or anyhow a fuller, impression of the background to British policy can be gained than emerges from the Blue Books themselves.

The archives preserved in the India Office Library include two especially important sets of documents: the Curzon–Hamilton Correspondence and the Ampthill Papers. The first consists of the confidential correspondence exchanged between Lord Curzon, as Viceroy, and Lord George Hamilton, who was Secretary of State for India until September 1903; the second, of letters written by and to Lord Ampthill, who deputised as Viceroy while Curzon was on leave in the summer of 1904. A complementary collection of Lord Curzon's correspondence during his six months' absence from India was kindly lent me by Mr T. S. Blakeney. I must thank Mr N. C. Sutton and the staff of the India Office Library for their unfailing helpfulness.

I am grateful, too, to Mr D. W. King, the War Office Librarian, for exhuming a number of reports and other documents dealing with the military aspects of the expedition: to Mr J. S. Maywood, until recently head of *The Times* Intelligence Department, for tracing in the records at Printing House Square several letters from *The Times* Correspondent in Tibet: and to Mr Hugh Richardson, CIE, OBE, the last British representative at Lhasa, for his wise counsel.

In the transliteration of place-names I have adhered, in the maps as well as in the text, to the usage of the period.

I should like, in conclusion, to acknowledge my indebtedness to a source which has nothing to do with documents and is not to be found in libraries. The historian, living in the present, can have no experience of the past, but it may be of service to him to know at first hand something of the background against which the events which it is his aim to reconstruct took place; to a sailor, for example, the interpretation of naval history probably presents fewer problems than it does to a landsman. With the Central Asian setting of my narrative—the plateaux and the mountains, the lamaseries and the salt lakes, the bitter winds, the shaggy ponies, the rough people, the rumours round the yak-dung fires—I can claim a peripheral acquaintance.

SOURCES AND ACKNOWLEDGEMENTS

Rightly or wrongly, I believe that this small store of experience has been, at times, a help.

Not all the individuals who were concerned, directly or indirectly, with the Tibet Frontier Commission emerge from my account of it with credit. I much regret any pain or annoyance which may thereby be caused to their descendants. But it is no easier to write history without criticising some of those who made it than it is to make an omelette without breaking eggs; and the posthumous verdicts passed in these pages on certain of Younghusband's superiors are neither as harsh nor as unjust as the verdict which they passed on him, officially, for his conduct in Tibet.

P. F.

CHAPTER ONE

The Great Game

To the world at large, and to England in particular, Russia's *Drang nach Osten* seemed at the end of the nineteenth century to be one of those world-forces which nothing can deflect, nothing sublimate, nothing mollify. It was impossible to imagine an Asia across which this juggernaut would not be slowly but inexorably grinding. Every precedent, every probability suggested that St Petersburg's imperialist aspirations were a permanent and minatory part of the landscape. To see beyond them, to suppose them capable of atrophy, or to prescribe for the problems which they posed any but a violent and perilous solution was not within men's power: any more than, today, we find it feasible to visualise a world in whose destinies international Communism will play a negligible part.

Throughout the nineteenth century Russia's Asiatic policy had been canny, successful and (within a framework of opportunism) consistent. Four Tsars—Alexander I, Nicholas I, Alexander II and Alexander III—had between them reigned for ninety years; each was a man of character and ability. Moreover, for eighty-three years—from 1812 to 1895—the Foreign Ministry had changed hands only twice, and the three incumbents Count Nesselrode, Prince Gortchakoff, M. de Giers evolved a tradition remarkable for its continuity.

One after another the crumbling Khanates were swallowed —Khiva, Bokhara, Khokand and the rest. The hill-tribes of the Caucasus were painfully subdued, and their ancestral valleys added to the Tsar's more desirable holdings in Transcaucasia, where the petty kingdoms between the Black Sea and the Caspian had been forced to acknowledge Russian sovereignty. The territory of the Tekke Turkomans was conquered, and railways—the first to be built in Asia outside India—were reviving the economic life and the strategic significance of far-flung, forgotten oases which had had little of either for several centuries.

Here and there upon the dun or charcoal-coloured desert the white bones of thousands of soldiers and tens of thousands of camels and horses, scattered in an untidy swathe across some unusually waterless expanse, marked a failure in administrative planning; but although the Russians deployed a prodigious military effort, the actual fighting was seldom severe, and their victories—attended by much ruthlessness—were not costly in their soldiers' lives. In Genghiz Khan's time it had been Asia's armies that were better armed, better trained, better led than any they encountered on the periphery of Europe; now the boot was on the other foot.

For Russia the tide had begun to turn at the end of the fourteenth century, when Tamerlane after reaching the banks of the Oka called off the advance on Moscow and wheeled his horde southward for Delhi and Bagdad. He was the last of the great invaders to come up out of Asia, across the mountains and the deserts, on to the glacis of the steppes, behind which in their swamps and forests the Russians acted, involuntarily and with varying success, as a flank-guard to Christendom. After Tamerlane the balance shifted and the pattern changed. The Russians, growing in strength and unity, threw off the Tartar yoke and passed gradually to the offensive. Europe counter-attacked Asia.

By the nineteenth century this historical process was at its apogee. The impetus given to it by Peter the Great showed no signs of flagging; it had even carried the outposts of an ebullient Empire across the Pacific to Alaska. What started as a quest for security, dictated by the need to drive back and contain the forces of Asiatic barbarism which had threatened Russia's very existence for so long, had become a gigantic foray into empty or ill-defended lands.

Hallowed—in her own eyes—by a sense of national destiny, Russia's expansion had behind it a diversity of impulses, ranging from the serfs' need for land (the serfs, to the number of twenty-three million, were liberated in 1861) and the piratical instincts of the free-ranging Cossacks, to a natural desire to keep up with the Joneses; for in Africa and Asia Russia's European rivals were carving out for themselves new and enviable domains.

Russian policy, then, was an inevitable product of the times, part of the rhythm of history. Her actions were based, perhaps, as much on instinct as on reason; the interests which they were designed to further were, by the standards of the nineteenth century, legitimate; her belief that she was fulfilling her destiny may be called specious but it can hardly be called mistaken, for it is inconceivable that she could have behaved otherwise than she did behave.

To those, however, who were injured or threatened by Russia's aggrandisement, its inevitability, if they apprehended it, brought no comfort; an understanding of the laws of gravity does little to lessen the misgivings of people who find themselves in the path of an avalanche. Of the European Powers, Great Britain was the most directly affected by this tempestuous overspill. By the end of the nineteenth century Russia's position in Central Asia conferred on her, vis-à-vis England, advantages of a peculiarly disturbing kind.

Not only had the extension of her frontiers until they were all but contiguous with India's created a dangerously inflammable situation for which a solution would become increasingly difficult to find, but the consolidation of her conquests in the East gave her an important lever in the West. 'The stronger Russia is in Central Asia, the weaker England is in India and the more conciliatory she will be in Europe.' Skobeleff, the victor of Geok Tepe, had said that, and it was roughly true.*

* Cf. Letter written by Nicholas II to his sister on 2 November 1899 on the outbreak of the Boer War: 'My dear, you know I am not proud, but I

THE BROKEN COVENANT.

"WE CANNOT CLOSE THIS BOOK, AND SAY WE WILL LOOK INTO IT NO MORE."

See Mr. Gladstone's Speech, April 27th.

THE GREAT GAME

There was a marked air of insatiability about Russia's Asiatic policy; for four hundred years (according to calculations made by Nansen in 1914) the Russian Empire had been growing at the rate of fifty-five square miles a day, or roughly 20,000 square miles a year. Few Englishmen seriously entertained the hope that her eastward progress would be halted by prudence, by exhaustion or by any other cause. Even if it were, her dominant position, so swiftly and ferociously achieved, challenged British prestige and British interests all over Asia, and notably in India, still haunted by memories of a Mutiny which might not be the last of its kind. At the close of Queen Victoria's reign a clash, sooner or later, between the two Empires seemed highly probable to all, unavoidable to some. Twice in the 80's—over Merv and over Penjdeh—such a clash had been narrowly averted; during the Penjdeh crisis in 1885 the Stationery Office printed, as a precaution, documents announcing that a state of war existed between Great Britain and Russia.* There was a general feeling that things could not go on like this for much longer.

No one, or at least no one with a first-class mind, held this view more strongly than the man who was appointed Viceroy of India in 1898. 'As a student of Russian aspirations and methods for fifteen years,' Lord Curzon wrote in 1901, 'I assert with confidence—what I do not think any of her own statesmen would deny—that her ultimate ambition is the dominion of Asia;' and he went on to argue that 'if Russia is entitled to these ambitions, still more is Britain entitled, nay compelled, to defend that which she has won.'

---

do like knowing that it lies solely with me in the last resort to change the course of the war in Africa. The means is very simple—telegraph an order for the whole Turkestan army to mobilize and march to the frontier. That's all. The strongest fleets in the world can't prevent us from settling our scores with England precisely at her most vulnerable point.' The Tsar however went on to admit that this *coup de foudre* could not be delivered until more railways had been built in Central Asia.

Quoted from *Krasny Archiv* in B. H. Sumner: *Tsardom and Imperialism in the Far East and Middle East, 1880–1914.* (Raleigh Lecture on History, 1940.)

* R. L. Greaves: *Persia and the Defence of India* (1959).

It was on no merely academic studies that these convictions were based. A tireless traveller (despite the injured spine which caused him constant pain) and a keen observer, Curzon had watched Russian policy at work all round her Asiatic frontiers from Persia to Peking. He had been among the first foreigners to jolt along the new strategic railway from the Caspian to Samarkand, noting as he did so (in 1888) that the whole of Russian Central Asia was 'one vast armed camp,' and that in the Russian newspapers photographs of this line were invariably captioned 'On the Road to India.' He had driven the last two hundred miles to Tashkent by *tarantass*, a 'sorrowful and springless vehicle.' From the breached ramparts of Geok Tepe he had looked down on the long, livid trail of bones which, winding away into the desert for eleven miles, marked the path of the victorious Cossacks after the stronghold fell. He had pondered the words of Skobeleff, the man who unleashed them on a pursuit which cost the lives of twenty thousand men, women and children: 'It will be in the end our duty to organize masses of Asiatic cavalry and to hurl them into India as a vanguard, under the banner of blood and rapine, thereby reviving the times of Tamerlane.'

Curzon's experience of Asia was large, his knowledge of her history encyclopaedic; but his theories about the role which Russia meant to play upon that continent had been formed, at least in outline, before he acquired either. These theories thus had an element in them which was instinctive or emotional rather than purely intellectual. All students of his complex character agree that, as Sir Harold Nicolson puts it, 'most of Curzon's basic convictions, the articles of his faith, were absorbed before he left Eton in 1878;' and it would not be unduly fanciful to suppose that the story of Britain's violation of Tibet began on, or anyhow not later than, 7 May 1877, when the Reverend Wolley Dod's House Debating Society met to discuss the question: 'Are we justified in regarding with equanimity the advance of Russia towards our Indian frontier?'

'The President [Curzon wrote in the Society's Minute Book after the debate] expressed the opinion that the policy of Russia

24

was a most ambitious and aggressive one. It dated its origin from the time of Peter the Great, by whom the scheme of conquest had been first made. He did not imagine for a moment that the Russians would actually invade India, and were they to do so we need have no fear of the result; but . . . a great question of diplomacy might arise in Europe in which the interests of England were opposed to those of Russia. It might then suit Russia to send out an army to watch our Indian frontier. In such a case as this England's right hand would obviously be tied back.'*

Two decades later the premises from which, as a schoolboy, he had thus argued had become much stronger. The 'scheme of conquest' continued to be implemented; and during his Viceroyalty Britain's military commitments in South Africa, North China and elsewhere made India a still more tempting target for diversionary activities, or even (as many feared) for a full-scale invasion.

Curzon's views on the Russian menace were well-known. He deplored the attitude of 'those who decry British interference anywhere and extol the odious theory of sedentary and culpable inaction.' 'Whatever be Russia's designs on India,' he wrote in 1889, 'whether they be serious and inimical or imaginary and fantastic, I hold that the first duty of English statesmen is to render any hostile intentions futile.' His advocacy of a forward policy was persistent, sonorous and didactic.

In the circumstances it was hardly surprising that, as his official biographer puts it, 'beneath the general chorus of approval' which greeted his appointment as Viceroy at the age of thirty-eight 'there existed a thin but perceptible current of uneasiness, which tended to crystallize into a fear of a policy of adventure beyond the Indian frontier.' Sir William Harcourt ended his letter of congratulation with a postscript: 'Let me beg as a personal favour that you will not make war on Russia in my life-time.' 'Campbell-Bannerman,' wrote Labouchere, 'spent this morning conclusively proving to me that you will

* Ronaldshay, Vol. I.

drag us into a war with Russia.' The fire-eating Sir Bindon Blood, who in the previous year had commanded the Malakand Field Force, struck the same note: 'It will amuse you to hear that I am being told by the Anti-Forward-Policy people . . . that now I shall have as many wars as I want.'

'It cannot,' his biographer comments, 'be said that these apprehensions were altogether without justification.' The passage of five years did nothing to diminish them; they powerfully influenced the events with which my narrative deals.

'The boundaries of the British Empire in Asia,' Curzon wrote two years after his resignation, in painful circumstances, of the Viceroyalty, 'had always exercised upon me a peculiar fascination;' * and soon after he arrived in India he set in motion administrative reforms (the most notable being the sequestration from the Punjab of the territory thenceforward known as the North West Frontier Province) which brought matters of frontier-policy directly under the Viceroy's control. Upon this 'Land Frontier 5700 miles in length, the most diversified, the most important, and the most delicately poised in the world,' † Afghanistan was the most explosive sector, Persia the weakest. Britain had already fought two unsatisfactory wars in Afghanistan, in 1841 and 1880; each was to a large extent provoked by Russophobia. As for Persia, the Russian railway network in Central Asia was steadily enhancing the military threat from that quarter.

Tibet, by comparison, was a backwater. But its borders, in those days as in these, were disputed and ambiguous, and for some years the Government of India had been endeavouring, with a complete lack of success, to regularise affairs on the distant watersheds separating Tibetan territory from the British feudatory states of Sikkim, Nepal and Bhutan. This unsatisfactory situation had arisen from the following causes.

In 1886 the Tibetans debouched from the Chumbi Valley, a corridor of fertile land flanked by the territory of Nepal on

* Romanes Lecture, 2 November 1907.
† Ibid.

the one side and Bhutan on the other, and occupied a strip
of Sikkimese territory some twenty miles deep. In 1888 a
small British expedition expelled the intruders without difficulty. British casualties were one officer killed and three
other ranks wounded; Tibetan losses were estimated at two
hundred killed, four hundred wounded and two hundred
captured. In 1890 a Sikkim–Tibet Convention was concluded
with China, whose suzerainty over Tibet Britain recognised,
and this was supplemented in 1893 by a set of Trade Regulations. The main purpose of these instruments, as far as Britain
was concerned, was to secure formal Chinese recognition of her
paramount rights in Sikkim; but they dealt, in detail, with
matters of commerce, frontier-delimitation and so forth.

China's hold over Tibet, precarious already, was further
weakened by her disastrous war with Japan in 1894–95; this
followed on the heels of a bloody Moslem rebellion in her north-
western provinces which cut one of the main lines of communication with Tibet. The Tibetans, who detested their Chinese
overlords, found it easy to take the line that, since they had not
been party to the Convention or to the Trade Regulations, the
provisions of neither were binding on them; and from this
obdurate attitude, which the Chinese were powerless to modify,
stemmed an endless series of vexatious incidents. Grazing rights
were infringed, trade obstructed, boundary-pillars overthrown;
British attempts to negotiate a settlement of these matters were
greeted with the cheerful contumacity of which the Tibetans
are masters.

These then, in brief outline, were what may be called the
tactical considerations which obliged the Government of India
(and would have obliged it under any Viceroy) to do *something*
about Tibet. Although the British grievances, when, promoted
almost to the status of a *casus belli*, they were in due course
published in a Blue Book, have a petty, parochial air, they
cannot be regarded as frivolous, let alone trumped-up.

The pasturing of a few score or a few hundred yaks on the
'wrong' side of an inadequately surveyed watershed, the
destruction by ignorant and superstitious hillmen of boundary-

pillars whose modern counterparts on a Surrey common would be unlikely to survive two fine week-ends—these were not the things that mattered. What mattered—what always matters on a frontier—was prestige. The Government of India was a tiny oligarchy controlling a huge sub-continent. Once it had asserted its rights on the Tibetan frontier, there was a point beyond which its neighbour's intransigence and its own forbearance could not be allowed to go. In the Indian Empire, as in all others, this was one of the rules of the game, one of the facts of life; and to ignore it on the North East Frontier involved jeopardy to the tenuous bonds which bound Sikkim, Nepal and Bhutan to the British connexion.

As a tactician on the Indian Frontier Curzon showed an unlooked-for streak of caution. His admiration for and his understanding of soldiers were limited, and he was quick to suspect them of wasting money on huge, elaborate fortifications and small, superfluous expeditions. 'On the North West Frontier and the North East Frontier alike he was constantly vetoing proposals for advances across the borders and reducing commitments urged on him by his military advisers.' * As a strategist, on the other hand, he was visionary and audacious. Circumspect in his use of pawns, he liked a board which offered possibilities for a sudden, paralysing *coup* by his queen. He had not been long in India before he began to discern in Tibet an opportunity—the only opportunity within the realm of practical politics—for just such a deployment.

Britain's tactical interests in Tibet have been summarised above. Of her wider, long-term interests this is the picture—nebulous but challenging—which had begun to emerge during the last decade of the nineteenth century.

Construction of the 3500-mile-long Trans-Siberian Railway, put in hand in 1891, unmistakably portended an intensification of Russian activities in Manchuria, Mongolia, China and Korea; in the last two countries Russia's interests were already in direct and on the whole successful competition with Britain's.

* Ronaldshay, Vol. II.

Four years later the Manchu Empire, pole-axed by Japan, appeared to be on the point of disintegration. It seemed that a great power-vacuum was about to be created, into important parts of which Russia, if only by virtue of her geographical position, was destined to expand.

Sinkiang, the huge Chinese dependency immediately to the north of Tibet, was one of the territories most likely—again for geographical reasons—to be annexed. Russia had occupied the Ili Valley in the 70's and still held a useful bridgehead there. In Kashgar her Consul-General, impressively attended by a Cossack escort, enjoyed greater prestige than Macartney, the British representative, whose consular status Peking declined to recognise. Rumours of a projected military railway which would link the Trans-Siberian line with Eastern Sinkiang and North West China were crystallised in a despatch to the Foreign Office in which, on 1 January 1898, the British Ambassador at St Petersburg recorded an interview with Count Witte, then the most powerful politician in Russia:

> Producing from a carefully locked desk a map of China, the Minister proceeded to draw his hand over the Provinces of Chihli, Shansi, Shensi and Kansu, and said that sooner or later Russia would probably absorb all this territory. Then putting his finger on Lanchow, he said that the Siberian Railway would in time run a branch line to this town.*

'Essentially,' Prince Ukhtomski, who was active in Far Eastern affairs, declared two years later, 'there are not and there cannot be any frontiers for us in Asia.'

When Curzon assumed the Viceroyalty nothing that could be called a British policy towards Tibet had been formulated. As long as Sinkiang remained under Chinese control, India's North East Frontier was insulated from Russia by two buffer-states, one on top of the other; but among the few experts who had studied the matter the consensus of opinion was that, if Sinkiang was annexed by Russia, some assertion of British

* Dallin: *The Rise of Russia in Asia.*

influence in Tibet would be desirable, if not essential. An invasion of India across the inhospitable plateaux of the Changtang was not seriously feared; but nobody liked the idea of Russia establishing a hold over the religious centre of the Buddhist world (which included the whole of Mongolia), and, as Bower, a British soldier-explorer, pointed out, 'two hundred men and a couple of mountain guns could take Lhasa and that number of Russians there would be sufficient to cause restlessness among the natives of Calcutta.' 'Unless we secure the reversion of Lhasa,' wrote Sir John Ardagh, the Director of Military Intelligence, in 1898, 'we may find the Russians there before us.'

Despite the cold clarity of his mind, Curzon took a romantic view of the Great Game,* the semi-clandestine duel in which the agents of two Empires contended in the desolate Asiatic uplands; 'its incidents,' he once wrote in words which might almost have come from the pen of John Buchan, 'and what I may describe as its incomparable drama are the possession of a few silent men, who may be found in the clubs of London, or Paris, or Berlin, when they are not engaged in tracing lines upon the unknown corners of the earth.' Line-tracing, as part of a rather cloudy *Kriegspiel*, appealed to the strategist in him. 'South of a certain line in Asia,' he wrote in 1899, 'her [Russia's] future is much more what we choose to make it than what she can make it herself.'

In this pronouncement the hard core of practical meaning is no longer readily to be detected; but perhaps it helps to illustrate the strong attraction which a Tibetan problem, once he got his teeth into it, was bound to have for Curzon. Here, on the Roof of the World, there was space for manoeuvre, scope for brilliance and boldness. Further west the Great Game was becoming inhibited by the terrible consequences of a false step. The grey and khaki pawns, if they were not yet jostling each

* This expression made its first appearance in print in Kaye's *History of the War in Afghanistan* (1843). It seems, however, to have been coined by Captain Arthur Conolly, a daring but in the end an unlucky player of the Great Game, who was beheaded after torture at Bokhara in 1842 (Davis).

other, could no longer make a move of any significance without endangering world peace. Only in Tibet, where neither side's pieces were as yet committed, might an adroit stroke thwart the adversary's plans before he could put them into effect.

Throughout the first two years of Curzon's Viceroyalty the Government of India—seconded, when it was deemed necessary to bring pressure to bear on the Chinese, by the Foreign Office in London—continued its patient attempts to settle affairs on the Tibetan frontier. These attempts had now been going on since 1890; they proved no more efficacious in the last two years of the century than they had in the previous eight. The far from exigent terms of the Convention of 1890 and the Trade Regulations of 1893 were ignored. An illegal tariff continued to be levied on the trickle of trade entering Tibet from India. The boundary remained undemarcated. From meetings arranged between Tibetan and Chinese representatives and the only British official in an area roughly the size of Yorkshire it was normal for the Tibetans to absent themselves without explanation, while the Chinese emissary would excuse himself on the grounds that the Tibetans, a people 'naturally doltish and prone to doubts and misgivings,' had failed to provide him with transport. Any hope that the Chinese might be induced to take a more serious view of their treaty obligations was dispelled by the outbreak of the Boxer Rebellion. A situation had arisen—had, indeed, existed without showing any improvement for ten years—which the Government of India could not, without dereliction of its duty, tolerate any longer.

On 11 August 1900 the Viceroy dispatched a letter to the Dalai Lama.

CHAPTER TWO

Emissaries and Agents

THE best part of three years was to elapse between the date on which Lord Curzon sent his first letter to the Dalai Lama and that on which the spearhead of the Tibet Frontier Commission entered the latter's domains. From this period there survives a vast mass of official correspondence dealing, or attempting to deal, with the Tibetan problem. It may however be hazarded that this extensive *paperasserie* includes no documents of greater significance than the two personal letters sent by the Viceroy to the Dalai Lama. Since neither, so far as is known, was read by its intended recipient, this statement requires elucidation.

Curzon's decision to place himself in direct communication with the Dalai Lama was taken after the failure of every attempt to enter into negotiations with the Tibetan authorities through less exalted channels; 'this solemn farce,' he wrote of these rebuffs, 'has been re-enacted with a frequency which seems never to deprive it of its attractions.' By his own intervention he was not, as he saw it, drawing a bow at a venture; he was bringing up a big gun. For it so happened that, when it came to writing letters to Oriental potentates and achieving the purpose for which they were written, the Viceroy had some excuse for regarding his qualifications as exceptional.

In 1894 Curzon, who although a Member of Parliament held no official position, determined upon a visit to the Amir of Afghanistan, a country to which access was by no means easy. In London efforts were made to dissuade him from this project, in India obstacles were placed in his path; but Curzon pressed

Curzon

The Thirteenth Dalai Lama

on regardless of opposition and eventually, riding into Kabul with an escort of two hundred Afghan cavalry, was lodged in a suite of the Amir's palace where the sheets were of cerise-coloured silk, the quilts of gold and silver brocade, and the chandeliers innumerable.

This favoured treatment Curzon owed, at least in part, to a letter covering seven large pages of vellum which he had addressed to the Amir. For a long time, he informed this blood-thirsty autocrat, 'it has been my principal and incessant desire to be permitted to visit the dominions of Your Highness; so that I might offer my salaams to the powerful and liberal-minded Sovereign of whom I have so often written and spoken [and whom, five years later, he was publicly to describe as 'cruel, vindictive and overweeningly proud'*]. Khorasan I have seen and visited; I have been in Bokhara and Samarkand. I have ridden to Chaman, and sojourned in Peshawar. But the dominions of Your Highness, which are situated in the middle of all these territories like unto a rich stone in the middle of a ring, I have never been permitted to enter; and the person of Your Highness, which is in your own dominions like unto the sparkle in the heart of the diamond, I have not been fortunate enough to see.' And so on.

Curzon had in a marked degree what Sir Harold Nicolson has called 'a tendency to approach all public questions from a personal point of view.' † It can scarcely be doubted that when he wrote his first letter to the Dalai Lama he had in mind the auspicious results produced by that earlier essay in Benares-ware prose; and there is ample evidence that the churlish treatment accorded to both the missives which he addressed to Lhasa produced on the Viceroy's mind a sense of personal affront which thereafter exerted upon his handling of the Tibetan problem an invigorating and at times a slightly un-balancing effect.

The first letter, which in firm but courteous terms invited the Dalai Lama to use his authority in securing a settlement of the

* *Russia in Central Asia.*
† *Curzon: The Last Phase.*

matters at issue, was taken by a British officer stationed at Leh to Gartok, in the confines of North Western Tibet, and was there delivered to the joint Governors of that region, known as the Urkhus, for onward transmission to the capital. It was dated 11 August 1900. Six months later the letter was returned to Leh; the seals were broken but nobody, it was explained, had dared to forward it. Curzon was exceedingly annoyed; 'the action taken by the Urkhu of Gartok seems to me to have been both improper and insulting.' He embarked on a second letter.

The prospects that this would be delivered appeared rosier. It was entrusted, in June 1901, to a Bhutanese official called Ugyen Kazi, who had already made one unsuccessful attempt to act as an intermediary with the Dalai Lama and who was about to return to Lhasa with a consignment of two elephants, two peacocks and a leopard which that dignitary had ordered for his private zoo.

Curzon's second letter was a good deal less urbane than his first. 'I wish,' he wrote, 'to impress on Your Holiness that, whilst I retain the desire to enter into friendly relations with yourself, and to promote a better understanding between the two nations, yet if no attempt is made to reciprocate these feelings, and if, on the contrary, they are treated with rudeness and indifference, my Government must reserve their right to take such steps as may seem to them necessary and proper to enforce the terms of the Treaty, and to ensure that the Trade Regulations are observed.'

Bearing this stern communication in a silken envelope covered with sealing-wax and honorifics, Ugyen Kazi disappeared into the mountains at the head of his menagerie.*

Four months later he returned, still bearing the letter. Its carapace of seals was intact. It was impossible to establish with accuracy whether the Dalai Lama had refused to receive it or

* One of the elephants died on the way. The leopard, although its transport must have presented serious problems, and the second elephant survived the journey.

whether Ugyen Kazi, losing his nerve, had made no attempt to deliver it. What was clear was that the epistolary approach, which five years ago had unlocked the gates of Kabul, was no Open Sesame at Lhasa. Lord Curzon was in the position of a brilliant golfer who, at a hole which he did in one last time, has just sliced two powerful drives into the rough.

He was not unprepared for this second disappointment. On 25 July 1901 he had telegraphed to the Secretary of State for India, Lord George Hamilton: 'Should this letter meet with the fate of its predecessor, we contemplate, subject to the approval of His Majesty's Government, the adoption of more practical measures with a view to securing the commercial and political facilities which our friendly representations will have failed to procure. As to the exact form which our altered policy should assume, we shall, if necessary, address your Lordship at a later date. But we may add that, before long, steps may require to be taken for the adequate safeguarding of British interests upon a part of the frontier where they have never hitherto been impugned.'

Lord George's reply reflected the misgivings aroused in London by the slightest symptom of viceregal bellicosity. The Government of India, the Secretary of State was ready to admit, 'would be justified in adopting strong measures. At the same time any such move . . . would be viewed with much disquietude and suspicion. . . . The character of the country, rugged and sparsely inhabited, is against the conduct of important military operations.' (Nobody had mentioned military operations.) The message ended by requesting that the Secretary of State should be consulted 'before any steps are taken that may involve a risk of the complications I have indicated.'

As one follows the long trail of official correspondence which led, deviously and hesitantly, up to the British invasion of Tibet, it is impossible not to feel that Curzon's two letters to the Dalai Lama were a landmark in it. 'His approach to external problems,' Sir Harold Nicolson has observed, 'was frequently coloured by prejudices deriving from some unpleasant personal experience, often so trivial as to escape conscious notice.' There is no avoiding the impression that Curzon's failure to communicate with the Dalai Lama was such an experience, that it rankled, and that he placed a disproportionate emphasis on it. He had, after all, no reason to believe that he had been deliberately insulted. The first letter, as far as anybody in India knew, had never got further than a subordinate official in a border-town; there was no proof that anyone in Lhasa, other than the Bhutanese elephant-coper, knew of the existence of the second.

Yet Curzon chose to take the view that a slight had been offered to the Viceroy, both in his own person and as the representative of the King-Emperor. Allusions to the matter recur throughout the documents with which he built up against Tibet a case that was strong enough without this small and hypothetical grievance. With the 'rejection' of his letters the Tibetan frontier ceased to be merely one of those small, untidy, aggravating problems which a dynamic Viceroy was impatient to clear up; the Tibetan hinterland was no longer a chess-board on which fascinating if perhaps rather academic possibilities of discountenancing Russia could be plotted. Tibet became something about which that strange human being, George Nathaniel Curzon, minded very much, without quite knowing why.

The intelligence which at this period reached India from Central Tibet was scanty, unreliable and difficult to evaluate; 'in 1898 . . . the Indian Government knew less of what went on in Lhasa and Shigatse than it did at the time of Warren Hastings.'* Its main regular sources of enlightenment were:

(a) The Government of Bengal forwarded periodical reports from its frontier-officers at Darjeeling, Kalimpong and elsewhere. These were normally based on information volunteered by or elicited from travellers and traders coming out of Tibet; the information was seldom less than several weeks old and,

---

* Lamb: *Britain and Chinese Central Asia*, Vol. I.

even when not deliberately fabricated, was often confused and misleading.*

(*b*) The British Minister in Peking repeated to India telegrams in which he apprised the Foreign Office of such news about Tibet as was current, from time to time, in Peking or filtered through to British Consulates in Western China, mainly from missionaries stationed in the Tibetan borderlands.

(*c*) Colonel Ravenshaw, the British Resident at Katmandu, sent in extracts from the despatches received by the Government of Nepal from their representative at Lhasa. This man, who seems to have been intelligent and pertinacious, reported frequently and at great length. Of the three regular sources he was easily the most illuminating; but most of his reports took the form of verbatim transcripts of his conversations with Tibetan and Chinese officials, and from these dreamlike disputations it was not always easy to distil any very clear meaning. This passage, for instance, taken from an account of an interview with the Four Kazis † early in 1904, illustrates not unfairly the difficulty of gauging the trend of affairs in Lhasa from the Nepalese Agent's reports:

'*I*. It is not only by taking the leavings of one affected with catarrh that one catches cold; but one may catch cold by taking such unwholesome food as brings on that disease. If one drinks cold water or takes sweets or fish, the cold gets worse. A matter can only be settled amicably when you speak for both sides, dealing justice evenly. I need scarcely have mentioned these facts so well known to you.

'*The Kazis*. What you say is true. Medication is necessary, and we are discussing the treatment.

'*I*. Please administer medicine quick. Should the catarrh grow worse it may turn into ozina, and in that case the ulceration in the nose will disfigure the countenance.'

* "The local English officers of these districts are very desirous of knowing anything about Tibet, and they would write down any tidings brought them, not distinguishing whether they were true or not." Ekai Kawaguchi: *Three Years in Tibet*. The writer is referring to this period.

† The Kazis, known to the Tibetans as Shapés, formed a kind of Privy Council on whose advice the Dalai Lama was in theory supposed to rely.

There were other obstacles, too, to the interpretation of Tibetan intelligence garnered from these diverse sources. Names of people and places were transliterated in so many different ways that they were often impossible to identify with any certainty. A close student came in time to realise that 'the Prefect Ho Kuang-hsi' referred to in the telegrams from China was none other than 'the Fapoon Hotarin' with whom the Nepalese Agent held intermittent and allusive converse; but many proper names which featured less regularly in the reports were devoid of any save the most conjectural significance. Dates, too, helped to blur the picture, since (for instance) the Tibetan, the Chinese and the Nepalese calendars differed not only from the Gregorian but from each other, and the knowledge that it had been composed on 'Monday, the 29th Marga, Sambat 1960' did nothing to clarify the obscurities contained in a Nepalese despatch.

When Curzon reached India on the last day but one of the year 1898, the long-standing Tibetan frontier-dispute was not among the matters which made immediate claims upon his boundless energy and his zeal for reform. He first addressed the Home Government on the subject on 30 March 1899, in terms which echo the desire to dispose of a minor irritant rather than any particular sense of urgency.

'We seem,' wrote the Government of India in the Foreign Department to the Secretary of State, 'in respect of our policy towards Tibet, to be moving in a vicious circle. If we apply to Tibet, we either receive no reply, or are referred to the Chinese Resident. If we apply to the latter, he excuses his failure by his inability to put any pressure upon Tibet. As a policy this appears to us both unproductive and inglorious. We shall be grateful for your Lordship's opinion as to the advisability of any modification of it in the near future.'

It was in this minor key that Tibetan affairs continued to be discussed for the next eighteen months. Although China was involved in its solution, the problem was seen as a quasi-domestic one. No wider implications loomed, as yet, behind the grazing-rights, the boundary-pillars and the trade-facilities which had been for ten years in dispute. In the tumescent files of official correspondence only fleeting references to Russia occurred: as when, on 30 April 1899, the Political Officer in Sikkim quoted a Chinese official as saying that 'if the Indian Government insisted on the Convention boundary, as understood by us, the Tibetans would fall back on the support of Russia, who had already offered them assistance.'

Curzon must have read this report, for he read everything. At about the same time rumours reached the Government of India from a private source in Darjeeling that a party of Russians had visited Lhasa during the previous winter. On 24 May 1899 Curzon wrote to Lord George Hamilton: 'There seems little doubt that Russian agents, and possibly even someone of Russian origin, have been at Lhasa, and I believe that the Tibetan Government is coming to the conclusion that it will have to make friends with one or other of the two Great Powers.'

The Viceroy's interest had been aroused; but it cannot be said that even in his receptive mind the spectre of a Russian threat to India through Lhasa had yet been conjured up.

In October 1900, far from the boundaries of Tibet, an event occurred that drastically altered the perspective through which the British viewed the North East Frontier of India.

On the 22nd of that month a short despatch reached the Foreign Office in London from H.M. Chargé d'Affaires in St Petersburg. 'I have the honour,' wrote Mr Hardinge, 'to enclose an extract from the official column of the *Journal de Saint-Pétersbourg* of the 15th instant, announcing the reception by His Majesty the Emperor on the 30th September of Aharamba-Agyan-Dorjief, who is described as "first Tsanit Hamba to the Dalai Lama of Tibet." ' The audience had taken place in the Livadia Palace, at the Black Sea resort of Yalta. 'I have not been able, so far,' Mr Hardinge added, 'to procure any precise information with regard to this person or to the mission on which he is supposed to have come to Russia.' It later transpired that Dorjieff (to use the commonest version of his name*) had delivered to the Tsar a letter from the Dalai Lama.

Although at this, his first appearance on the international stage, Dorjieff aroused in India and in England no more than a suspicious curiosity, it is scarcely possible to exaggerate his importance, over the next four years, as a formative influence on British policy towards Tibet. In June 1901 he was back in Russia (having, it was discovered with chagrin, made a clandestine transit of India on his way from Lhasa to St Petersburg), and this time he was at the head of what the Russian Press described as an 'Extraordinary Mission of eight prominent Tibetan statesmen,' which was said to have as its object the 'strengthening of good relations between Russia and Tibet' and the 'establishment in St Petersburg of a permanent Tibetan Mission' for this purpose. The Tibetan envoys had audience of both the Emperor and the Empress, to whom they presented gifts and a letter from the Dalai Lama. They had a letter, too, for the Foreign Minister, Count Lamsdorff.

They were a nine days' wonder in the Russian capital, where the newspapers drew the obvious conclusions from their unheralded but gratifying visit. The *Novoe Vremya* saw it as a logical consequence not only of the favourable impressions formed by Dorjieff in the preceding year but of the renown attending Russian victories in Manchuria and North China. 'Under the circumstances, a *rapprochement* with Russia must seem to the Dalai Lama the most natural step, as Russia is the only Power able to counteract the intrigues of Great Britain, who has so long been endeavouring to obtain admission to Tibet, and only awaits an opportunity to force an entrance.' Unkind things were said about the ill-success of British arms in South Africa, 'where England has striven in vain to deprive a small but valiant people of its independence. Perhaps [mused

---

* Variants included Doroshiyeff, Dorzhievy and Darjew. In reports from Lhasa Dorjieff was generally referred to as 'the Tse-nyi-ken-po', which was the designation of his official Tibetan appointment and means 'Abbot of Metaphysics.'

the *Novoe Vremya*] rumours of the Boers' heroic struggle have penetrated to Tibet.'

For the authorities in London and in India a vista of ominous possibilities was opened up by the news from St Petersburg, and what little could be learnt about the background of the 'Extraordinary Mission' was the reverse of reassuring. Dorjieff, it appeared, was a Buryat Mongol by birth and thus a Russian citizen by nationality.* A Captain Ulanov, of the 1st Regiment of Don Cossacks, had, according to the *Messager Officiel*, been attached to the Mission as an interpreter. How many more Cossacks, wondered British students of the Great Game, could speak Tibetan? The whole mysterious episode, without precedent in Tibetan history, might have been specifically designed to convince trained and already suspicious observers that Russia harboured designs on Tibet.

Count Lamsdorff did what he could to allay the British Ambassador's misgivings; it was not much. The idea, he told Sir Charles Scott in early July, that 'these Tibetan visitors were charged with any diplomatic or political mission' was 'ridiculous and utterly unfounded.' He understood that Dorjieff 'occasionally' came to Russia to collect monetary subscriptions from his fellow-Buddhists, of whom there were a large number in the Tsar's domains; thus 'the Mission was of the same character as those sent by the Pope to the faithful in foreign lands.' Dorjieff was a member of the Russian Geographical Society who 'at present held some post of confidence in the Dalai Lama's service.' As for the letter addressed to the Russian Foreign Minister from Lhasa, 'it was found on translation to be very concise and simple. It merely expressed a hope that Count Lamsdorff was in the enjoyment of good health and prosperous, and informed him that the Dalai Lama was happy to be able to say that he himself enjoyed excellent health.'

* The Buryats, a tribe of nomadic Mongols whose homelands lie at the southern end of Lake Baikal, were subdued and absorbed into Russia in the eighteenth century. After the Bolshevik Revolution Buryat Mongolia became an Autonomous Soviet Socialist Republic in 1923.

Captain Ulanov was a Buryat who chanced to be conversant with Tibetan. There was, in a word, no cause for alarm.

The British Government did what Governments often do when given assurances whose value they regard as dubious. They desired their Ambassador to inform Count Lamsdorff that his explanation had been received 'with satisfaction,' and at the same time to point out that 'His Majesty's Government could not regard with indifference any proceedings which might have a tendency to alter or disturb the existing status of Tibet.' These instructions Sir Charles Scott carried out on 2 September 1901, receiving from the Russian Foreign Minister a renewal of his former pledges.

Dorjieff is said to have been born in 1853. At the age of nineteen he made his way to Tibet and entered the monastery of Drebung near Lhasa. He seems to have been a diligent and gifted student of metaphysics and by 1888 had achieved a position which brought him into close contact with the Dalai Lama. Mongols, however pious, had in theory no right of entry into the Tibetan priesthood, but Dorjieff used his influence at court to overcome the prejudice against his fellow-Buryats. Since these were Russian citizens, Dorjieff could not plead their cause without at the same time disarming suspicions of, and perhaps arousing curiosity about, Russia; and it may well have been in this semi-fortuitous way, rather than as the convinced advocate of closer Russo-Tibetan relations, that Dorjieff came to be employed as an intermediary.

On his first visit to St Petersburg in 1898 (no details of which were made public) he was received with 'restraint and distrust.'* The Tsar said that if Tibet wanted Russian help the Dalai Lama must ask for it officially in writing; 'only in the imperialist "great-power" circles was the idea of a Russo-Tibetan *rapprochement* treated favourably and Dorjieff

* *Novy Vostok.* No. 3, 1923. 'Towards Tibet's Struggle for Independence.' This early Soviet source appears to be based, at any rate in part, on Tsarist archives.

promised help.'* But on his second visit, in 1900, he found a warmer welcome; partly perhaps owing to the Boer War, Russia's interest in Tibet had quickened. The Tsar gave him a gold watch studded with diamonds to present to the Dalai Lama, together with vague assurances of Russia's willingness to help Tibet. A third visit in the following year established closer but still undefined relations between the two countries.

Younghusband, years later, was given an account of Dorjieff's status which is interesting and plausible. On 21 April 1939 he wrote to the Marquess of Zetland (who as Lord Ronaldshay had been Curzon's biographer): 'The acting Russian Ambassador during the Great War told me that he was a Secretary in the Russian Foreign Office during my Mission to Tibet and could assure me that the Russian Government were in no kind of communication with the Dalai Lama. What, he said, did happen was that the Dalai Lama's tutor, Dorjieff, through Rasputin, got in personal touch with the Tsar and Tsarina. There was an interchange of presents between the Tsar and the Dalai Lama. The Tsar seemed to acknowledge some kind of spiritual guidance from the Dalai Lama; and the latter thought he was under the political protection of the Tsar.' Although uncorroborated, this version of affairs may well be close to the truth.

Historically the importance of Dorjieff lies, not in what he was, but in what he appeared to be. He had undoubtedly much influence with the Dalai Lama; in some Russian circles—adventurous rather than influential—he was regarded as a useful catspaw; and he represented possibilities which made a strong appeal to the combination of vanity with mysticism which formed part of Nicholas II's character.† But all these

---

* *Ibid.*

† Cf. Letter from Sir Cecil Spring Rice to Sir Charles Hardinge, dated St Petersburg, 15 March 1906: 'I expect that the Emperor is immensely pleased by the compliments lavished on him by the Dalai Lama. . . . He likes being called the stepson of Heaven and the 169th incarnation. . . . Lamsdorff and the Foreign Office don't approve. . . . The Emperor has had a sad disappointment. There was an inscription on the embroidery

attributes, though they were real enough, could not have produced upon the march of events a small fraction of the influence exerted by the far more potent, but largely chimerical, status with which Dorjieff came to be invested in the imaginations of the British. If his comings and goings between the Dalai Lama and the Russian Court had been kept secret (as was his first interview with the Tsar in 1898)—if he had been, in other words, the sort of sinister *éminence grise* which the British saw in him—his impact on the history of twentieth-century Tibet would have been small. As it was, this impact proved considerable.

It is necessary to recall in what kind of a light, against what kind of a background, the portent of Dorjieff presented itself to the British authorities. He was, as Lamb has pointed out, 'the sort of agent whom Curzon would dearly have liked to possess.' His debut as a go-between occurred two months after the despatch of Curzon's first letter to the Dalai Lama, which was itself the sequel to numerous and unsuccessful attempts to open a more normal channel of communication with Lhasa;* his second appearance in St Petersburg almost exactly coincided with the departure of Ugyen Kazi and his elephants, bearing the Viceroy's second letter.

The Tibetans had explained in a variety of ways their traditional tabu on entering into correspondence with foreigners. The Dalai Lama, for instance, told Ugyen Kazi in the summer of 1901 that 'he was precluded from writing any letter to any

---

presented to him and he thought it was one of his new titles. It turned out to be the Chinese advertisement of a Shanghai firm. . . . The real reason [for the Emperor's Tibetan aspirations] is the idea which he has fixed in his mind that, if he assumes or is given the right to act as temporal protector of the chief centre of the Buddhist faith, he will become the moral chief of the continent of Asia.' (*The Letters and Friendships of Sir Cecil Spring Rice.*)

* In a private letter written to the Secretary of State in November 1900 Curzon, uncharacteristically and for the last time, scouted the importance of Dorjieff, whom he described as probably 'a fraud' who 'does not come from Lhasa at all. . . . Tibet is, I think, much more likely to look to us for protection than to look to Russia, and I cherish a secret hope that the communication which I am trying to open with the Dalai Lama may inaugurate some sort of relation between us.'

Foreign Government,' as one of his predecessors had made an agreement 'that no letters should be written without first consulting the [Chinese] Amban;' while in the previous year the Urkhus of Gartok had excused themselves from forwarding Curzon's letter to Lhasa on the grounds that it was 'contrary to regulations.' Dorjieff's mission to a Power with whom Tibet shared no common frontier and had no commercial or treaty relations exhibited in a new and most disquieting light the façade of unapproachability behind which the Lhasa authorities had been sheltering from the British. Since the Dalai Lama could write letters to the Emperor of Russia, it was not easy to place a charitable interpretation on his refusal to read letters from the Viceroy of India. Dorjieff's jack-in-the-box appearances at the Imperial Court in 1900 and 1901 proclaimed—or seemed to proclaim—an active and reciprocated Russian interest in Tibet; and thereafter it was inevitable that the mysterious Buryat should bulk larger and larger in the minds of all concerned with India's North East Frontier. The Tibetan problem, for so long a petty administrative–diplomatic imbroglio, began to assume a strategic significance.

After December 1901, when he was reported as having had audience of the Russian Empress, Dorjieff vanished from the British view; but in August of the following year intelligence reached the Foreign Office which seemed all too likely to be a sequel to his activities behind the scenes.

On 2 August 1902 the British Minister at Peking, Sir Ernest Satow, reported by telegraph that rumours were current of a secret agreement between Russia and China over Tibet. A few days later he forwarded an extract from the *China Times* summarising the alleged terms of this agreement. Of the twelve clauses, these were the most important:

> 1. China, conscious of her weakness, undertook to relinquish her interest in Tibet to Russia, in return for Russia's support in maintaining the integrity of the Chinese Empire.

2. Russia pledged this support, which would be forthcoming 'so soon as her interests in Tibet have been secured.'

3. Russia would suppress any disturbances in the interior of China with which the Chinese Government found itself unable to cope.

4. Russia would 'establish Government officers in Tibet and control Tibetan affairs.' China would have the right of stationing Consuls in the country.

5. Russia would abstain from introducing Christianity into Tibet, and in the construction of railways and fortifications would avoid the desecration of 'temples and other sacred spots.'

6. China would be allowed to participate in mining and railway enterprises, and Chinese imports would be either duty-free or very lightly taxed.

It was hardly possible to dispute the newspaper's contention that its report 'furnished interesting reading.' It might be incomplete, or premature; it might contain inaccuracies, distortions or ommissions. But it had so plausible an air that it was difficult to reject it, *in toto*, as without foundation. It appeared, Satow reported, to have originated in a newspaper in Soochow, a town which (he might have added), though traditionally famed for the beauty of its women, contained no foreign settlement or consulates and was therefore an unlikely launching-ground for a *ballon d'essai*.

In London the story of a secret Russo-Chinese treaty was taken seriously—the more so since other and strikingly similar versions of the same story were coming in from a wide variety of sources. Satow was instructed to warn the Chinese Government against concluding any such arrangement and to tell them that, if they did, His Majesty's Government would be 'certainly forced to take steps for protecting the interests of Great Britain.' The Chinese denied vigorously that a transaction of this kind had even been discussed with Russia. A parallel *démarche*, backed by the threat that any Russian interference in Tibet would provoke a strong British reaction,* elicited from the Russian Government, after some delay, an equally categorical disclaimer.

The Russian assurances were comprehensive and unequivocal. But there were precedents—the seizure of Merv in 1884 provided one—for equally fervent diplomatic protestations being followed by the very deeds from which the Imperial Government had undertaken to abstain. In London, moreover, it was believed, with reason, that the Russian Foreign Office had sometimes imperfect knowledge, and almost always imperfect control, of the activities of other ministries. 'Trustworthy engagements with Russia,' Lord Salisbury had publicly pointed out in 1885, 'are not things which we can count upon obtaining'; he went on to observe that the promises of a bankrupt, who failed to honour them, were worth no more than the promises of a swindler, who broke them deliberately. 'Unless,' as a British diplomat wrote from St Petersburg a year or two later, 'an agreement is made direct with the Emperor, it is of no avail: one department (e.g. the Foreign Office) cannot bind another (e.g. the War Office): the Emperor alone has the power to bind the country.' On 7 November 1903 Count Benckendorff, the Russian Ambassador in London, in an interview with Lord Lansdowne 'dwelt upon the peculiar situation which had been created by the establishment of the new Far Eastern Viceroyalty [under Admiral Alexeieff, in July 1903]. The result had been that the foreign policy of Russia at this point was no longer one and undivided. He evidently [Lord Lansdowne commented] wished me to understand that many things happened for which Count Lamsdorff could not be held responsible.'

In these circumstances it is hardly surprising that smoke continued to hang thickly in the air long after the existence of a fire had been officially denied. The story of the secret treaty

* 'If they sent a mission or an expedition,' Lord Lansdowne told the Russian Ambassador in London on 18 February 1903, 'we should have to do the same, but in greater strength.' The Russian Government's formal denial that it had designs of any kind on Tibet was received in London on 8 April.

came altogether too pat upon the revelation of Dorjieff's role as a high-level intermediary between Lhasa and St Petersburg. The two bogeys were complementary; each lent to the other a verisimilitude which it was beyond the power of the most solemn *démentis* to dispel. 'The story of the Russo-Chinese agreement as to Tibet,' Lord Lansdowne minuted on 1 October 1902, 'is supported by a good deal of evidence.' 'I am myself,' Curzon wrote six weeks later, 'a firm believer in the existence of a secret understanding, if not a secret treaty, between Russia and China about Tibet; and, as I have said before, I regard it as a duty to frustrate their little game while there is yet time.'

On the massive files marked TIBET, borne lethargically by uniformed *chaprassis* from one office to another in Calcutta or in Simla, the name of Russia, which during the last decade of the nineteenth century had made only sparse and random appearances, now figured with a growing regularity.

Dorjieff

Monks and Nuns

CHAPTER THREE

The Unknown Land

To Asia, of which it forms a part, Tibet's uncouth and lofty fastnesses seem never to have issued any particular challenge. Officials of the Manchu Empire regarded a tour of duty there as a thankless penance, normally the consequence of flagrant misdemeanours or a heavy fall from grace. Buddhist pilgrims from Mongolia and elsewhere occasionally embarked, from motives of piety, on a pilgrimage to Lhasa; there was a small Nepalese community and a sprinkling of Kashmiri traders in the capital. But for the generality of Asians Tibet held no more attractions than did the Scottish Highlands for the eighteenth-century Londoner.

On the West, however, its mysteries exerted a fascination which endures today. By the end of the nineteenth century there were few major enigmas left on the African continent. Save for Antarctica, whose austere secrets were already arousing the competitive instincts of explorers, Tibet was the only region of the world to which access was all but impossible for white men and concerning which the small sum of existing knowledge served rather to tantalise than to instruct.

Western contacts with Tibet began in 1627, when a Jesuit mission was established at Shigatse; more Jesuits, coming from Peking, reached Lhasa in 1661. Capuchins later took over the Lhasa mission, and these two outposts of an alien faith, whose rivalries did nothing to improve their security of tenure, retained—though not continuously—some sort of foothold in the country until 1745. During this period an enterprising Dutch traveller called van der Putte resided for thirteen years in

Tibet, which in 1720 had come under a loose form of Chinese domination.

Thirty years later the Chinese tightened their grip on the country. The last of its lay rulers was deposed, and thereafter the Dalai Lama, whose office had come into being at the end of the sixteenth century, became the temporal as well as the spiritual head of the state. He exercised his power through a Chief Minister and a cabinet of four councillors known as Shapés; but his authority was curtailed and his actions supervised by the Chinese Amban, a resident political agent representing the interests of Peking. The Dalai Lama was selected in infancy by a process of divination, each incumbent being supposedly a reincarnation of his predecessor, and for the first eighteen years of his life his temporal powers devolved upon a Regent. The attractions of the Regency were great, a fact which may partly explain the high mortality rate—one in three —among Incarnations during their minority. These casualties caused no distress to the Chinese, who may well have had a hand in bringing them about; a reigning Dalai Lama was always liable to weaken the Suzerain Power's position by providing a rallying-point for the forces of Tibetan nationalism.

The first British visitor to Central Tibet went there, surprisingly, in response to a Tibetan invitation. In 1774 the Tashi Lama,* who was acting as Regent during the infancy of the Dalai Lama, wrote to Warren Hastings to intercede for the Bhutanese, whose turbulence on the frontiers of Bengal was being severely punished by the forces of the East India Company, and who were then regarded by the Tibetans as their vassals. Warren Hastings immediately despatched George Bogle, a young man of twenty-eight, to Shigatse (where the Tashi Lama lived) with wide discretionary powers to open diplomatic and if possible commercial relations with Tibet.

The Tashi Lama was an unusually intelligent and open-minded man; Bogle was candid, tactful and determined. The Lhasa authorities, however, sheltered behind the same pre-

* Nowadays known as the Panchen Lama.

judices and suspicions which were in evidence 130 years later, and nothing very concrete came of Bogle's mission. But he himself was enchanted by the Tibetans ('Farewell, ye honest and simple people! May ye long enjoy the happiness which is denied to more polished nations!'); and his visit, by breaking the ice and sowing the seeds of goodwill, laid foundations on which, in time, some form of intercourse between Tibet and India might be established.

In 1782 (both Bogle and the Tashi Lama having, most unfortunately, died in the interim) Warren Hastings, who hoped among other things to get at the China trade by the back-door, sent a second emissary into Tibet. Captain Samuel Turner, like his predecessor, came no nearer to Lhasa than Shigatse, but he too managed partially to dismantle the barriers of suspicion, only to discover, as Bogle had and as Curzon would, that behind them stood the still more formidable obstacle of Chinese influence, which, whether invoked as a valid reason or as a facile pretext, was always capable of blocking diplomatic or commercial approaches from India.

Ten years later the Nepalese invaded Tibet and sacked Shigatse; they were driven out by a Chinese army of unexpected prowess. By an unlucky coincidence the first British envoy to Nepal had arrived in Katmandu at about the time of this incursion; the sinister though unwarranted deductions drawn in Tibet from this concatenation led to the effectual severing of all connexion with India.

This deadlock (which owed much to the fact that Britain had as yet no properly established diplomatic relations with China) was broken in 1811 by an eccentric called Thomas Manning. He had been a friend of Charles Lamb, had left Cambridge without taking a degree in order to study Chinese, and, having failed to obtain recognition or assistance from the Indian authorities (to whom he may well have appeared a lunatic), embarked on his Tibetan adventure as a private individual, accompanied only by a Chinese servant whom he detested.

Perfunctorily disguised as a 'Chinese gentleman,' bearing 'two large handsome phials of Genuine Smith's Lavender

Water' as a present for the Dalai Lama, befriended by a flute-playing Chinese general, and selling as he went along personal effects which included gauze gowns, a fan and an opera glass, Manning minced across the Tibetan landscape like some character in Edward Lear. Yet he reached Lhasa; was received by the ninth Dalai Lama, then a boy of seven ('sometimes,' Manning credibly reported, 'particularly when he looked at me, his smile almost approached to a gentle laugh'); and came back unscathed, prostrating himself before every official he met, quarrelling pettishly with his servant, and recording in idiosyncratic terms his often ludicrous adventures. On his return to Calcutta he refused, from pique, to divulge any particulars of his singular excursion, and the journals in which he described it did not come to light until long after his death.

Manning was the last Englishman who is known to have reached Lhasa until the troops escorting the Tibet Frontier Commission marched into the city with fixed bayonets in 1904. In 1846 two French priests of the Lazarist order, the Fathers Huc and Gabet, entered Tibet from the Chinese side and were permitted to spend some months in Lhasa. After their departure the Forbidden City, as it came to be called, relapsed into a state of inaccessibility which lasted, as far as Europeans were concerned, for more than half a century.

By the end of this period Lhasa represented for the adventurous a goal as unique, in its own way, as the peak of Everest was to become for mountaineers. Like flies buzzing round a meat-safe, more and more travellers launched themselves into the sparsely inhabited no man's land which, to the west, to the north and to the north-east, formed a huge, desolate glacis masking the closely guarded passes which alone gave access to the heart of the country and its capital.

From Britain came Bower, Carey, Littledale (with his hardy wife), Wellby, Deasy, Rawling and others; from France Bonvalot, Prince Henry of Orleans (whom the British did not take seriously), Grenard and Dutreuil de Rhins, who was murdered; from Sweden the vain, audacious Sven Hedin; and from Russia a series of well-found parties under leaders of whom Prjevalsky was the exemplar. The Russian expeditions, with their Cossack escorts and their Buryat or Kalmuk guides, had a less amateur, more military aspect than the others. Captain Kozloff, for instance, entered North Eastern Tibet in 1899 at the head of an armed band mustering three officers and nineteen men of the Moscow Grenadiers and the Transbaikal Cossacks and fifty-six camels; when he emerged in 1901 he had fought three actions with hostile Tibetans, in one of which he killed twenty-eight and wounded nineteen.

None of these parties reached Lhasa; to have penetrated to within two hundred miles of the capital was accounted a creditable achievement.

In 1901 a Japanese traveller, Ekai Kawaguchi, got through to Lhasa from Nepal and was received by the Dalai Lama. He passed himself off as a Chinese, and was greatly helped by his intimate knowledge of the Buddhist scriptures and his acquaintance with medicine, a science of which the Tibetans practised only a ghoulish caricature. But in the end he had to make a hasty and unobtrusive departure, and the Tibetans who had befriended him were severely punished for doing so.

There was, finally, a small but important category of explorers in the shape of the 'Pundits.' These were native agents who, from 1866 onwards, were sent into Tibet by the Survey of India to carry out clandestine reconnaissance, mainly of a topographical nature. They were known only by code-names or initials and travelled in disguise. Nain Sing, the first of them, measured distances along his route with the help of a rosary which, comprising 100 beads instead of the statutory 108, made it easier to pace out the miles; and his successors used a variety of simple expedients, such as compasses hidden in prayer-wheels, to facilitate their formidable task.

Loyal, brave, patient and conveniently inexpensive, these humble spies covered thousands of miles of Tibetan territory, and thanks to them the main geographical features of Central Tibet were recorded with a general accuracy by the Survey of India. One at least—Sarat Chandra Das, on whom Kipling based the character of Hurree Chunder Mookerjee in *Kim*—

reached the capital; and Sven Hedin paid a compliment (which he probably meant to be back-handed) to the native agents employed by both sides in the Great Game when he wrote:

> Truly it was a crazy project to risk so much, my life included, mainly for the pleasure of seeing Lhasa, a city which, thanks to the descriptions of Indian Pundits and Russian Buryats, their maps and photographs, is far better known than most other towns in Central Asia.*

From this brief summary it will be apparent that in 1900 Tibet differed subtly but unmistakably from other empty squares on the international chessboard. It had about it a mystery, an allure, which were lacking (for instance) from Afghanistan, for so long a cockpit of Russo-British rivalries. It stirred men's curiosities, aroused their sporting instincts; it had a brighter lustre than the other counters in the game. And the British attitude to it was, if not dog-in-the-mangerish, at least faintly proprietorial. There was no impulse to intervene in Tibet as long as Tibet remained a vacuum; but, as Curzon reminded the Secretary of State early in 1903, 'the policy of exclusiveness to which the Tibetan Government has during the last century become increasingly addicted has only been tolerated by us because, anomalous and unfriendly as it has been, it carried with it no element of political or military danger.' This situation had now, to all appearances, changed.

Though striking and voluminous, the evidence on which the British based their increasingly lively distrust of Russian intentions towards Tibet was not conclusive. Time has shown that it was misleading. The rumour of the secret treaty with China was false; nor was Dorjieff an agent in the employ of the Russian Government. But when men believe that witches and goblins exist, or that the works of Shakespeare were written by Bacon, they seldom have difficulty in accumulating proofs that their convictions are well-founded; and British intelligence,

* *Central Asia and Tibet.*

hypnotised by a fundamental illusion, built up in support of its validity an elaborate dossier of clues from which the element of truth was almost wholly lacking, and to which plausibility was lent only by the sponsoring fallacies.

It would however be quite wrong to suggest that the British had no cause to worry. Although it was not, as they persuaded themselves, imminent, Russian intervention in Tibet boded dangers which they had strong grounds for wishing to avert. Of these dangers they took an objective, not an alarmist view. A direct military invasion of India through Tibet was at no time feared. Lhasa was more than a thousand miles from the nearest frontier-post in Russian Central Asia, from which it was separated by virtually impassable natural barriers; 'a large [Russian] force would starve and a small one could be easily driven out or crushed by a superior force from India,' Major Bower had reported to the Director of Military Intelligence in 1898.

The British fear, which in the climate of those times cannot be dismissed as morbid, was of political infiltration which would establish Russian influence at Lhasa. A Russian 'protectorate' over Tibet was often spoken of; and although this, as the British would have realised if they had known more about the Tibetans, was an overstated conception, the possibility of Russian agents gaining a quasi-diplomatic status in Lhasa was clearly on the cards. To hold a bridgehead, however circum-scribed, at the acknowledged centre of the Buddhist faith would greatly enhance Russia's prestige in Asia, and notably in Mongolia, whose annexation she showed signs of contemplating; and the Government of India, which for years had striven to prevent Afghanistan from becoming a base for licensed Russian intrigues, viewed with extreme disfavour a parallel contingency in Tibet. 'We can, and ought to, prevent Russia getting a position which would inevitably cause unrest all along the North East Frontier,' wrote Lord Roberts in October 1902.

Over the past ten years India's relations with Tibet—in so far as relations could be said to exist at all—had been as un-satisfactory as possible; the assertion of Russian influence at

Lhasa could be relied upon to obliterate all prospects of improvement. There was moreover the important problem of the border states—Bhutan, Sikkim and Nepal, the last a recruiting-ground from which the Indian Army drew the flower of its infantry, the Gurkhas. Nepal was an independent kingdom; the other two enjoyed an autonomy which was qualified by their treaties with the British. But all three states had ancient ties with Tibet and, through Tibet, with China. In this sector the opportunities for mischief-making open to a Russian diplomatic outpost at Lhasa would be almost unlimited and might, if skilfully exploited, disintegrate the delicate system of subventions and allegiances upon which, rather than upon costly garrisons and strategic railways, the security of the North East Frontier depended.

Faced (as it believed) with these threats, the Government of India was clearly obliged to devise some form of remedial or preventive action. Throughout 1902, from St Petersburg, from Peking and from the frontier listening-posts, more and more reports poured in of secret agreements, of Russian agents and mining engineers and even military expeditions converging on Tibet. By the end of that year the Viceroy had become convinced that there was only one thing to do: send a mission up to Lhasa.

CHAPTER FOUR

The Pot and the Kettle

THE only surprising thing about the Viceroy's project was that neither he nor anybody else had suggested it before. In a private letter to the Secretary of State written in July 1901 he had indeed mentioned a mission to Lhasa, but only as a remote and almost academic possibility, one of the 'ideas which have hardly yet taken shape in my mind, and which are certainly by many stages removed from action.' This letter, which dealt severely with the failure of counter-intelligence in Bengal to prevent Dorjieff from twice travelling across the breadth of India on his way to Russia, visualised a blockade of the Tibetan frontier as a more practical method of bringing pressure to bear on the Tibetans.

Yet, without going back to Warren Hastings, there were precedents showing that in 1874, and again in 1885, the British Government had concerted arrangements for sending a commercial mission to Lhasa; both schemes, the second in particular, had reached an advanced stage before being abandoned for extraneous reasons. With these precedents Curzon made considerable play when urging upon London, early in 1903, the adoption of his new policy. It seems strange that they had not attracted his attention before, and that an expedient which, though it might prove difficult of execution, was in conception extremely simple, took nearly four years to enter his mind.

Once there, it became almost an obsession. The Tibetan problem was twofold. On the tactical level there was the old, humiliating deadlock over the frontier, the Trade Regulations and the flouted Convention; on the strategical level there was the need to forestall or sterilise the designs of Russia. By the end of 1902 it had become clear that only by gaining access to the Tibetan capital could the British hope to achieve their objectives in either field.

In the summer of that year, with the approval of the Home Government, a further step was taken towards the settlement of the frontier disputes, which resulted at least in a clearer definition of the issues involved. J. C. White, the Political Officer in Sikkim, was despatched to the Giaogong plateau (the scene of the most flagrant Tibetan trespasses) with an escort of a hundred and fifty Gurkhas; he was instructed not to cross the boundary as laid down by the Convention of 1890, but to evict any Tibetan guard-posts stationed on the wrong side of it.

White carried out these orders without provoking any serious incident; some valuable survey-work was done, and the Sikkimese grievance about grazing-rights was discovered to be at least partly illusory, since there was reciprocal use of pastures on both sides of the frontier. The Chinese however took umbrage, partly because they had not been informed of White's mission, and partly because of its military escort. They appointed two Commissioners to meet White and co-operate with him (one was an Englishman in the Chinese Customs Service, Captain Randall Parr); but these delegates were prevented, by various threadbare excuses, from reaching the frontier. So nothing of moment was achieved, and the only faint ray of hope that emerged from the proceedings was a report, telegraphed from Darjeeling after White's party had returned, that the Dalai Lama had 'asked Captain Parr to procure for him some artificial flowers, a trivial request, but one showing that the objection to Europeans must be on the decline.'

Thus matters stood when on 8 January 1903, in a luminous, forceful and closely reasoned despatch, the Viceroy recommended to the Secretary of State a radical departure from the policy of forbearance which, four years earlier, he had described as 'unproductive and inglorious.'

THE POT AND THE KETTLE

Curzon began by recapitulating, with none of the prolixity which was a besetting weakness of his style, the recent history of India's relations with Tibet. He recalled the failure of his attempts to communicate with the Dalai Lama. He described White's mission to the frontier; pointed out that, although successful, its outcome 'has not been materially to improve our position upon the border, or to effect anything more than a timely assertion of British authority upon the spot;' and found it probable that 'the chief advantage of Mr White's mission up to the present time consists in the fear inspired among the Tibetans that it is the prelude to some further movement—an advantage which would be wholly sacrificed when the discovery was made that no such consequence was likely to ensue.'

He turned next to the reports of Russia's designs upon Tibet. There was 'much circumstantial evidence' of their truth. In the light of this evidence, wrote the Viceroy, 'what we are concerned to examine is not the mere settlement of a border dispute, or even the amelioration of our future trading relations with Tibet, but the question of our entire future political relations with that country, and the degree to which we can permit the influence of another great Power to be exercised for the first time in Tibetan affairs.'

He then rehearsed the various declarations of their interest in Tibet which the British Government had been prompted to make, in St Petersburg and Peking, by the appearance of Dorjieff and by rumours of the secret Russo-Chinese treaty. He emphasised the dangers implicit in 'the creation of a rival or hostile influence in a position so close to the Indian border and so pregnant with the possibilities of mischief.' The time had come, he urged, for Britain to take the initiative.

A cue for doing so was provided by a recent Chinese affirmation of their desire to reach a settlement of the Tibetan affair; the Peking Government, in appointing a new Amban and ordering him to proceed to Lhasa without delay, had proclaimed their readiness to reopen negotiations. On this *démarche* the Government of India had been asked to give their views.

These, the Viceroy now revealed, were that the Chinese proposal should be welcomed, but that the re-opening of negotiations should be made conditional on their taking place at Lhasa, with a Tibetan representative participating. Here followed references to the precedents mentioned above, which showed that the idea of a mission to Lhasa had been accepted in principle by at least two British Governments in the recent past.

Curzon went on to provide as far as possible for a situation in which China declined to acquiesce in these arrangements. 'We regard,' he wrote loftily, 'the so-called suzerainty of China over Tibet as a constitutional fiction—a political affectation which has only been maintained because of its convenience to both parties. . . . We hope that it will not be thought necessary to seek the permission or the passports of China for a British Mission to Lhasa.' Here the Viceroy's argument, whatever its *de facto* merits, was scarcely tenable *de jure*; on the publication of his despatch a year and a half later the American Ambassador in London was instructed to remind the Foreign Office that Chinese suzerainty over Tibet, however pejoratively Lord Curzon might describe it, had been recognised by Great Britain in the Chefoo Convention of 1876, the Peking Convention of 1886 and the Calcutta Convention of 1890.*

A further inducement to ignore or by-pass the nominally suzerain Power was seen in the fact that the Dalai Lama, 'having successfully escaped from the vicissitudes of childhood' (his four immediate predecessors had failed to inconvenience their Regents by coming of age), was now, at the age of twenty-eight, an effective power in the land; 'there is for the first time in modern history a ruler in Tibet with whom it is possible to deal instead of an obscure junta masked by the Chinese Amban.'

The despatch ended by recommending that the Peking Government should be informed that a commercial mission would start for Lhasa in the spring; that negotiations there should have the widest possible scope; and that they 'should

* Tieh-Tseng Li: *The Historical Status of Tibet.*

culminate in the appointment of a permanent British representative, Consular or Diplomatic, to reside at Lhasa.' Although 'the military strength of the Tibetans is beneath contempt,' the mission would require an escort to 'overawe any opposition that might be encountered on the way.' Finally, the Government of India proposed to act throughout in close concert with that of Nepal, which had been alarmed by recent developments and would, it was believed, be only too anxious to co-operate. If the whole plan commended itself to His Majesty's Government, the Viceroy requested the earliest possible notification, since the construction or repair of roads leading to the frontier would have to be put in hand without delay.

This able despatch, every line of which bears the impress of a fine, hard mind at work in a mood of dedication and resolve, reached London on 24 January 1903. It had hardly arrived there when a small thing happened which had a prejudicial effect on the reception of Curzon's proposals by the Cabinet.

On 2 February the Russian Ambassador transmitted to the Foreign Office a short and rather sharp note. The Imperial Government, Count Benckendorff wrote, had learnt from an authoritative source that a British military expedition had reached Komba-Ovaleko and was making northward for the Chumbi Valley. The Imperial Government took a grave view of this development, which might oblige it to take steps to safeguard its own interests in those regions; it drew the British Government's attention to the matter in order to avoid any misunderstanding.

No evidence survives to show that anyone in London, when they heard of the Russian note, instinctively assumed that George Curzon had taken the bit between his teeth and was implementing the preliminaries of his plan without waiting for it to be approved; but so pervasive was the view taken—on the evidence of the past four years, unfairly—of his adventurism and his impatience of control that it would have been surprising indeed if no such suspicions were, however fleetingly, entertained by some members of Mr Balfour's administration.

The Secretary of State for India lost no time in cabling to enquire whether there was any foundation for the Russian allegations.

The Viceroy replied promptly that there was—'it is needless to say'—none, and asked for permission to go ahead with his preparations for the Lhasa mission. A few days later Lord Lansdowne passed his denial on to the Russian Ambassador, whose recent communication, he added severely, struck him as being 'unusual and, indeed, almost minatory in tone.' Research had failed to disclose the existence of any such place as Komba-Ovaleko; but a political officer with a small escort had been endeavouring to regulate affairs on the Sikkim–Tibet frontier some time previously.

Count Benckendorff deplored the prevalence of exaggerated rumours. Russia, he said, had no designs upon Tibet; he presumed that Great Britain had none? Lord Lansdowne, hedging slightly, affirmed that Great Britain had no desire whatever to annex Tibetan territory; he could give no sweeping assurances about her future relations with a country where so many local questions affecting trade and treaty-rights remained unsettled.

The timing of this Anglo-Russian exchange, trivial but brusque, was unfortunate for Curzon's new Tibetan policy. The pot, long accustomed to calling the kettle black, was disconcerted by a counter-denigration; and although for the moment the *tu quoque* was unfounded, it would not, if the Viceroy's project was adopted, be wholly so next time. The small, fortuitous incident was a reminder of the high stakes for which the Great Game was played, and of the uncertain temper in which it was apt to be conducted.

Caution was the keynote of the reply to Curzon's proposals which was cabled from the India Office on 20 February. The dangers of the Tibetan situation were recognised by His Majesty's Government. However, in the course of Lord Lansdowne's conversations with the Russian Ambassador about the Komba-Ovaleko note, Count Benckendorff had been asked, and had undertaken, to make 'specific enquiries' in St Petersburg as to whether Russia had any secret treaty with China or intended, as had been reported, to establish an agent at Lhasa. A reply to these enquiries was awaited; and 'while discussions between the two Governments are in progress, the despatch of an expedition to enter Tibet by force would, in the opinion of His Majesty's Government, be most undesirable.' The Viceroy should inform the Chinese Amban that he was ready to resume negotiations; that a Tibetan representative with full powers must be a party to them; and that the time and place of the meeting were still under his consideration.

The correspondence between Lord Curzon and the India Office (which was often voicing the views of the Cabinet) produces, over and over again, an effect of unbalance, of anti-climax. There is a lack of equipoise between the cogent and always admirably marshalled arguments advanced by the Viceroy and the less than masterly, sometimes slipshod, responses which they evoked from Whitehall; it is as though a brilliant student were submitting essays to a tutor whose comments on them betrayed his second-class mind.

The Home Government, after taking a month to reach an interim decision, overlooked the one practical matter on which the Government of India had requested the earliest possible guidance: its road-building programme. On 24 February the Viceroy repeated, by cable, his request for authority to go ahead with this; the roads were 'necessary to precaution in any case.' This request was approved.

It was not until 8 April—five weeks after they had been asked for—that the Imperial Government's assurances about Tibet were received at the Foreign Office. Russia had no treaty with Tibet, or with China about Tibet, or with anyone else. She had no agents in Tibet, and no intention of sending agents there. Count Lamsdorff expressed a rueful surprise that His Majesty's Government should have given credence to *canards* of this nature. Russia however, since she regarded Tibet as forming part of the Chinese Empire in whose integrity she took

63

an interest, 'could not remain indifferent to any serious disturbance of the *status quo* in that country.' If one occurred, she might find it necessary to safeguard her interests in Asia—not in Tibet, since her policy *'ne viserait le Thibet en aucun cas;'* but she 'might be obliged to take measures elsewhere.'

This firm and rather tart disclaimer ended the moratorium which for a few weeks had, not very usefully, absolved the British Government from deciding what to do about Tibet. On 14 April they asked the Viceroy for his suggestions.

Curzon's reply was prompt and workmanlike. The idea of a mission to Lhasa must, he realised, be abandoned for the time being; he lowered his sights. He proposed to open negotiations with China and Tibet at Khamba Jong, the nearest inhabited place on Tibetan territory to Giaogong. The Chinese delegates had already been appointed; they should be instructed to bring with them a duly accredited Tibetan representative of the highest rank. The British representative would be accompanied by an escort of two hundred rifles; reinforcements would be held in reserve in Sikkim. If the Chinese and Tibetans failed at the rendezvous, the British representative would move forward to Shigatse or Gyantse, to accelerate their arrival from Lhasa. As the season was short and the negotiations were likely to be long, the Viceroy asked for an early decision on his plan.

He got one on 29 April. His Majesty's Government had no objection to Khamba Jong as a *venue* and they approved the proposed military arrangements. Under no circumstances, however, was any advance from Khamba Jong to be made without reference to them. A week later, in a telegram amplifying his project, Curzon announced his choice of the British representative at the tripartite negotiations. 'As Commissioner,' he wired, 'I propose to appoint Major Younghusband, Resident at Indore, who should receive temporary rank of Colonel. I can confidently rely on his judgment and discretion and he has great Asiatic experience.'

We are now on or very near the crest of the slope—a gentle one at first—down which the British Government, propelled in the first place by the Viceroy of India, and later sucked inexorably by those forces of gravity which are liable to be generated by even the mildest-mannered foray across a frontier, was to slither, with gathering momentum and acute misgivings, until its armed forces entered the Tibetan capital more than a year later. It is time now to learn something of the man who was to lead them there.

CHAPTER FIVE

The Man on the Spot

FRANCIS EDWARD YOUNGHUSBAND was born on 31 May 1863, the second son of a Major-General in the Indian Army, in which his four uncles had served and his two brothers were to serve. His mother was a sister of Robert Shaw, a notable explorer of Central Asia. He had deep roots in his own country (the Younghusbands trace their descent back to Saxon free-holders at Bamburgh in Northumberland) and inherited traditions which had led his family through times of turbulence and danger. It may not be over-fanciful to suggest that these attributes lay at the foundation of that sympathy to which Younghusband, and others like him in the service of the British Empire, owed their success in handling primitive peoples.

The problems and prejudices of a tribe in Africa or Asia differed only (though often startlingly) in degree from those which had at one time or another preoccupied its counterpart, an old-established family in the British Isles. In the outlook of both the same patterns had recurred—the same over-riding need for security, the same conflict between loyalty and opportunism in the quest for it, between distrust of strangers and the desire to offer them hospitality, the same faith in precedent. The petty chieftain and the squire's younger son were both products of the same process—a successful exercise in the arts of survival. Perhaps this helped them to understand each other.

Francis Younghusband was a small man, only five foot six in height, with a wiry frame, penetrating blue eyes and a moustache vaguely resembling Lord Kitchener's. His upbringing had been conventional. Clifton College, under the redoubtable

THE MAN ON THE SPOT

Dr John Percival, was a forcing-house for those qualities of character and leadership of which an expanding Empire discovered an increasing need. It was a hard, homespun place where little store was set by scholarship but which (as Younghusband afterwards recalled) 'produced the type of public servant that was needed for the times.' If it could not prevent Henry Newbolt—who was Younghusband's contemporary and friend—from becoming a poet, it left its somewhat daunting influence upon his Muse:

> The victories of our youth we count for gain
> Only because they steeled our hearts to pain,
> And hold no longer even Clifton great
> Save as she schooled our wills to serve the State.

Younghusband went on to the Royal Military College at Sandhurst, where he worked hard and won distinction as a long-distance runner. In 1882 he was gazetted to the King's Dragoon Guards and joined them in the sweltering heat of Meerut. He had been drawn to the cavalry because he was by nature a 'thruster' with an innate taste for patrol-work and reconnaissance, for proving ahead of the main body into the blue. Inevitably he found little satisfaction in the hot-weather routine of a cantonment in the Indian plains, and although he liked his brother-officers he was disenchanted by their offhand attitude to their profession. The regiment, moreover, was a smart one, and Younghusband lacked the financial means to keep up with its standards in the mess and on the polo-field. His first months as a Dragoon were unhappy.

But he was an efficient, hard-working officer, with a deep sense of dedication; 'the thought,' he wrote, 'of what the regiment had done in the past and what it might do in the future made me sometimes almost cry with pride.' He settled down and before long was appointed Adjutant at the early age of twenty-one.

After two years there came the sort of opportunity which his destinies demanded; the divisional commander sent him up to reconnoitre the Kohat frontier, across which (for this was at the time of the Penjdeh Incident) there was more reason than usual to apprehend a Russian invasion. Younghusband became a pawn in the Great Game; thereafter the King's Dragoon Guards had only fleeting glimpses of him.

In 1886 Younghusband was given six months' leave to go to Manchuria and travelled along much of the frontier across which covetous Russian forces confronted the outposts of the debilitated Chinese Empire. Then, with the connivance of the British Minister in Peking, who suppressed a telegram recalling him to India, he carried out, alone, a remarkable journey through Inner Mongolia and Sinkiang which brought him down to Kashmir over an unexplored pass through the Karakoram. He had been away from India for more than a year and a half. At twenty-five he had achieved fame; for all his modesty and self-effacement he relished it.

After a few weeks' leave in England, where he lectured to the Royal Geographical Society, and a short tour of duty with his regiment, he was seconded to the Foreign Department at Simla in 1889 and sent off to explore the passes leading into the small, remote state of Hunza, which borders Chinese and Afghan territory to the north of Kashmir, and whence came reports of trouble with Kanjuti brigands and rumours of Russian infiltration. With an escort of six Gurkhas he penetrated the Kanjuti stronghold and by sheer force of personality restored order. Somewhere on the Pamirs he met one of his opposing pawns, a celebrated Russian traveller called Captain Grombtchevski. Visits were exchanged between the two lonely camps, toasts drunk. The Englishman put his Gurkhas through their paces;* the Russian showed off his Cossacks. Before they parted, Grombtchevski told Younghusband that 'although we English might not believe the Russians really intended to invade India, he could assure me that the Russian Army—officers and men—thought of nothing else.'

This journey, which earned him the personal congratulations

* Grombtchevski was a huge man, and the Gurkhas begged Younghusband to explain to him that they were unusually small members of their race, most of whom were much larger than the Russian.

of the Viceroy, Lord Lansdowne, was followed by others, in all of which geographical exploration was combined with counter-intelligence. In 1891, again in the Pamirs, he had an encounter with another Russian party, under a Colonel Yonov, who with the utmost cordiality explained that he was in the process of annexing to the Tsar's dominions a large tract of territory, much of it demonstrably within the Chinese or Afghan frontiers and the rest of it debatable. Younghusband 'merely remarked that the Russians were opening their mouths pretty wide' and accepted an invitation to dinner.

Four days later he was awakened in the middle of the night by the clatter of hoofs. Colonel Yonov, profuse in apologies but at the head of thirty Cossacks, had received orders that Younghusband was to be expelled from 'Russian' territory. Younghusband yielded with a good grace to *force majeure*. He undertook to return to Chinese territory (as defined by the Russians) and not to leave it by certain specified passes, a list of which included all those through which access to India was known to be possible. Younghusband, scrupulously keeping his parole, struggled with great difficulty through an un-suspected crack in the mountains and reached India two months later.

Meanwhile news of his predicament had filtered through to London, where the Press reported that he had been killed. A stiff protest against his illegal detention was delivered in St Petersburg, and eventually elicited an apology from the Russian Government. The Viceroy was full of sympathy and praise. The Commander-in-Chief, Sir Frederick (later Lord) Roberts, revealed that he had mobilised the Quetta Division. The little incident blew over, leaving its youthful protagonist enveloped in a becoming haze of legend. In the Great Game Francis Younghusband, not yet thirty, was now regarded by both sides as something more potent than a pawn.

In 1893 he became the first Political Agent in Chitral, then in a volcanic state following a dynastic crisis. It was here, in 1894, that he met the itinerant Curzon and formed, rather surprisingly, a friendship which though not intimate was enduring. 'We resented Curzon's cocksureness,' he wrote: adding, perhaps over-sanguinely, 'it might have been toned down if he could have been for a time with a regiment or served on the frontier. . . . But irritating though this manner was, it was yet compatible with remarkable tenderness of heart. In friendship he was warm and staunch.'

In 1895 he was home on leave when the uneasy situation in Chitral exploded. A British mission was besieged in the capital; a relief force met with disaster. Younghusband offered to return at once to duty but was told that there was no immediate need for his services. *The Times* asked him to go to Chitral as their Special Correspondent. The Government of India forbade this, on the grounds that Captain Younghusband was still their Political Agent in the area, but eventually withdrew their objection on the understanding that it might be impossible for them to re-employ him in Chitral. With Major Roddy Owen, the finest gentleman-rider of his day, Younghusband galloped on ahead of the relieving column and was the first man to reach the beleaguered British garrison.

After this the tempo of his remarkable career slowed down. In 1895–96, still on leave, he went to South Africa for *The Times*; a series of able despatches covered, among other things, the Jameson Raid. In 1897 he married Helen Augusta Magniac, the daughter of a Member of Parliament. She was of lighter calibre than he—witty, cultured, worldly, lacking his spiritual depths and perhaps only dimly aware of them. Younghusband's biographer wrote: 'They were too profoundly different, both in temperament and upbringing, to be suited to each other, yet he was the light of life to her, while he gave to her a protective love and loyalty which went far beyond conventional affection.' * It was not an ideal marriage ('I was not really suited to my wife', he recorded in old age) but it lasted until his death. Their only son died in infancy; their daughter, Miss Eileen Younghusband, CBE, carries on with distinction, and in many fields, the long family tradition of public service.

* Seaver.

THE MAN ON THE SPOT

On his return to India in 1898 'the Government showed no marked enthusiasm in welcoming me back,' and Younghusband was posted as third assistant to the Political Agent in Rajputana, 'the lowest appointment they could give me.' The Indian hierarchy was always apt to look with disfavour on officers who indulged in extramural activities, and it seems at least possible that Younghusband's connexion with *The Times* (as whose representative he had been received in Simla, after the Chitral campaign, with a deference out of proportion to his rank) had aroused some prejudice against him.

But after a year a better posting came his way, though he had to cope with the horrors of a famine, and early in 1902, after Younghusband and his wife had stayed as Lord Curzon's guests at Viceregal Lodge, he was made Resident in Indore. It was here that, in May 1903, he received a telegram summoning him urgently to Simla.

Younghusband was enchanted with the prospect of leading a mission to Tibet. 'This is a really magnificent business I have dropped in for,' he wrote to his father on 21 May. The enterprise might have been specially designed as a vehicle for his personality and talents. In 1889 he had put forward a plan for a single-handed journey, in disguise, to Lhasa, but his commanding officer had refused to give him the requisite leave. He now discovered, from the files in Simla, that on two previous occasions the Lieutenant-Governor of Bengal had asked for his services on the Tibetan frontier, where it was thought that his Chinese experience would come in useful; the Government of India had turned down both requests, on the grounds that Younghusband, then a subaltern, was about to sit for a promotion examination.

In Simla, that curiously suburban eyrie, the final arrangements for the mission to Khamba Jong were concerted in secrecy, and at the highest level. Younghusband stayed with Dane, the Foreign Secretary, a man—like his guest—with a streak of impetuosity in his make-up. One afternoon, after a luncheon at Viceregal Lodge, Younghusband sat with Curzon

and Kitchener (whose monumental feud was still in the cold
war stage) * under the deodars at Annandale. While they simu-
lated polite interest in a gymkhana—the Simla season was at its
height—the Viceroy unfolded his views about Tibet. 'He had,'
Younghusband recalled, 'his whole heart and soul in the undertaking.' Kitchener he found 'a little more cautious than the
Viceroy but thoroughly in earnest about the business.'

This was far from being true of the British Government,
who were still nervously insistent that the scope of the negotiations should be limited to the settlement of local questions; in
deference to their qualms Younghusband's orders included a
strict injunction that he was not to say or do anything which
might commit Britain to any definite course of action without
first obtaining the sanction of the Government of India, who
were similarly bound to consult Whitehall. But no last-
minute hitch occurred to prevent the departure of the mission
for Tibetan territory, and Younghusband left Simla early in
June 1903. He gave out, truthfully enough, that he was going
to Darjeeling.

In addition to Younghusband the original members of the
Tibet Frontier Commission (as it came to be designated) were
J. C. White, who had had fourteen years' experience of the
Tibetan frontier and who, if he felt any chagrin at being passed
over in favour of a younger man with no local knowledge, was
too loyal to show it: Major (later Sir) Frederick O'Connor, an
imperturbable gunner who had learnt the Tibetan language:
and Ernest (later Sir Ernest) Wilton, a humorous and resourceful sinologue borrowed from the China Consular Service.

At Darjeeling, the hill-station where the Government of
Bengal took refuge from the ordeals of a summer in Calcutta,
Younghusband was uneasily conscious of being an interloper.
Since the days of Warren Hastings Tibetan problems had been
primarily the concern of the Lieutenant-Governor of Bengal,
upon whose territory they impinged and by whose officers they

---

* A definitive—and fascinating—account of the Kitchener–Curzon
vendetta is to be found in *Kitchener*, by Sir Philip Magnus (London, 1958).

were handled; it was only recently that the increasing cen-
tralisation of frontier affairs (which Younghusband deplored on
principle) had diluted Bengal's authority in this field, and
Younghusband had some reason to fear that an outsider's
intervention would be looked at askance.

He received, however, the fullest co-operation from the
authorities in Darjeeling: 'it was more than I could expect of
them,' he wrote to his father, 'for the Viceroy treats this and all
other local Governments in a very high-handed way. In this
Tibet business they have been absolutely ignored.' On 19 July
he set off northward into Sikkim, riding down through torrential
rain into the luxuriant, stifling valley of the Tista River, only
700 feet above sea-level. Beyond Gantok, where he stayed a
few days in White's well-appointed bungalow in the territory
of the chaste and gentle Lepchas, he found the camp of the
32nd Pioneers, a jack-of-all-trades Sikh unit, equally apt at
fighting or at building roads, which with two sister-regiments
had been specially formed for service on the Frontier. Here he
picked up an escort of two hundred rifles, under Captain
Bethune.

Before leaving Gantok he had received a cipher telegram
modifying his orders; he was not, now, to enter Tibetan territory until he was assured that Tibetan delegates of suitable
rank were awaiting him. Younghusband did not like this, and
decided, characteristically, that the Nelson touch was called
for. 'I am,' he confided to his father, 'taking these orders as
personal to myself—that is to say, I am going to read the "you"
in the telegram as meaning F.E.Y. only and I am going to send
on the escort and O'Connor and probably White too to
Khamba Jong, while I remain with the support of 300 men at
the head of the Sikkim valley. I shall give out that my camp
equipage has been detained by the rains (which it has) and
that I cannot proceed beyond the last inhabited place till it
arrives: that in the meanwhile a portion of my escort (really the
whole) has been sent to prepare the camp and make all preliminary arrangements. That is what I shall give out. It is not
quite as I should have liked to have done things myself.' This

pattern of conduct—mildly insubordinate, very slightly devious, and followed in complete confidence that it was the right thing to do—was to recur more than once in Younghusband's handling of the Mission to Tibet.

The precarious track began to climb. Gradually the little expedition drew away from the leeches, the mosquitoes and the oppressive heat, and on 26 June reached Tangu, a pleasant, flowery place at an altitude of 12,000 feet. Here, within a week, they were joined by the 'support'—a further three hundred men of the 32nd Pioneers under the regiment's commanding officer, Lieutenant-Colonel Brander. They had had an arduous seven-days' march—throughout the summer the monthly rainfall in Sikkim averaged nearly thirty inches—and exposure caused sixty casualties, of whom three died.

The Mission was now on White's old stamping-grounds, only ten miles from Giaogong, which was half that distance again from the Kangra La, a 16,900-foot pass leading into Tibetan territory due south of Khamba Jong.

Younghusband, conforming to the letter of his orders, stopped at Tangu and on 4 July sent White and O'Connor forward with Bethune's escort of two hundred men. There was a wall at Giaogong which the Tibetans claimed as their boundary and from which White had removed them in the previous year. Just south of this wall the British column halted and camped. They had already been intercepted by the Jongpen, or Commandant, of Khamba Jong;* he told White that two Tibetan delegates of high rank, who had come to discuss frontier matters, were encamped on the other side of the wall. White replied that he would be delighted to receive the delegates in his camp on the following evening, but that he could hold no discussions in Giaogong, where he did not propose to halt.

Next morning O'Connor rode forward to the wall, with White and the escort following. The Jongpen, beyond whom could be seen a large but unarmed cavalcade headed by the

* *Jong*, nowadays transliterated as *Dzong*, means a fort. *La* (as in Kangra La) means a pass.

two plenipotentiaries in yellow silk robes, implored him to dismount. So, when they came up, did the two delegates, who, getting off their ponies, invited O'Connor to their tent for refreshment and a parley. They were told, courteously, that no discussions could be held until the Mission reached Khamba Jong.

At this the Tibetans seized the Englishmen's bridles, and Sikhs had to be called up to clear the way. The column moved forward. The silk-robed delegates remounted and rode rue-fully back to their tents. Only the Jongpen, in a state of great agitation, continued for some distance to accompany White and O'Connor, renewing his importunities and hinting darkly that 'You may flick a dog once or twice without his biting you, but if you tread on his tail, even if he has no teeth, he will turn and try and bite you.'

But at length he was left behind, and on the next morning the Tibetan frontier was crossed without incident. Contact was established with the senior Chinese delegate, Ho Kuang-hsi, and the only untoward portent was the discovery, in a stream near the British camp, of several scores of dead fish. Earlier in the day the fish in this stream had been in perfect health, and poisoning was suspected. The small mystery was never cleared up.

Khamba Jong was reached on 7 July. The escort made, and began to fortify, a camp at the foot of the crag crowned by a great fort which was to be a familiar landmark on the route of the earlier Everest expeditions.* Supplies of fodder for the transport-animals were made available, after some demur, by the Jongpen. A fertile valley, containing good grazing, crops of barley and herds of sheep and cattle, was discovered three or four miles away. Gazelle provided sport and venison. Courtesies and presents were exchanged with the Chinese and Tibetan delegates.

The advance of the Mission into Tibet had been a leap in the dark, but it had landed on its feet. Younghusband joined

* Six of the seven parties which attempted Everest between the wars used Khamba Jong as a staging-post.

it from Tangu on 18 July. He found the political atmosphere inauspicious and blamed White's high-handedness. 'He has never been out of Sikkim; he is a little god there but he is absolutely useless and worse than useless in dealing with high officials of an independent nation. . . . If the Deputy Commissioner at Peshawar treated the Afghan officials at Jellalabad as he treats his own *teshildars* [headmen] there would be a row, and though we may pull through without a row here because the Tibetans are a mild people it will not be thanks to White.' But though he wrote of these misgivings to his father he kept them out of his correspondence with Simla; 'I hope I shall be able to put political matters straight without hurting White's feelings.' Sneaking had been tabu at Clifton, and Younghusband was always punctiliously reluctant to report adversely on individuals. White was to render service of great value to the Mission before its work was done.

The Tibet Frontier Commission remained at Khamba Jong for five months. It was very much *en l'air*, but although there were recurrent rumours that the Tibetans were going to attack it, nothing of the kind occurred. The officers roamed widely over the surrounding countryside, surveying, visiting monasteries, shooting, and collecting geological, botanical and zoological specimens. But no negotiations took place.

It is needless to follow the frustrations with which the British Commissioner was met at every turn. The Tibetan delegates refused to receive written communications, to report oral communications to Lhasa, or to hold any discussions at Khamba Jong. If Younghusband wanted to negotiate he must go back to his own side of the frontier; this suggestion, unacceptable in any case, was rendered even more so by the Tibetans' insistence that the frontier was several miles south of the line—an obvious watershed—laid down in the Convention of 1890, of whose terms they pretended to have no cognisance. The Tibetan attitude was not in the least evasive or disingenuous; it was based four-square on infantile obstinacy. Having made this maddeningly clear at a long interview on 22 July the

Lhasa delegates withdrew into the Jong and had no further intercourse with the British Mission.

The Chinese attitude was more equivocal and harder to fathom. Mr Ho, Younghusband found, 'was not a very polished official and did not favourably impress me.' Wilton, the consul from China, reached Khamba Jong on 7 August and immediately established that Ho's rank was inferior to that required by protocol for a plenipotentiary. The Viceroy having written to the Chinese Amban pointing this out, Ho was recalled to Lhasa, where (he assured Younghusband) he was 'sanguine that his efforts to induce a more enlightened policy would not be barren of results;' but he was delayed on the road (as Chinese officials so often were, or claimed to be) by the Tibetans' refusal to provide him with transport, and his replacement, a Colonel Chao, turned out, though personally likeable, to belong to an even lower grade in the Imperial hierarchy. Meanwhile the new Amban, Yu-t'ai, who in December 1902 had been ordered to proceed post-haste to Lhasa, was still on his leisurely way, and did not reach his destination until February 1904.

In India it had been expected that negotiations might languish. It had not been foreseen that none would take place.

CHAPTER SIX

The Fate of Two Spies

THE stalemate at Khamba Jong was of great importance. The Tibetans' refusal to negotiate, or even to go through the motions of negotiating, and the Chinese impotence (if it was nothing more culpable) to make their vassals conform to the declared policy of the Peking Government, set several processes in motion.

Some of the Viceroy's impatience and indignation began to communicate itself to the British Government. The despatch of a Mission to Khamba Jong had been a compromise. It had failed; none of the objectives aimed at, limited though they were, had been achieved. Not one of Britain's long-standing grievances had been remedied, and now, in addition, she had suffered a rebuff. Her Commissioner had been ignored, cold-shouldered, sent to Coventry. He could not stay indefinitely where he was; to do so, apart from being futile, was dangerous, for reports were coming in that the Tibetans were only waiting for the onset of winter, which would gravely complicate the Mission's administrative problems, before attacking.

Was Younghusband to be recalled empty-handed? In London it began reluctantly to be accepted that the Tibetans would have to be taught a lesson. 'His Majesty's Government should realise,' Curzon cabled on 16 September, 'that the Lhasa Government have no conception of our power.' In his reply, four days later, the Secretary of State admitted the possibility of 'coercion' becoming necessary, but added that the 'proposal to advance far into the interior is regarded with grave misgivings by His Majesty's Government, who are disposed to think that the fact that we are in earnest may be sufficiently brought home to the Tibetans by the occupation of the Chumbi Valley in the first instance.'

On Younghusband, the thruster, the effect of the *impasse* in which he found himself was marked. He was a man of immense patience, and behind the armour of his self-control lay inner spiritual reserves. But when he wrote, six years afterwards, 'If the delegates did not choose to give me any work, I was quite content to do none, for I was thoroughly happy in camp there at Khamba Jong. . . . I did not care a pin how long these obstinate Tibetans kept us up there,' he was telling something less than the truth.

That he was happier than anyone else would have been in the circumstances is probable, for he had a deep, mystical love of all wild empty places and especially of mountains. He had a vivid apprehension of natural beauty and a vaguer (but ever-present) consciousness of some great abstract power or virtue of which such beauty was the expression. 'It is high up among the loftiest mountain summits, where all is shrouded in unsullied whiteness, where nothing polished dares pollute, that the very essence of sublimity must be sought for. It is there indeed that the grand and beautiful unite to form the sublime.'

But although there was solace in the sight of Kanchenjunga, and the more distant Everest, challenging a cloudless sky beyond a vast expanse of rolling upland, Younghusband had not come to Tibet to admire the view. Although by tempera-ment he was unusually well qualified to endure it, the dead weight of frustration lay irksomely on the strongest impulses in his nature—his sense of duty, his thirst for achievement, his perfectionism. The deadlock at Khamba Jong was the first of three periods of forced inaction to which Younghusband had to submit on the long road to Lhasa. Since each left its mark on his conduct of the Mission, an attempt must be made to assess the effect on this questing, dedicated man of situations in which he found himself thwarted, becalmed, unable directly to further the purpose in which his mind and being were absorbed.

Twelve years earlier, reflecting on the lot of an isolated

Russian outpost in the Pamirs, he had diagnosed with a curious exactitude the *malaise* from which, behind an imperturbable exterior, he suffered at Khamba Jong. 'How these Russian soldiers can support existence there is a marvel. . . . I can well imagine the joy it must be to them to return to more genial quarters. One can imagine that they must often long, also, to push on down to more hospitable regions *in front* of them. An officer shut up in these dreary quarters, with nothing whatever to do—week after week and month after month passing by in dull monotony, only the same barren hills to look at, the same stroll about the fort to be taken—must long to *go on*. . . . It is only human nature that he should wish so, and when he is in this frame of mind it obviously requires a very little inducement to move him on, and a pretty tight rein from behind to keep him still.'*

At Khamba Jong the question of 'going on', of taking some rash or unauthorised action, did not arise; but Younghusband found release from his sense of impotence by assiduously collecting and sending back to India every scrap of evidence he could lay his hands on which was calculated to strengthen the case for a more adventurous Tibetan policy. He believed, as firmly as he knew Curzon to believe, that half-measures would achieve nothing; only by an advance to Lhasa could Tibetan intransigence be overcome. It was natural that his reports should tend, directly or indirectly, to bear out this view, which events were to prove correct.

It was natural, too, that these reports should reveal him as a partisan, whose devotion to his cause was so strong as to raise doubts about the soundness of his judgment. Younghusband, almost inevitably, overplayed his hand: almost inevitably, because a strong-willed leader, marooned in a tent sixteen thousand feet above sea-level and faced with insuperable obstacles which only his distant superiors can overcome, cannot help trying to put the maximum pressure on them, for that is the way that men are made.

It was of course Younghusband's duty to telegraph to India

* *The Heart of a Continent.*

rumours of impending attack on the Mission, symptoms of Tibetan contumacity or Chinese prevarication, reports of growing Russian influence; nor is it to be inferred that he exaggerated evidence which supported his own convictions, or suppressed any that did not. But he supplemented his tele-grams with several long written reports, and in these, on occasion, deductions so large and so far-fetched were based on such small and dubious clues as to compromise their author's pretensions to objectivity.

In one such report, for instance, a remark once made to Younghusband by a French explorer provided almost the entire basis for a theory that from her possessions in Indo-China France might one day join hands with Russia across the pros-trate body of Tibet. The same report, dated 17 August 1903, stated as a fact that 'the net result of Russian activity in Tibet is that Russian influence is now so strong in Lhasa that, directly we begin to negotiate with the Tibetans over matters of trade and an insignificant boundary question, we find the Tibetans arraying the Russians against us and fully confident of their support.' It is small wonder that when this document came at last to rest in the archives of the Foreign Office its margins were liberally illuminated with question-marks.

The bureaucrats in Whitehall were wholly incapable of visualising, let alone making allowances for, the stresses under which Younghusband's eager mind was working when, tethered to a remote and inconvenient rendezvous which the Tibetans had not kept, he relieved himself by writing down everything which might conceivably improve his Mission's prospects of success. 'It will all depend,' he had written to his father in June, 'upon Government—especially the Home Government— and my own idea is that I shall have much more delicate work in managing *them* than with the Chinese and Tibetans. I shall have to carry them with me step by step.' This intention was more obvious, and the methods by which he sought to im-plement it less unobtrusive, than Younghusband supposed; and in Whitehall he began to be suspected as unsound, a bit of a fanatic. When, in due course, he became aware that this was so, he was not only distressed but puzzled. 'The Secretary of State,' he complained in a letter to Curzon on 18 June 1904, 'is under the impression that I am a sort of rampant adventurer.' He never understood that he himself had created this impression.

Meanwhile the chimera of Russian influence in Tibet continued to thrive. Just before Younghusband left Simla in June a report from Sikkim quoted a Chinese newspaper (of unspecified date) which had published an 'official telegram' to the effect that there were '143 Russians, attired mostly like military engineers,' on the eastern frontier of Tibet. On 10 August the Mission at Khamba Jong heard rumours of Cossacks entering Tibet from the north; and similar *faits divers* included a circumstantial account, received via Darjeeling in December, that two thousand Russians had arrived within a few miles of Lhasa. Their uniforms were described in detail and they were credited with having some means of intercommunication corresponding roughly to a telephone; they were also said to 'consume a large amount of pork.'

Of greater significance (or so it was believed) than these fables was the discovery that Dorjieff was not the only Buryat who came and went between Tibet and Russia. One Tsybikoff delivered, in May 1903, a lecture in St Petersburg on his experiences at Lhasa and was given a medal. Another, Norzanoff, who had been detained at Darjeeling and deported from India in 1900, also cropped up in the intelligence reports; the fact that he had had a letter of introduction to the French Consul at Calcutta was felt to be vaguely sinister, as was his connexion, established by the Darjeeling police, with 'a very rich lama called Darjilicoff.'

From St Petersburg and other sources came reports suggesting that these elusive, gnome-like characters were controlled, from Urga in Outer Mongolia, by a master-mind variously known as de Groot and von Grot, who was sometimes described as 'nominally' an inspector of mines and sometimes as belonging to the Chinese Customs Service. 'If neither Dorjieff nor

Norzanoff nor Tsybikoff,' wrote Younghusband in October, 'are at present in Lhasa encouraging the Tibetans with hopes of Russian assistance, we must credit the Russians with much less enterprise than they usually display.'

Naturally there were quarters where both the authenticity and the importance of these reports were scouted; but the proponents of a forward policy could always turn the sceptics' flanks by pointing out that what immediately influenced the attitude of the Tibetans was not the amount of support they actually got from Russia (which might, indeed, amount to very little) but the amount of support they thought they could rely on getting. A parallel was sometimes drawn between Tibet and South Africa. 'It is exactly the same position,' Younghusband was to write, in May of the following year, to the Acting Viceroy, Lord Ampthill, 'as Kruger's with the Germans. Kruger was assured he had the support of Germany and drifted headlong into a struggle with us fully relying on this support. Similarly the Dalai Lama thinks he has Russia behind him.' In the building up of a case against Russia in Tibet there was at times an element of heads-I-win-tails-you-lose.

It soon became clear that the deadlock at Khamba Jong was creating a situation which, unsatisfactory and exacerbating though it was, the British could do little or nothing to alter in their favour. The delegates from Lhasa would have no truck with the Mission, who could get no change out of the Chinese. Meanwhile harmonious relations existed between the British officers and the local inhabitants, and during August a senior abbot from Shigatse, a man of charm and affability, was a frequent and a welcome visitor to the Mission's tents.* The little expedition was under no sort of pressure or threat, and although its position was in the abstract humiliating and even

* 'Whatever intellectual capacity he may have had was not very apparent to the casual observer,' Younghusband recalled afterwards, 'and he corrected me when I inadvertently let slip some observation implying that the earth was round, and assured me that when I had lived longer in Tibet, and had had time to study, I should find that it was not round, but flat, and not circular, but triangular, like the bone of a shoulder of mutton.'

ridiculous, its day-to-day existence was placid and uneventful to a degree. What was needed—though nobody said so, at any rate officially—was an Incident, something which would provide the pretext for positive action.

It was at this stage that a pair of humble, anonymous figures, known to the official archives as 'the two Lachung men,' made their providential appearance. They were first mentioned in the Mission's Political Diary on 2 August, when O'Connor, who kept this diary and ran the primitive intelligence service which provided much of the material for it, wrote: 'The two Lachung men sent to Shigatse on 18 July have not returned. I despatched another man, a Tibetan, to Shigatse this morning to see if he can get word of them.'

It is abundantly clear from the context that these two men from Lachung—a small town in Sikkim not far from Khamba Jong—were low-grade spies working, like several others, for O'Connor. The Political Diary is full of similar entries; on 17 August, for instance, 'I sent out three Lachung men to reconnoitre towards Kangma.'

On 6 August, and again two days later, rumours reached the British camp that these particular agents had been captured, beaten and imprisoned by the Tibetans. An immediate protest was lodged by White; the men, he told a Tibetan official in the presence of Ho, the Chinese delegate, must be released and returned to Khamba Jong within ten days. On 19 August, this demand not having been complied with, an indemnity of a thousand rupees for each of the Lachung men was levied, and Colonel Brander, at Tangu, was instructed to seize all Tibetan-owned livestock found grazing on the Sikkimese side of the frontier near Giaogong; two hundred yaks and fifty sheep were impounded. On the same day Younghusband sent a report of the affair to India, suggesting that if, as appeared probable, the Lhasa Government and not merely the local authorities were behind 'this unfriendly act,' the Government of India 'may wish to take more special notice of the case.' The hint was not lost on the Viceroy.

On the 20th Younghusband followed this report with two

petitions from the families of the spies, humbly imploring the intervention of the British Government on their missing relatives' behalf. In these documents, whose wording is so similar and so succinct as to cast doubts on their spontaneity, the Lachung men were stated to have gone to Shigatse 'for trading purposes,' a fiction which was maintained throughout the references to them in British official correspondence.

By 2 September the pair of unfortunates were well on their way to attaining an international significance; the Tibetans were to be informed, cabled the Foreign Secretary from Simla, that 'unless immediate reparation is made, we shall exact restitution as we think fit.' The Viceroy drew the Secretary of State's attention to the matter in a telegram, and strong diplomatic protests were made in Peking about the two Lachung men. Only in Younghusband's weekly letters to his father, in which he described all developments of importance, was no mention of them made.

Anxiety about the detainees was revived on 10 October, when Younghusband telegraphed that missionaries at Lachung, which was largely dependent on its trade with Shigatse, had represented that the town was 'paralysed with fear' by reports that its two long-lost citizens had been tortured and cut in pieces. But their finest hour came when, in a long despatch to the Secretary of State dated 5 November 1903 and enclosing eighty-four supplementary documents, Lord Curzon made their supposed martyrdom the spearhead of his attack on the iniquities of Lhasa. 'Perhaps, however,' he fulminated, 'the most conspicuous proof of the hostility of the Tibetan Government and of their contemptuous disregard for the usages of civilisation has been the arrest of two British subjects from Lachung at Shigatse, whence they have been deported to Lhasa, and, it is credibly asserted, have been tortured and killed.'

For a brief period the two Lachung men evoked the wrath and pity of *désorientés* leader-writers and, if they cannot be said to have deeply affected the emotions of their fellow-subjects in Great Britain, at least caused more of a stir than generally falls to the lot of individuals so obscure that nobody knows their names. Very soon, however, they dropped out of the running and were forgotten. They had, after all, played their part; and five days after Lord Curzon had written his despatch a circumstantial Nepalese report revealed that the 'two spies sent by the British to Shigatse on a pretence of making some purchases' were confined in a Lhasa gaol, where they were being well treated.

CHAPTER SEVEN

The Telegram of 6 November

IN the autumn of 1903 the fortunes of Mr Balfour's Conservative administration were at a low ebb. The British Government was in no mood to grasp the nettle so insistently proffered by the Viceroy, and he knew it. 'Not until we move forward will any progress be made,' he wrote to Sir Hugh Barnes, the Lieutenant-Governor of Burma, on 20 September 1903. 'But will a tottering Home Government ever commit themselves to this?' *

It seemed unlikely; but weak Governments, like weak men, are sometimes subject to a kind of spasm which nerves them momentarily to hardihood, and on 1 October Curzon was notified that, in the event of a complete rupture of negotiations, not only the occupation of the Chumbi Valley but an advance to Gyantse would be sanctioned. This was the course which he had urged in a forceful telegram on 16 September. Its adoption was not attended in London by any marked enthusiasm; after showing the telegram to the Prime Minister, the Foreign Secretary, Lansdowne, recorded in a minute that Mr Balfour 'is incredulous as to the importance of Tibetan trade, and dislikes the idea of allowing ourselves to be permanently entangled in Tibet.' But an advance into the interior had been authorised.

Things began to move. A second regiment of Pioneers, the 23rd, were ordered up to repair the track leading out of Sikkim over the Jelap La into the Chumbi Valley. On 11 October Younghusband left Khamba Jong for consultations in Simla, and on the same day the Mission's escort was ostentatiously strengthened by a hundred rifles from the support-group at

* Barnes MSS.

Tangu. This caused a frenzy of speculation among the Tibetans and Chinese at Khamba Jong, and couriers galloped off to Lhasa with the news.

Meanwhile there were developments, ominous from the Tibetan point of view, in Nepal. This independent kingdom still paid triennial tribute to the Chinese Emperor and was bound by treaty to come to Tibet's aid if she was attacked; but although British influence at Katmandu was asserted only through a Resident, Nepal valued the British connexion highly and showed much zeal in furthering, or trying to further, the Viceroy's Tibetan policy. In September the Nepalese Prime Minister had written to the Lhasa authorities a long letter in which he urged them to behave reasonably, to fulfil their treaty obligations, and to trust the British, of whose honourable and humane behaviour Nepal had long experience. 'Thinking,' he sagely concluded, 'that to bring about unnecessary complications with the British Government is like producing a headache by twisting a rope round one's head when it is not aching, I have written to you my views, and I see it clearly that, if you disregard my advice, a serious calamity is likely to overtake you.'

No response was evoked by this attempt at mediation, and the Nepalese Government followed it up with an offer to supply the Mission and its escort with a large number of yaks—five hundred during September and a further eight thousand in the following month. The offer was accepted, and great droves of these useful pack-animals were already moving up from Nepal when Younghusband left Khamba Jong for Simla. It was a clear indication that Tibet could expect no succour from her neighbour.

Younghusband could not help being gratified by his reception in Simla. He had been conscious, while he was at Khamba Jong, that the Government of India were treating him with a respect and consideration not normally accorded to a comparatively junior officer of the Political Department; 'literally not the smallest move is made without consulting me,' he wrote to his father on 2 October, 'and I get two or three cypher telegrams from Government every day now.' In Simla he found that he was the man of the moment. 'As you know, Governments invariably have an "only man." For the present I am in that fortunate position and from being neglected I have been raised to a pinnacle of trust. But I know Governments well enough to be aware that this does not last.'

Another letter to his father, dated 28 October 1903, gives a revealing snapshot of Curzon as a moulder of Imperial policy. The Viceroy was in bed after a riding accident. Younghusband was summoned to the presence with Dane, the Foreign Secretary. 'The Viceroy was very cordial in his reception; but the interview which lasted nearly two hours was rather formal. He asked me to state the present situation and took notes as I spoke. Then he asked me for proposals for the measures I thought necessary and my reasons for making them: and took down each as I gave it. Then he spoke against everything I had said, threw cold water on each of my proposals and flouted my reasoning. This I knew was all put on, so I stuck to my arguments and would not budge. At the end of the interview he said the question would be placed before Council the next day and he asked me to attend. . . .

'Next day I attended Council and was given a seat at the Council table immediately on the left of the Viceroy. It was all most amusing. Kitchener beamed affably on me as I took my seat, and then the Viceroy began making a long speech, exactly like he might have in the House of Commons. He said he had summoned me to Simla to consult me personally: that he had been most anxious to avoid an advance but that the advice I had given him had made him reluctantly change his mind: and then he proceeded to spout out all the arguments I had used on the previous day and to adopt all my proposals. After mentioning each he turned to me and said "That is what you recommend, I think?" . . . Finally it was decided to telegraph my advice to the Secretary of State and to recommend its adoption.

'It was very interesting seeing the Council. I fancy from

what I saw and have heard that nobody says much against the Viceroy. He does not so much invite discussion as lay down the law and almost defiantly ask if anyone has any objection. If anyone *has* he is promptly squashed. Kitchener seems to treat the whole business as rather a bore and if the Viceroy asks him if he has any remarks to make throws himself back and says "Oh, no." '

Next day Younghusband had an interview with the Commander-in-Chief, whom he found 'most genial and jovial.' 'The main thing I asked for was some British soldiers. In the provisional scheme the Military had drawn up there was not a single British soldier. I said that politically we ought to have some white faces to show up there. Kitchener said "All right, you shall have the section of a *British* mountain battery and two Maxim gun detachments all of British soldiers and I will give orders that not a single man is to be under six feet." ' Younghusband thanked him and—perhaps remembering his little Gurkhas and Captain Grombtchevski—'said I would tell the Tibetans that we only sent *small* men with our guns.'

Kitchener told him to write to him direct if he wanted anything; 'this is really a great boon, and it is much to be in private correspondence with both Lord Curzon and Lord Kitchener.' People, he noted, were impressed by the confidence which Curzon placed in him, 'for nearly everyone else he sits on most desperately. . . . I am I believe one of the very few out here he unbends to. At the interview when Dane was present he always called him Mr Dane and was exceedingly stiff with him. I think he might with advantage unbend to others as well as me; but I suppose being a young man when he came out he stiffened himself up to assert himself and so keeps stiffened up. . . . He is absolutely *hated* here—this year worse than ever!'

It seemed at this stage that the die had been cast and that His Majesty's Government, though not prepared to send a force as far as Lhasa, were committed to a cut-down but still venturesome version of the policy which Curzon had been advocating for a year or more. But while plans for the advance to Gyantse were being worked out in Simla under Younghusband's supervision, the not very animated political scene in London underwent a mild convulsion which was to have far-reaching consequences for the Tibetan expedition.

This is not the place to anatomise the Cabinet crisis, provoked by a clash of convictions about fiscal policy and adroitly manipulated in his own favour by the Prime Minister, which led to the resignations of Mr Joseph Chamberlain, the Duke of Devonshire and Lord George Hamilton. It had however two important repercussions upon the project which was being mounted in Simla.

Its first, and more indirect, result was to produce in the reconstituted Cabinet a more favourable disposition towards France and her ally, Russia, and a less favourable one towards Germany, of whom Chamberlain in particular had been a partisan. As this feeling ripened, the British Government became increasingly tender toward Russian susceptibilities and increasingly reluctant to ruffle them by asserting a British interest, however legitimate, in Tibet.

But the Cabinet crisis had a more direct and less impersonal impact not only upon British policy in Tibet but upon the man who framed it and the man who carried it out; for it brought to the India Office, fresh from an inept tenure of the War Office, Mr St John Brodrick.

He replaced Lord George Hamilton, who had been there since 1895. Lord George's record as Secretary of State was not outstanding, but he knew India and for four years he had somehow contrived to keep the peace between His Majesty's Government and the King-Emperor's representative in India, who was not always successful in dissembling a tendency to regard Cabinet Ministers as insufficiently appreciative vassals. (Balfour once said that Curzon as Viceroy claimed a predominance for his views on policy which, if granted, 'would raise India to the position of an independent and not always friendly Power.') Lord George had been impotent to prevent the Viceroy from flaring up, but he had succeeded in limiting the scope of the conflagrations. While he was at the

India Office, the tether which bound the Viceroy to White-hall neither chafed unendurably nor came near to break-ing.

His successor was one of those figures who recur throughout the history of British party-politics: a man who, although remarkable neither for his talents nor his principles, is tacitly, perhaps even reluctantly, regarded as an indispensable pillar of his party's fortunes and, when it is in power, is automatically given a portfolio. Brodrick's 'never-failing gaucherie,' Lord George had written to Curzon in August, 'will prevent him from ever becoming either a popular or a really capable minister,' and in the following month Kitchener wrote to Lady Salisbury from Chitral: 'I also had a letter of abuse from Brodrick [then still Secretary of State for War] of which I have taken no notice. What he will do to us if he comes to the India Office is too dreadful to contemplate.' *

But though Brodrick had his enemies, the Viceroy of India was not among them. The two men, contemporaries at Eton and Oxford, had up to now been exceptionally close friends. They were members of the same circle, and when Curzon was in England met frequently and exchanged confidences. When Curzon was on his travels they kept up a regular correspond-ence, in which loyalty, affection and something akin to adula-tion supplied the keynotes in Brodrick's letters. 'You have been the good genius of my life for twenty years!' Curzon wrote to him before leaving to assume the Viceroyalty; and when Brodrick's first wife died in 1901 Lady Curzon, who was in London, wrote to her husband: 'I shall stay here for the funeral because he is your dearest friend.' †

Such was the relationship existing between the Viceroy and the new Secretary of State when the latter took office at the end of October 1903. Men who knew them both might have pre-dicted that their lifelong friendship would not emerge altogether scatheless from the stresses to which the tug-of-war between India and Whitehall was bound to subject it. No one could

---

* Salisbury MSS.
† Ravensdale-Metcalfe MSS.

have foreseen that exactly two years later Lady Curzon would
be writing to her mother 'Our life here under St John Brodrick
has been perfect hell—you would not treat a dog as he has
treated George:' to which Curzon added that the Secretary of
State had been 'unsleeping in his malevolence.' *

Simla was made promptly aware that, as far as Tibet was
concerned, its hard-won snaffle had been replaced by a curb.
Sir Arthur Godley, the Permanent Under-Secretary at the
India Office, recalled in the following year that 'on his very
first appearance in his room at this office [St John Brodrick] had
to take a line about Tibet—yes or no.' The line he took was
disagreeably apparent from his first telegram to the Viceroy,
despatched on 29 October: 'Though I fully appreciate the
force of the reasons which cause you to urge an immediate
advance to Gyantse I see from my predecessor's telegram to
you of the 1st October that the advance was contingent on a
rupture of negotiations which has not yet taken place. Please
let me have a full estimate of the expenditure involved, and a
statement of the troops necessary to maintain communications.'

This was a callow telegram. It was perfectly clear that, as
the Viceroy hastened to point out, 'the rupture of negotiations
with Tibet (if, indeed, negotiations can be said to have ever
begun) is not only inevitable but has taken place.' The probable cost of the expedition and the number of troops involved
were not questions which could be usefully raised by the Home
Government at this very late stage. The message boded
obstruction and interference.

Curzon was obliged to fight all over again a battle which
he thought he had already won. On 4 November a long
telegram recapitulated the main factors in the situation and
the cogent arguments against withdrawal or inaction; only a
small force would be needed, and the total cost of the expedition was calculated at £153,000. Simultaneously a long
despatch—the one in which the supposed fate of the two

* Ravensdale-Metcalfe MSS.

93

Lachung men played a role analogous to that of Jenkins's Ear
—was put in the mails, together with a large miscellany of documents dealing at first hand with the frustrations of the last five
months.

Luck gave the Viceroy the opportunity of adding a small
bombshell to this barrage. His main telegram was followed on
the same day by a stop-press item: '*Tibetan affairs*. An overt act
of hostility has taken place, Tibetan troops having, as we are
now informed, attacked Nepalese yaks on the frontier and
carried off many of them.' This report of aggression against an
independent state (or rather against its livestock) was not, perhaps, likely to stiffen the sinews and summon up the blood of
Mr Balfour's Cabinet; the fact of its despatch, and its dramatic
wording, reflect Curzon's anxiety to arrest the backsliding
tendency in British policy of which Brodrick's telegram had
made him newly aware.

What the message from the Assistant Resident in Nepal had
in fact revealed was that the yaks and their unarmed Nepalese
escort (five of whom were frozen to death in a snowstorm which
coincided with the encounter) were entering Tibetan territory
when they were stopped by a strong party of armed and
mounted men, who proceeded to disperse the yaks with the aid
of rattles. This was not a friendly proceeding; it could fairly be
described as uncouth. But to call it 'an overt act of hostility'
(by implication committed against the British) was an example
of the mild intellectual dishonesty into which—as with the two
Lachung men—Curzon allowed himself to lapse when striving,
against formidable odds, to impose his will on Whitehall. His
tactics here remind one, not for the first time or the last, of an
advocate attempting to sway a jury; it was a role which,
probably because it ill became his probity of intellect, he played
less effectively than he imagined.

In London the question was considered, or reconsidered, by
the Cabinet on 6 November, and that evening Brodrick summarised their decision in a telegram which, since the oddly
nebulous statement of policy contained in it was ever thereafter

treated as definitive and sacrosanct, requires to be quoted in full:

'In view of the recent conduct of the Tibetans, His Majesty's Government feel that it would be impossible not to take action, and they accordingly sanction the advance of the Mission to Gyantse. They are, however, clearly of opinion that this step should not be allowed to lead to occupation or to permanent intervention in Tibetan affairs in any form. The advance should be made for the sole purpose of obtaining satisfaction, and as soon as reparation is obtained a withdrawal should be effected. While His Majesty's Government consider the proposed action to be necessary, they are not prepared to establish a permanent mission in Tibet, and the question of enforcing trade facilities in that country must be considered in the light of the decision conveyed in this telegram.'

Although it laid down firmly what the Government of India was *not* to do, this directive was both vague and inconsequent in its more positive aspects. What was meant by 'obtaining satisfaction' and 'obtaining reparation?' What was meant by 'enforcing trade facilities?' Taken literally, these expressions seemed to imply that a diplomatic mission with a specific purpose was now regarded in London as a punitive expedition with undefined objectives. 'The view,' Curzon complained on 24 November (in a telegram omitted from the Blue Book), 'that we are going to Gyantse simply in order to secure from the Tibetans legal reparation or satisfaction is not quite understood by me.' Surely, he went on, the object of sending the Mission into Tibet was to negotiate a new Convention?

But neither then nor later was he able to shake the Government's almost mystical faith in the lapidary status of the telegram of 6 November as a declaration of British policy. It is impossible not to agree with Younghusband's comment, made six years later, on this 'curious telegram': 'It is remarkable that a document which was so often quoted to the Russian Government, to the Indian Government, to the Chinese Government, and which the Indian Government on one occasion quoted to me in terms of admonition, should have described with so little precision the real purpose of the advance.' *

* *India and Tibet.*

The Curzonian adventure to which, in however gingerly a fashion, it was committed had never appealed to the British Government. The project, distasteful while it was still a State secret, became doubly so now that it was about to emerge into the limelight as a *fait accompli*. 'I hardly think,' Brodrick wrote to Curzon in the following spring, 'you can realise how little appetite there is in England at this moment for another little war of any description.'

A Blue Book, containing a collection of State papers going back to 1889, was already being printed for presentation to Parliament. 'From the diplomatic point of view,' wrote a senior civil servant in the India Office to his opposite number in the Foreign Office at the end of October, 'I understand that it is desirable to indicate that the Government of India had ~~good~~ sufficient reason to be alarmed by the reports they received as to Tibetan missions to Russia in 1900 and 1901 and as to a secret Agreement between Russia and China as to Tibet in 1902.' A reluctantly conspiratorial atmosphere pervaded the handling in London of a delicate matter which very few felt strongly about and none completely understood.

The Russian Government were notified in general terms, on 7 November, of the impending advance into Tibet and of its limited and legitimate objectives. So were the Chinese Government. Both protested, the Chinese feebly, the Russians less forcibly than had been feared. There were signs that the matter was being officially played down in St Petersburg, whence the British Embassy reported on 12 November that, although 'the news of the British expedition has caused much hostile comment,' only one newspaper had attacked it editorially; 'it may therefore be supposed that a warning has been conveyed to the Press.'

The reactions of the British Press were cool at best. A military expedition, which has been prearranged behind the scenes by the politicians, the reasons for which are complex and difficult to explain, and which no correspondents are allowed to accompany, never makes a strong *prima facie* appeal to

Brodrick

Khamba Jong

editors or, indeed, to their readers. 'It is really about time,' grumbled the *Westminster Gazette* on 2 December, 'that the Government should tell us what they are doing in Tibet and why they are doing it.' It would have been difficult to select from among the members of Mr Balfour's Cabinet a spokesman willing or competent to comply with either demand.

CHAPTER EIGHT

The Commander of the Escort

THE difficulties attending an advance into Tibet from Indian territory were very great; the diagram on the opposite page gives some idea of the geographical foundations on which they were based.

It had at first been assumed that the physical obstacles were insuperable during the winter. In September Curzon cited this assumption as one of the factors which made speed imperative: 'a further complication is that any sort of action will be difficult after November.' But six weeks later his thinking on this important point had changed, and he was cabling to the new Secretary of State that 'though cold, the season of the year is entirely favourable, and we anticipate no difficulty in carrying through the operation and maintaining communications and supplies.'

It was Younghusband—sanguine, indomitable, above all experienced—who during his October visit to Simla had convinced the Viceroy and the Commander-in-Chief that an old tradition on the North East Frontier was rooted in fallacy. He had questioned White closely about local conditions, and had come to the conclusion that what had been done on the high passes of Gilgit and Chitral was feasible on the even higher passes of Tibet. 'We do not hesitate,' he wrote later, 'when there is real necessity, to send troops and missions into unhealthy and hot places in the hottest season of the year. Why, then, should we be put off by cold? . . . I know that passes which are closed for single men or small parties are not necessarily closed for large parties, which can organize regular

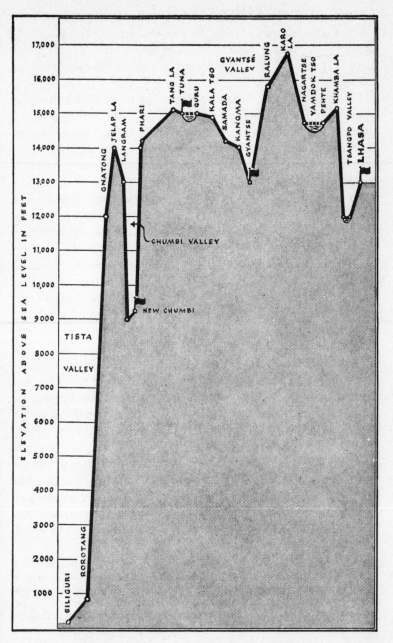

Diagram illustrating Altitudes on Route.
Horizontal distances are not to scale. The distance from Siliguri to Lhasa is roughly 400 miles.

shelters and trample down paths in the snow.' He admitted, nevertheless, that a winter advance was 'a risk to take, and Lord Curzon and the Government of India were courageous in taking it.' *

No military force, before or since, has faced such vehement opposition from climate and terrain; nature seriously complicated the basic problem of supply, which was comparable to that confronting an old-fashioned Antarctic expedition.

Railhead was at Siliguri, a wayside station whence a narrow-gauge offshoot of the Bengal Railway branched off to zigzag 7000 feet up the mountainside to Darjeeling. There was nothing at all at Siliguri except the little railway-station—no cantonments, no go-downs, no nucleus of accommodation which could be expanded to meet the requirements of a military base. Tents for the staff, transit-camps for newly detrained units, mule-lines, bullock-lines, hovels for hundreds of coolies, latrines, a water-supply—everything had to be improvised. There was no other source from which supplies could reach the expedition.

They reached it on the backs of animals or men.† This method of transport is subject to the law of diminishing returns, since the animal must carry its own fodder and the man his rations, cooking utensils, blankets and so on. If, for instance, a mule's standard load is 160 lbs and the mule needs 10 lbs of fodder a day, it can carry 80 lbs of ammunition for four days, after which it must return to base. A coolie's carrying-power is similarly limited, and when man and beast form part of a force advancing in what amounts to single file through inhospitable country, neither can rely on supplementing their rations from local resources, because the head of the column consumes whatever poor perquisites, in the way of grazing or fuel, are to be found

* *India and Tibet.*

† Or sometimes women. One Coolie Corps, recruited from the natives of the Tista Valley, embodied large numbers of the weaker sex. The winter clothing issued to this Corps included warm pyjamas, which were intended to be worn at work. At first the ladies objected strongly to these unfeminine garments; but they were reconciled to them, and before long pyjamas were the height of fashion on the banks of the Tista.

in its path. In Tibet this age-old problem was complicated by the fact that above the tree-line no firewood was available; since in that climate men could not survive without at least a cooking-fire, this often meant a further readjustment in the loads between the sinews of war and the necessities of life, always in favour of the latter. And the further the spearhead of the expedition advanced, the greater—and the more nearly self-defeating—became the administrative effort required to nourish it.

A campaign which is, or which is felt by the soldiers to be, primarily the concern of politicians always starts under a handicap; the advance into Tibet was no exception. Officially, at the outset, it was not a military operation at all. The troops were there only to act as escort to the Mission; Kitchener and GHQ were playing second fiddle to Curzon and the Foreign Department. There was thus a natural tendency for senior staff-officers to drag their feet. In the mounting of the expedition this lack of wholeheartedness, combined with the underestimation of some problems and the failure to foresee others, sponsored a number of false economies.

There were, to begin with, not enough pioneers and engineers, not enough coolies and pack-animals, and not enough junior officers and non-commissioned officers to supervise transport and stock-piling. The units already in Sikkim worked feverishly, but the best they could do was to half-solve every problem they tackled, and along the line of communication these half-solutions, like mathematical errors in a column of figures, snowballed and produced fresh problems of their own. 'Transport has broken down,' a staff officer wrote to his wife on 21 October, 'and the supply depots are a mass of chaos which it will take months to straighten out.'

It may be doubted whether any military expedition, in any age, pressed into its service a wider variety of quadrupeds. In the *Report on the Supply and Transport Arrangements with the late Tibet Mission Force*, a paragraph headed 'Animals' includes the following statistics:

Animals	Number Employed	Casualties	Percentage of Casualties on Number Employed
Mules	7,096	910	12·8
Bullocks	5,234	954	18·2
Camels	6	6	100
Buffaloes	138	137	99·2
Riding Ponies	185	24	12·9
Pack Ponies	1,372	899	65·5
Nepalese Yaks	2,953	2,922	98·9
Tibetan Yaks	1,513	1,192	78·7
Ekka Ponies	1,111	277	24·9

The final entry on the list dealt with two-legged animals:

Coolies	10,091	88	0·87 *

Except for the Tibetan yaks, which were acquired by purchase or capture on their native uplands, the whole of this menagerie had to pass through the Tista Valley, where anthrax, rinderpest and foot-and-mouth disease were rife. As the improvised track climbed into the mountains, many animals died from eating aconite, a poisonous plant better known in the British Isles as monkshood or wolfsbane. The Nepalese yaks, whose adventures while in transit had helped in a small way to launch the campaign, were completely wiped out; the thirty-one who on paper survived were in fact slaughtered and eaten. They were mostly half-breeds, and included many cows and young animals unfit for pack-work. The very heavy casualties among the Tibetan yaks were due mainly to undernourishment. During the winter, when the force was immobile, grazing was scarce, and inevitably became scarcer, around its quarters; and in the spring, when the advance was resumed, the stages proved

* This list was incomplete in at least one respect. A young subaltern serving with the 7th Mountain Battery wrote in his diary: 'In my Section are two Zebrules, half zebra and half donkey, which the Government of India insisted on being taken on this show and thoroughly tested out as gun-mules. They are more trouble on the march than the whole section put together. They cannot carry any load at all and even bareback have to have men told off to haul them up the slopes. The men hate them.'

too long for a slow-moving animal whose disconsolate progress is best interrupted after five or six miles so that *Bos grunniens*, the grumbling ox, can restore his energies. The mules, outnumbering any other category of animals and yet suffering negligible losses, reasserted with their usual bad grace a reputation for dependability on even the most outlandish form of active service.

The construction and maintenance of a pack-trail (for it could hardly be called a road) presented appalling difficulties; these were increased by divided responsibilities, remote control and parsimony. The route as far as the Tibetan frontier was theoretically under the jurisdiction of the Public Works Department, Bengal (for the first thirty miles), and the Public Works Department, Sikkim. A company of Sappers and Miners, later assisted by the 32nd Pioneers, had begun to repair it in the early summer of 1903. Floods, mud, landslides and disease hampered work in the Tista Valley; in the mountains stiff gradients, intractable boulders, and ice (which caused many casualties among the animals) had to be coped with. It was obvious from the first that a large labour-force was required.

But military labour was cheaper and easier to control than an army of coolies, whose need to be housed, clothed and fed would clutter up an already overburdened line of communication. Estimates of the cost of all work undertaken had to be approved by the Government of India before the work was sanctioned; and on at least one occasion sanction was withdrawn after the work had been put in hand, so that the coolies engaged on it had to be paid off and disbanded. The following extract from the official *Report on Engineer Operations of the Tibet Mission Escort 1903–04* gives some idea of the bureaucratic imbroglio which hung like a distant thunder-cloud over the pioneers who were striving to open a way to Lhasa:

On 26 March the Quartermaster General conveyed the orders of Government to the effect that when sanction was originally given to the construction of a mule path, Government understood that one already existed, and that it could be improved and kept open for a small outlay; that there was no intention of constructing a permanent road; that economy was the first consideration; that work was NOT to be entrusted to the Public Works Department; that arrangements were to be made to construct it by military labour; and that the total expenditure was to be limited to 20,000 Rupees.*

Setbacks recurred throughout the mounting of the operation; the most serious were the wholesale losses of pack-animals from disease, but countless others, including delays in the supply of winter clothing for the troops and coolies, plagued the small, hard-pressed staff in Sikkim. Nevertheless, by early December 1903 preparations were as complete as they were ever likely to be, and the Tibet Frontier Commission was poised at Gnatong for an advance over the Jelap La, 14,390 feet high, into Tibet. The detachment still left at Khamba Jong under Captain Ryder, the Survey Officer, were meanwhile carrying out a withdrawal which promised to be hazardous but proved un-eventful; they rejoined Younghusband in the Chumbi Valley.

The Mission's escort mustered at this stage roughly 1150 fighting men, with four guns and two Maxims. It was made up as follows:

One section of the 7th Mountain Battery, Royal Garrison Artillery, with two ten-pounder screw-guns.

Two seven-pounder guns manned by men of the 8th Gurkhas and carried by coolies. Known as Bubble and Squeak, these two cannon had seen more than forty years' service on the frontier and possessed small military value.

8th Gurkhas (six companies).

23rd Sikh Pioneers (eight companies).

2nd Sappers and Miners (half-company).

Maxim-gun detachment of the 1st Battalion, the Norfolk Regiment.

Field hospital, engineer field park, telegraph, postal and sundry detachments.

* £1333 6s. 8d.

THE COMMANDER OF THE ESCORT

In immediate reserve were the 32nd Pioneers, with the remaining elements of the 8th Gurkhas and the 23rd Pioneers. It was not a very formidable expedition to launch, in midwinter, into hostile and unknown territory on the Roof of the World.

There was in the manning of this enterprise an element of duality; it is of cardinal importance to bear in mind the distinction between the Tibet Frontier Commission, which was a small diplomatic delegation composed partly of civilians and partly of soldiers seconded to the Foreign Department, and its much larger military escort. The troops forming the latter were not technically on active service; * their role was in theory limited to protecting the persons of the Mission and ensuring its safe passage to whatever rendezvous should be appointed for negotiations; their commander's status was ancillary.

This delicately poised relationship between military and political interests forms a pattern which recurs throughout the history of British rule in India. The two interests are seldom easily compatible. The outlook of a political agent and a commander in the field are almost bound to differ, and to demarcate their respective spheres of responsibility in unforeseeable contingencies is impossible. Their partnership is full of the seeds of conflict. Where, in the decision to arrest a tribal leader, to bombard a fort, or to burn down a village, is the border-line between political and military action? Who should have the say when it comes to taking a calculated risk—the man who is carrying out a political directive, or the man who is worrying about the safety of his troops? Friction, or worse, is all but inevitable when control is shared between the military and the civil power in a difficult adventure. The only hope of averting it is to ensure that each is represented by an individual who is likely to get on well with his opposite number. This was not done in Tibet.

* By a special dispensation they were granted field service allowances in June 1904.

Colonel J. R. L. Macdonald, CB, of the Royal Engineers, was on 29 September 1903 appointed 'Commandant Royal Engineers on the road from Siliguri onwards under the orders of the Director General Miscellaneous Works. He will assume command of all troops employed on the road from Siliguri onwards, with the exception of the actual escort of the Mission and its support.' At this date the 'actual escort of the Mission' would have meant the 32nd Pioneers, who were out in the blue at Khamba Jong and Tangu and whom it would have been practical to exclude from Macdonald's command on geographical grounds. But from the fact of his subordination to the Director General Miscellaneous Works it seems certain that he was originally destined for administrative duties on the lines of communication. A month later, however, the 'Sikkim Force News Summary' * recorded that 'Colonel Macdonald was informed that the troops under his command in Sikkim had been placed directly under the orders of the Commander-in-Chief, India.'

Although, since Kitchener had started his career in the Corps of Royal Engineers, a very slight element of military nepotism may have been involved, the general impression gained is that Macdonald (who shortly afterwards was promoted Brigadier-General) slipped almost fortuitously into command of the Tibet Mission Escort. He was not specially selected for a widely coveted appointment; he simply happened to be the only officer of suitable seniority in Sikkim at the time.†

It was remiss of GHQ to act so casually in an obviously important matter; and it is very strange that from the depths of the Viceroy's capacious memory Macdonald's name evoked no warning signals. For it was not the first time that this officer had been in the public eye.

* The Sikkim Force was redesignated the Tibet Mission Escort in November.

† For a keen Sapper with more than twenty years' service, the Directorate General of Miscellaneous Works in India must have been something of a backwater: and the fact that, in the British force sent to North China during the Boxer Rebellion three years earlier, Macdonald held the appointment of Director of Balloons rather suggests that he was not regarded as an outstanding officer.

THE COMMANDER OF THE ESCORT

As Under-Secretary of State for Foreign Affairs, a post which he held from 1895 to 1898, Curzon had been closely concerned with the Uganda Railway. In May 1892 Macdonald, then a thirty-year-old captain, arrived at Kampala in Uganda with a detachment of Indian troops; these formed part of an expedition under his command which had been surveying a route for the railway from the coast to Lake Victoria. The situation at Kampala was insecure. A wide area of East Africa was plagued by a civil war in which Protestant converts, Roman Catholic converts and Muslims were the chief though by no means the only contenders.

At Kampala Macdonald found Captain Lugard, a dynamic, dedicated servant of Empire. For months Lugard had been striving, with little to help him save the force of his personality, his long African experience and his flair for handling barbaric situations, to restore order in Uganda. He now urgently needed to return to England, where the situation in East Africa, and the international rivalries behind it, was viewed with considerable disquiet and very little comprehension.

It was a three months' march to the port of Mombasa, and to Lugard the appearance of Macdonald, with a contingent of well-armed, British-officered troops, was at first sight a godsend; for it meant that he could start for the coast—whither Macdonald also was bound—without denuding the weak Kampala garrison of rifles and riflemen. Macdonald readily agreed to afford Lugard and his retinue of some two hundred unarmed camp-followers protection on a dangerous journey.

It was perhaps inevitable—since Macdonald was Lugard's junior in age, in the *Army List* and in African experience—that in the course of a long and difficult march there would be some friction between the commander of the escort and the man he was escorting. In travel, as in all other human activities, mono-poly generates conflict; the man who holds the purse-strings, speaks the language, owns the car or (as in this case) controls the rifles, automatically becomes, at times, a target for the resentment of his less well-found companion.

But this simple rule of human nature provides no diagnosis

for Macdonald's conduct towards Lugard. Animated, on the face of it, by a mixture of paranoia and puerility, he sought every occasion to assert a *de jure* supremacy over the senior officer who was *de facto* dependent on him. 'He is a charming fellow whom I like immensely,' Lugard wrote in his diary on the eve of their departure from Kampala, 'but this question of command is his bugbear, and he is very sensitive about it.'

Throughout their arduous trek Macdonald's attitude was overweening and his behaviour pettish. He forced Lugard to acknowledge him, in writing, as his commanding officer. He insisted that Lugard's party should bring up the rear, thus exposing them to the maximum of heat, exasperation and delay. He required Lugard to dine in his mess-tent and then affronted him by reading a book at table. He accused Lugard's servants of looting and other misdemeanours and humiliated Lugard by publicly asserting his own right to flog them. He wrote—from a tent pitched within a biscuit-toss of the other man's—peremptory notes to Lugard, summoning him to an interview as though he were a subaltern or (as Lugard put it) 'a governess.' He badgered him, insulted him, kept him waiting and in general went out of the way to make life intolerable for perhaps the most distinguished of his compatriots then serving in East Africa.*

Reliable news of the disturbances in Uganda was scarce in Europe. Serious charges were being levelled against Lugard by French and German missionaries; he was accused of provoking the civil war, of committing atrocities, of high-handedness and gross injustice. His own version of events had not reached London, and the Government, disturbed by the controversy of which he was the centre, decided to appoint a commission of enquiry. As Commissioner—to Lugard's horror—they nominated Macdonald.

Macdonald's report reached the Foreign Office in 1893, a year and a half after the events which formed its theme. It was,

* For a full though necessarily partisan account of the extraordinary relationship between Macdonald and Lugard, see *The Diaries of Lord Lugard*, edited by Margery Perham, Vol. III; and for an assessment of that relationship, *Lugard: The Years of Adventure*, by the same author.

in the main, a damning indictment of Lugard. Its contents were unwelcome to the Government and its impartiality was suspect (Macdonald had among other things enlisted, as a sort of co-Commissioner, a German journalist of questionable reputation). The report was suppressed, and the charges against Lugard were ignored.

But (and this is the point here) the Lugard–Macdonald controversy dragged on behind the scenes, and left traces, both in the Foreign Office files and in the minds of officials who dealt with African affairs, which could hardly have escaped Curzon's notice when he was concerned with Uganda (in which, according to his biographer, 'he took a particular interest'). Lugard, for instance, deposited in the Foreign Office a sealed envelope dealing with Macdonald's shortcomings which was not returned to him until August 1895; and as late as March 1898 the conflict between the two men was discussed in a House of Commons debate. Lugard, who was not a man to suffer in silence, knew Curzon and was intermittently in touch with him during these years. One would have expected that in Curzon's mind Macdonald's name would have had, if not a black mark against it, at least a question-mark. This does not seem to have been so.

When, in the course of the expedition, Macdonald's fitness for his duties as Escort Commander came to be called in question, Curzon's references to him in private correspondence betray no previous knowledge of his career, though he admitted to doubting his suitability on general grounds. 'I should have doubted whether Macdonald is a big enough man for the job,' he wrote in June 1904 to Ampthill. 'I only selected him [*sic.* Curzon's responsibility must have been limited to approving the appointment] when we were looking to roads and communications. To what extent he is a soldier, strategist or commander I have no idea.' It is curious that he failed to identify the Royal Engineer who (as Lord Rosebery told the House of Lords in 1894) 'happened to be on the spot' in Uganda with the Royal Engineer who happened to be on the spot in Sikkim nine years later.

Among Younghusband's papers a letter survives which must be one of the first communications received by the British Commissioner from the man who was to command his Escort. It is dated 27 August 1903 from Gantok in Sikkim; at this stage Younghusband was still up at Khamba Jong and Macdonald was acting under the orders of the Director General Miscellaneous Works.

My dear Younghusband,

The Military Member [of the Viceroy's Council] is forcing on the despatch of the 23rd Pioneers, and I have said I will arrange for them, but no one will tell me where to put them.

I wired General Christopher about this, and he said I should ask you. I then wired Mr Dane,* as I knew you had made proposals to the Foreign Department; but he maintains a discreet silence. Last night Sir E. Barrow wired to me to arrange 'such details' with you and OC 23rd Pioneers.

The easiest place from a supply point of view is Siliguri, where depots already exist and supplies are stocked. If they go to Kalimpong or Padong I can manage also, but this would entail building depots and laying out a new line of transport. However there is no trouble about this *if only I can get orders.*

It is clear that when this letter was written—several weeks before an advance into Tibet was sanctioned—Macdonald regarded his own status as subordinate to Younghusband's; soldiers will recognise the plaintive tone of an officer engaged on administrative duties who is called on to solve an operational problem which he regards as lying outside his province. And it cannot be said that the letter reflects those qualities of initiative and resource which one would hope to find in an officer selected for independent command on, and beyond, the Indian frontier.

When the two men first met we do not know, but Young-

* There was at yet no telegraphic communication with the Mission at Khamba Jong; Macdonald could not therefore wire to Younghusband.

husband's first impressions of his colleague were—like Lugard's —favourable. Before he left Simla at the end of October he must have been aware that Macdonald was to command the Escort, and he wrote to his father: 'Macdonald is an excellent, sound, solid fellow and we shall get on capitally. Of course in actual military operations I have nothing to say. But otherwise I am to be the senior officer to him.' He wrote again from Calcutta on 11 November, reporting that Kitchener had accepted *in toto* his plan for the advance and adding: 'At the same time I have told Macdonald that from now till I reach Gyantse he must regard me simply as a precious parcel of goods to be carted from one place to another and taken the greatest possible care of on the way.'

Younghusband was essentially a generous-minded person, always determined to see the best in men and to get the best out of them. The first hint that his relations with his escort-commander were proving less harmonious than he had hoped came in a letter to his father written from Darjeeling on 24 November. The matter at issue was the future movements of the rump of the original Mission, still marooned at Khamba Jong. In Younghusband's plan, which had been accepted by GHQ, this small party with its escort of Pioneers was to move directly eastward across country to Kala Tso on the Tibetan tableland, where it would rendezvous with the main body, approaching via the Chumbi Valley and the Tang La. 'Macdonald, who is an exceedingly cautious, methodical Scotchman thought this plan too risky, and after arguing for three days I consented to recommend the change.' It seems probable that in this instance Macdonald's judgment was sound; there were obvious military risks, and no discernible political rewards, in committing the Khamba Jong detachment, which was under close surveillance, to an unsupported advance through Tibetan territory. But that it should have taken three days to resolve this minor dispute boded ill for the times ahead, when larger issues were certain to be in question.

At this stage, however, Younghusband still found Macdonald 'an exceptionally pleasant man to work with;' and when at dawn on 11 December 1903 the long straggling column moved off from Gnatong for a short first stage to the foot of the Jelap La, the two men rode side by side, following a mounted orderly bearing the Union Jack along the winding, snow-mantled valley. No one, then, could have foretold how great a part was to be played in the enterprise by the conflict between their irreconcilable outlooks.

Macdonald

The Fort at Phari

CHAPTER NINE

Over the Top

THE Jelap La, the pass which leads from Sikkim into Tibet, is 14,390 feet above sea-level. It was undefended, and this was fortunate for the expedition, as it clambered painfully up the southern face of the mountain range and slithered down the far side where, after the leading troops had trampled the snow, the track, 'as steep as the side of a house, became a regular slide, as slippery as glass. . . . I believe [wrote an officer afterwards] there was not a single load that was not thrown at least once. Somebody said that it reminded him more of the retreat from Moscow than the advance of a British army.' Because of the height, animals as well as men found themselves distressingly short of breath. The troops were partially equipped against the cold, but the ponies and mules, fresh from the sweltering Tista Valley, were not; many of their native drivers were inexperienced, much of their harness was ill-fitting or otherwise unsuitable. There were, and had been for some time, desertions among the indispensable coolies; Younghusband recalled that 'a curious feeling was prevalent on the frontier that we were advancing to our doom.' On the first stages of its march the force was in no shape to meet opposition.

This, in point of fact, was not expected. Immediately ahead of them lay Yatung, the chief of the places along the frontier which had been designated as trading-marts in the Treaty of 1890. The Tibetans had effectually prevented the use of these marts and, as at Giaogong, had built walls across the tracks leading in from India. But at Yatung there was an office of the Chinese Customs Service, and this was manned by that same

Captain Parr who had figured abortively as one of the Chinese delegates at Giaogong. Through him Younghusband had made it known to the local Tibetan commander that the British had no intention of fighting unless they met with resistance, and although this assurance had not been acknowledged, the invasion of Tibet began in the atmosphere of an armed truce, with both sides equally anxious to avoid firing the first shot.

'Ubiquitous' was the epithet which Younghusband used to describe Captain Parr, and it is a matter for regret that we do not know more about a minor actor who appears, always in a slightly equivocal role, in so many scenes of the Tibetan drama. His seems to have been the fate often reserved for the European who enters the service of an Oriental Power; neither his employers nor his compatriots ever wholly trusted him. 'I am unable to repose great confidence in Captain Parr,' the Chinese Amban wrote to Younghusband from Lhasa. By Miss Annie Taylor, an indomitable Scots missionary residing—dressed as a Tibetan—in Yatung, the Lieutenant-Governor of Bengal was warned that 'Englishmen in the Chinese Customs Service must be expected to look more after the interests of their Chinese masters, from whom they draw very high pay, than after the interests of their own countrymen.' As the advance continued, with Parr hanging on its flanks or popping up in its path, the wisdom of allowing him to transmit and receive cypher messages to and from Peking over the British telegraph-line came to be questioned, and the matter was the subject of several exchanges between Tibet, India, London and the British Legation in Peking. The privilege was never withdrawn, nor is there the slightest reason to suppose that it was abused.

At Yatung, Younghusband recorded, Captain Parr was 'in many ways extremely helpful at this time.' It would be possible to infer from this that at other times, and in other ways, Parr was unhelpful; but 'loquacious' is the worst pejorative which survives in the letters and diaries of the officers who met him and who were impressed (as far as Regulars would allow themselves to be) by the fact that he had obtained special leave from the Chinese Customs to go and serve his Queen with a volunteer regiment of Mounted Infantry in the Boer War.

The odds are that Parr was a lonely man, to whom the British expedition was like a passing ship to a castaway. He clung perhaps too closely to it, strove perhaps too officiously to serve it, exchanged perhaps prematurely his status as the local expert for that of the predictable intruder into ill-provided mess-tents. But at least (we may believe) he did his best to help; and at least the short British aggression upon Tibet interrupted the long hostilities between Captain Parr and the eccentric Miss Taylor, who once appealed to a relative in some faraway branch of the Public Works Department to induce the Government of India to 'dissuade the Commissioner of Customs from drowning his illegitimate children in my well.'

The force halted for the night at Langram, in a pine-forest some 2000 feet below the pass; they were relieved to be back within the tree-line, and huge fires blazed as the rearguard limped in well after dark. Here Younghusband was visited by Tibetan emissaries from Yatung. They pressed him to go back over the pass to Gnatong, where delegates would come to discuss matters with him. Younghusband refused. Would he then please wait where he was for two or three months? Younghusband said that he would not. What, the Tibetans asked, would the British do if they found the gate in the Yatung wall closed against them? Younghusband replied that they would blow it open. The Tibetans vanished disconsolately into the night.

Next morning—13 December—the force, throwing out scouts and flank-guards, advanced cautiously down the wooded gorge. In due course, rounding a bend, they found their path blocked by a stout wall, beyond which showed the mean roofs of Yatung. As a skirmishing party moved up to the wall the delegates of the night before reappeared, repeating their demands that the British should withdraw. But the gate in the wall was left open and the advance-guard passed through it, followed by Younghusband, Macdonald and their staffs.

Once inside the gate Younghusband dismounted and sat down on a rock. A large and curious crowd collected, mainly for whose benefit (it appeared to Younghusband) the Tibetan general made a speech of protest. The British Commissioner replied in firm but conciliatory terms, the assembly broke up in an atmosphere of bemused jollity and everybody of consequence went to luncheon with Captain Parr, at whose house they were soon joined by a party of Chinese and Tibetan officials bringing an assortment of their respective national dishes, so that in the end three meals had to be eaten, one on top of the other.

This was an auspicious beginning; and for the next few days, as they advanced up the Chumbi Valley, Younghusband's hopes of a peaceful settlement ran high, while the soldiers morosely discussed the receding prospects of a campaign medal. The people of the valley (called Tromos and not of pure Tibetan stock) were friendly and co-operative. The British paid as handsomely as Indian Government regulations allowed for everything they bought or hired; supplies of fodder, mules and ponies were readily obtained; the women and children, who had taken to the hills, returned to the filthy, stone-built villages. Blood pheasants and monals promised sport and a change of diet; despite the stringent restrictions on the weight of an officer's personal kit, a surprising number had brought shotguns with them.

Beyond Yatung the route over the Jelap La joined the main axis of the Chumbi Valley, down which flowed the Ammo Chu,* and a few miles beyond the village of Chumbi, at a place to which they unimaginatively gave the name of New Chumbi, the expedition halted, shook itself out, and set about forming an advanced base. Here the Mission, which had been joined by the Khamba Jong party under Ryder, was to stay for a few days, while the Escort reconnoitred the way ahead and established the supply-dumps which were essential to further progress. Macdonald marched north with just under eight hundred rifles

* *Chu* means river.

on 18 December; their route, it was believed, had never before been traversed by a European.

On the third day out this advance-guard debouched from a narrow, highly defensible but unguarded gorge and moved across a desolate and fuelless plain to the great castellated fort of Phari. Here resistance was expected. When the fort came into sight 'our first impression was "If this is held it will take a good deal of taking;" ' * and the assurances of the Tibetan garrison-commander that he had no intention of fighting were initially suspected as a ruse. But it turned out that he meant what he said. The grimy, stout-walled, almost impregnable keep was occupied by two companies of the 8th Gurkhas with one of the obsolete seven-pounders and ten days' rations; and after the Mounted Infantry had reconnoitred without incident the 15,200-foot Tang La, separating the Chumbi Valley from the main Tibetan tableland, Macdonald took the remainder of his force back to New Chumbi. Here Christmas was celebrated, amid complaints that forty degrees of frost made champagne undrinkable.

Things had gone well—surprisingly well—thus far; Younghusband's reports to India, still laced with vague rumours of Dorjieff's activities and Russian influence at Lhasa, breathed a cautious confidence. But for him personally it cannot have been a very happy Christmas; although he as yet mentioned the fact to no one, he was finding his relations with his Escort Commander increasingly irksome.

'We were never started off right,' he wrote to Dane, the Foreign Secretary, on 4 June 1904 in a letter reviewing the origins of what was by then a sort of undeclared feud. It had not been explained to Macdonald that, unless fighting broke out, the Escort's role was ancillary. From the first 'he was very much "the General Officer Commanding." The Mission was a bothersome detail very much in the way. Even at Darjeeling he used to send for me to his room. And after we crossed the frontier he undoubtedly thought he was supreme. Though I

* Ottley: *With Mounted Infantry in Tibet.*

never complained about a detail of that kind I never thought well of him for pitching my camp to the left of his the whole march up here.' *

These, as Younghusband admitted, were trivial matters; but the advance to Phari produced two specific incidents, one of which irritated, while the other deeply angered him.

From New Chumbi Captain Ryder and Mr Hayden, the geologist attached to the Mission, sought and were given permission by Younghusband to follow the advance-guard up to Phari. Half-way there they met Macdonald, who was returning with the bulk of his force; he forbade them to go on, saying that they were under his orders and that it was unsafe to proceed without an escort. 'It was most silly rot stopping us,' Ryder wrote to his wife that night; 'I expect Colonel Younghusband will be a bit annoyed with the General.' This forecast was fulfilled. 'I told Macdonald [Younghusband wrote to Dane] that I was perfectly willing to *lend* him Ryder's services . . . but he was under my orders till transferred to the Military by the orders of Government.'

This breach of protocol, though its effect on nerves and emotions may have been enhanced by the altitude, was essentially a domestic tiff. Of far greater significance, in Younghusband's eyes, was Macdonald's decision to occupy the fort at Phari. This Younghusband regarded as an unforgivable departure from a policy which he had concerted, after full discussion, with his Escort Commander. Younghusband had assured the Tibetans at large, and specifically the Phari Jongpen, who visited him at New Chumbi, that the British would take no hostile action as long as the Tibetans took none. The Tibetans, leaving a succession of death-traps undefended, had scrupulously kept their side of the unratified bargain; 'I do not see how under the circumstances then can think us anything else but deceitful when under the guise of a peaceful Mission we quietly walked into one of their forts.' Younghusband's sense of chivalry was outraged; he felt that Macdonald had not only broken faith with him but had involved him in a breach of faith with the

* In all armies the right is senior to the left.

Tibetans, thereby prejudicing his status as a negotiator. 'I was very angry,' he told Dane, 'and I have never spoken to any man as severely as I did to Macdonald about that.'

The dilemma sketched in the preceding chapter is here seen very clearly. Which mattered most—the safety and comfort of the British troops, or the susceptibilities of the Tibetans? How, and by whom, should the risks of a military disaster be weighed against the prospects of a diplomatic success? The question is never easily resolved. Within four decades history was to reproduce this predicament several times, and on a much larger scale. Mobilise, or continue negotiations without mobilising? Heads or Tails? The coin has often been spun in Europe, and much ink has been spent in proving that those who called Tails should have called Heads, or vice versa.

It is difficult not to feel that Younghusband was unreasonable over the episode at Phari. The fort dominated the surrounding plain; 'we thought it impossible that the Tibetans would be such fools as not to hold this place,' wrote an officer with the advance-guard. To leave it ungarrisoned, with a tiny British force camped under its walls (and dependent on its water-supply), would have involved a risk which no military commander had the right to accept; 'the ground,' as Younghusband himself wrote afterwards, 'was frozen so hard that a working party of twelve men only succeeded, after two hours' hard work, in excavating some thirty-three cubic feet of earth, and as neither turf nor stones were available it was impossible to construct any entrenchments.' Moreover, the local Tibetan officials stayed in the fort, which was thus (as Curzon telegraphed to London on Christmas Day) under 'a joint occupation.' Younghusband was doubtless justified in feeling that Macdonald had gone back on his word; but he seems to have exaggerated the political ill-effects of his action at Phari and to have disregarded the sound military reasons which impelled him to take it.

'Dirt, dirt, grease, smoke;' thus Manning had summed up his impressions of Phari on 21 October 1811. A century had brought few changes to this uninviting town of some 2000 to 3000 inhabitants. 'Only a bargee could adequately describe the place,' wrote Edmund Candler, the *Daily Mail* correspondent; but his colleague of *The Times*, Perceval Landon, made a spirited attempt to do so:

Let it be said at once that in the best quarter of the town, that in which the houses are two-storeyed, the heaped-up filth—dejecta and rejecta alike—rises to the first-floor windows, and a hole in the mess has to be kept open for access to the door. It must be seen to be believed. In the middle of the street, between the two banks of filth and offal, runs a stinking channel, which thaws daily. In it horns and bones and skulls of every beast eaten or not eaten by the Tibetans—there are few of the latter—lie till the dogs and ravens have picked them clean enough to be used in the mortared walls and thresholds. The stench is fearful. Half-decayed corpses of dogs lie cuddled up with their mangy but surviving brothers and sisters, who do not resent the scavenging ravens. Here and there a stagnant pool of filth has partially defied the warmth, and carrion, verminous rags, and fur-wrapped bones are set round it in broken yellowish ice. In the middle the brown patch is iridescent. A curdled and foul torrent flows in the daytime through the market-place, and half-bred yaks shove the sore-eyed and mouth-ulcered children aside to drink it. The men and women, clothes and faces alike, are as black as the peat walls that form a background to every scene. They have never washed themselves. They never intend to wash themselves. Ingrained dirt to an extent that it is impossible to describe reduces what would otherwise be a clear, sallow-skinned but good complexioned race to a collection of foul and grotesque negroes.

And the disgust of all this is heightened by an ever-present contrast, for, at the end of every street, hanging in mid-air above this nest of mephitic filth, the cold and almost saint-like purity of the everlasting snows of

Chomolhari—a huge wedge of argent a mile high—puts to perpetual shame the dirt of Phari.

In the fort itself eighty coolies were employed for a week on refuse-disposal, and throughout the first stages of its occupation the accumulated dirt of generations continued to be carried away by the sackful from the warren of dark chambers and galleries over which the Union Jack now streamed in the wind alongside innumerable prayer-flags. But the old building was riddled with cracks and crannies, and in the dry, thin upland air the wind collected dust from noisome basements, armouries and storerooms and blew it through the quarters which had been cleared; so that each day a pall of fine, malodorous powder, 'the secretion of centuries of foul living,' overlay everything and brought on hacking coughs. A note of disillusion permeates the letters written home (mostly in pencil; ink froze) from Phari. Tibet, the land of mystery, was proving the reverse of glamorous; many officers, deriving their only preconceptions about Tibetan lamas from *Kim*, were shocked to find that in real life most of these sages personified a loutish depravity.

A story often quoted in the unofficial annals of the expedition is of two British soldiers toiling up a particularly savage gradient on the route to Phari.

> *First Soldier*. I thought they told us Tibet was a ——ing table-land?
> *Second Soldier*. So it ——ing well is, you silly ——. This is one of the ——ing table-legs.

From the diagram on p. 99 it will be seen that this homely diagnosis was not far out. Although the Tang La, eleven miles north of Phari, was nearly a thousand feet higher than the Jelap La, the approach to it was gradual and easy. The pass was not a narrow defile through a steep mountain-barrier, but a barely perceptible depression in a broad pamir; 'one might cross it,' Candler remarked, 'without noticing the summit, were it not for the customary cairns and praying-flags which the lamas raise in all high places.' Beyond the Tang La, though there were still obstacles to be surmounted, the advance would in the main follow a recognised caravan-trail across the plateau; road-making and road-maintenance ceased to be pre-requisites to further progress.

But when, the officers of the Mission found themselves wondering in the days after Christmas, would further progress be made, and how far would it take them?

Curzon's proposals for an advance—an 'immediate advance' —to Gyantse had been forwarded on 26 October and approved by the Cabinet on 6 November; the advance had begun on 11 December, and by 22 December Phari, at the northern end of the sixty-mile-long Chumbi Valley, had been occupied, garrisoned and victualled. So far so good.

But everybody was aware that momentum was being lost. On the day they moved off from Gnatong Younghusband had written to his father: 'If I am at Gyantse by the end of January I shall be surprised.' Three weeks later the original plan of pushing on to Gyantse (more than a hundred miles from Phari) and riding out the winter there had been abandoned. The main cause of its abandonment was the extreme caution of Brigadier-General Macdonald.

His circumspection was already attracting adverse comment throughout the whole expedition. 'Laughably cautious' ... 'The most cautious man I've ever met—just the wrong sort for this sort of show'—criticisms such as these, which recur in letters and diaries at this early stage, were to become harsher as the slow advance went on.

The penalty of prudence was delay, for Macdonald, abetted by an unimaginative staff, consistently over-insured. Until fighting started, supply was the only problem (and at all times the main problem) which the force-commander had to solve. All supplies were moved forward by convoys of pack-animals. If ten tons are loaded on a convoy, and one ton is going to be consumed by the animals and their drivers on the journey there and back, the amount delivered will be nine tons. But if the convoy is accompanied in both directions by a strong escort, which will consume a further two tons of the original load *en route*, the amount delivered will be only seven tons. This sort of arithmetic was already having a noticeable effect before the advance-guard left the Chumbi Valley; and as the lines of communication lengthened an over-solicitous policy for protecting them became increasingly a drag on progress.

The forward move from New Chumbi began on 4 January 1904, and four days later the Mission and its Escort, with the Mounted Infantry skirmishing ahead, crossed the Tang La, marching doggedly in the teeth of a bitter wind. Ahead of them the empty, snow-clad plain stretched endlessly to the foothills of Chomolhari, whose massive peak, rising to a height of 23,390 feet, began by filling them with awe and wonder but ended for many of them with something of a gaoler's status; for they were, it transpired, engaged only upon a token advance into Tibet proper, and the mountain was to dominate their lives for weeks to come.

As they entered this wilderness, rumours of an impending attack by hostile cavalry ran down the column. This was due to the sighting for the first time of the large wild asses known as *kyangs*, skirmishing in the middle distance in troops of ten or twenty. 'At first we mistook them for detachments of Tibetan cavalry, the wild horsemen of the Changtang, as they came galloping along in a whirlwind of dust, then executed a perfect wheel-round, then extended out in line at regular intervals, and advanced again; and as if at the word of command reformed into close order and came to an instant halt.' *

The column's destination was a place of no importance called Tuna, whose half-dozen mean houses were soon visible in what appeared to be the middle distance. All landmarks in Central Asia project this tantalising, mirage-like impression of pro-

---

* Waddell: *Lhasa and its Mysteries.* Cf. 'They ranged in hordes of anything up to fifteen, and in their manoeuvres achieved an uncanny unanimity of movement . . . no troop of cavalry was ever more symmetrically ranked, more precisely simultaneous in its evolutions.' (Fleming: *News from Tartary.*)

pinquity; it was in fact only after one of the most gruelling marches of the whole campaign that Tuna was reached. It was found deserted.

The official records throw curiously little light on the reasons for the choice of Tuna as winter-quarters for the Mission. The original plan for a swift, forceful advance to Gyantse was allowed, almost without comment, to slip into the limbo of impracticability; but it seems to have been felt that the British Commissioner should, as early as possible, place himself at least as far inside Tibetan territory as he had been at Khamba Jong. This small, rather *protocolaire* point would have been taken by the Chinese or the Russians; it may have been lost upon Lhasa.

On the earthy, superstitious, unplumbable minds of the Tibetan authorities it is impossible to guess what impression was produced by the British Government's decision to station their representative, throughout the most vindictive months of a cruel winter, in a corner of the country wholly devoid of material amenity, military advantage or political significance. If the Tibetans saw in the occupation of Tuna, which lasted for three uneventful months, no more than the symptoms of a baffling eccentricity, they were entitled to at least as much of history's indulgence as were the members of Mr Balfour's Cabinet, who, little though they knew of Tuna, were ultimately responsible for Younghusband's wintering there.

The unopposed march over the Tang La to Tuna began in an atmosphere of adventure, or at least of relief from frustration; it was remembered as long and thankless.

The head of the straggling column reached the desolate little hamlet towards dusk; but there were doubts—which perhaps precursors from the Mounted Infantry should have resolved— about the adequacy of the water-supply, and they moved wearily on to a stream three miles ahead.

When, in a cold country, the climate is the chief enemy, the tail of a column becomes, in a sense, its teeth; until the baggage-train, carrying tents, sleeping-bags, cooking-utensils, rations and other necessities for survival has arrived, the fighting men are in an unenviable position. Hungry, tired, no longer warmed by the exertions of the march, they light small fires and gather round them, grumbling and impatiently scanning the horizon for the mules. There is a sense of hollowness, of uncomfortably suspended animation. Nobody is at his best.

It was in this lacklustre interlude that the Escort Commander suddenly lost his head. Younghusband described the incident in a letter to his father written from Tuna three weeks later:

Two hours after we arrived here on Jan. 8th Macdonald came up to me and said we could not stay here and would have to retire the next day as there was no fuel and grass and the men would not be able to stand the cold. I told him I would never agree to retire, that I knew the style of country and would consider it abounding in fuel and grass compared with the Pamirs and that as to the cold if fifty men died of it that would be better than retiring. He appeared to give way.

But the next morning he came again to me and said that he found we had only seven days' rations and so we must retire. I told him I would absolutely refuse to move. He said I must give him that in writing and assume all responsibility. I said I would gladly do so. So it was decided to stay.

Later in the day he came to me and said he had not been well in the morning and not his proper self and said he would not ask me to give it in writing. So I have made no mention of the matter officially but only told Dane and the Viceroy about it privately—not to be placed on official record—and they have said I was 'entirely right.' But it was a close shave and to show what a terrible mistake it would have been to retire I may mention that a camp of 2000 Tibetans who were six miles off on our flank *themselves* retired on the very day that Macdonald wanted *us* to. We have found an inexhaustible supply of fuel and grass, enough for weeks yet.

Macdonald's proposals were, on the most charitable view, unsoldierly and pusillanimous; they amounted to a dereliction of duty. To march for one day into Tibet, and then to turn round and march out again without hearing a shot fired or even sighting a single hostile Tibetan would have been militarily disgraceful and politically disastrous. Here was something more culpable than over-caution; only a failure of the human spirit can explain this attempt to admit defeat without cause, to embrace failure at the first excuse.

After spending one day at Tuna Macdonald with the bulk of the force withdrew over the Tang La to his base in the Chumbi Valley, leaving the Mission adequately guarded and supplied at Tuna. On purely personal grounds Younghusband cannot have been sorry to see his Escort Commander's back; but it must have been with dubious feelings that the thruster contemplated the future of a difficult enterprise in whose conduct the laggard was to have so large a say.

CHAPTER TEN

'A Close Shave'

THE Tibetan expedition was gravelled for the next three months.

On 4 January, the day they crossed the Tang La, Curzon had telegraphed to London an outline of Younghusband's plan—which had been agreed with Macdonald—for the next phase of the campaign. 'A halt for one week will be made at Tuna; the Mission will then advance to Kala Tso and remain there for some three weeks. It is expected that by the middle of February Gyantse will be reached.'

This plan envisaged an advance of over a hundred miles in six weeks. Exactly a week later Macdonald telegraphed that he had returned to Phari; 'Colonel Younghusband is remaining at Tuna for political reasons.' The official archives, which are ample, contain no indication that Macdonald ever gave, or was ever asked to give, his reasons for abandoning the project to which he was committed. Private sources, compiled by individuals who may have known little or nothing of the original plan, make no comment on its cancellation.

Throughout the campaign there was continual telegraphic communication between the expedition in the field and the authorities in India and London to whose apron-strings it was tied. Many of the messages exchanged were trivial. 'Lieutenant Hodgson wounded in wrist,' the Viceroy cabled on 23 May 1904 to the Secretary of State for India, who a few days later continued their august correspondence with 'Your decision to send up an additional Native Mounted Infantry Company is approved.' With so close a degree of remote control in force, it is strange that a military decision which dislocated the whole time-table of the campaign should have been taken without previous reference to, or at least subsequent queries by, higher authority.

In the second week of January 1904 the situation, which did not alter in essentials until the end of March, was as follows:

The Escort Commander, with more than half his first-line troops and all his artillery except for one of the seven-pounders, was at New Chumbi, 10,000 feet above sea-level but below the tree-line and housed in reasonable comfort. Phari was held. At Tuna, sixty miles from New Chumbi and roughly half that distance from the nearest tree, the Mission squatted forlornly in the middle of a huge plain just over 15,000 feet above sea-level. It was guarded by four companies of the 23rd Pioneers, the Norfolks' Maxim-gun detachment, one of the Gurkhas' seven-pounders, ten Mounted Infantry and a detail of Madras Sappers and Miners who, coming from Southern India, were particularly vulnerable to the cold and soon had to be sent down the line; altogether there were about two hundred fighting men at Tuna. Less than ten miles away a Tibetan army several thousand strong (its numbers varied from time to time) was encamped, lymphatically, about Guru.

Younghusband's position at Khamba Jong, with an escort of roughly the same strength and improvised fortifications of roughly the same weakness, had always been precarious, though in fact it was never immediately threatened by attack. At Tuna he was even more perilously situated, mainly because of the cold. However carefully oil was wiped off them, rifle-bolts froze into the breeches. The Maxims were even more prone to stoppages from this cause, and Hadow, the subaltern in charge of them, used to remove the locks at night (when the cold was greatest) and take them to bed with him. The rifles of the Mounted Infantry froze to the bottom of their buckets* so firmly that both hands had to be used to extricate them.

Though lavish by the standards of those days, the protective

---

* 'Buckets' were the leather sheaths fastened to the saddle in which the cavalry of the period carried their carbines.

clothing issued to the troops—poshteens, Gilgit boots, thick underwear, and so on—bore no comparison with its scientifically-designed counterpart today. It was not wind-proof and it was so bulky that the soldiers had small chance of handling their weapons with precision. The thin air, too, was an enemy to marksmanship for riflemen and gunners; though it increased the maximum range of a bullet or a shell, it altered the trajectory, inducing a tendency to fire high. 'It seemed impossible,' Younghusband recalled, 'that the poor sentries at night would ever be able to stand against the howling storm and the penetrating snow, or that our soldiers would ever be able to resist an attack from the Tibetans in such terrific circumstances.' In the ranks of the 23rd Pioneers, eleven out of twelve cases of pneumonia proved fatal.* A young civilian in the Indian postal service died after having both feet badly frost-bitten and amputated; the soldiers gave him a military funeral, a ceremony which might not have been necessary had he been eligible, under the regulations, for an issue of Gilgit boots.

All in all, the little outpost was exposed to risks which on the North West Frontier would have been accounted suicidal. To leave it there, twenty miles from the nearest reinforcements, for three months, was to assume a total lack of bellicosity on the part of the Tibetans. It is surprising that the soundness of this assumption was never challenged by proponents of the theory that Russian influence was supreme in Lhasa; by the rules of the Great Game—if their theory was well-founded—Younghusband's vigil at Tuna should have been brought to an abrupt and ignominious end. From the fact that the British Mission was not molested nobody drew the obvious conclusion —that Russia's political influence in Tibet was either negligible or non-existent.

During the first few days at Tuna Younghusband, outwardly as impassive as ever, seems to have been under some strong

---

* The Sikhs, of which this regiment was composed, cremate their dead. The drain caused by these casualties on the supply of firewood, brought up by convoy over the Tang La, was viewed with misgiving at Tuna.

internal stress. His dealings with Macdonald had placed an increasing strain upon him; and Macdonald's retirement, leaving the Mission marooned in the middle of nowhere and still more than eighty miles from Gyantse, must have filled him with rancour and dismay. Something, at any rate—some impulse which, though far from foreign to his nature, he would have suppressed if he had been in a normal frame of mind—drove him to an act of staggering foolhardiness.

Contacts, official and unofficial, were quickly established between the two military forces, ill-matched in size, who shared the plateau over which Chomolhari brooded. From the British camp Mounted Infantry patrols rode out and, from a coign of vantage on a ridge, watched the Tibetan host at musketry practice. A Tibetan general's cook was captured, interrogated and released. A flock of sheep was rounded up and paid for at a generous rate. Meanwhile from the Tibetan side delegates rode frequently into the British lines. Their status varied, but not the burden of their proposals: the Mission must go back to Yatung before negotiations could begin.

The first of these deputations appeared on 12 January; it stopped short of the British perimeter and Younghusband sent O'Connor out to parley with it on the glacial plain. O'Connor reported that, although the Tibetans had at first been insistent on a return to Yatung, they later let fall a hint that discussions might be held at Tuna.

Some evidence that Younghusband was in a mood of intransigence, or perhaps of desperation, is provided by a dispatch which he had written to the Government of India on the previous day. In this he urged (in a passage omitted from the Blue Book) that 'we should throw aside the idea of advancing as a purely peaceful mission and definitely assume a militant attitude. . . . I hardly hope, however, for any good results until we advance to Lhasa itself.'

Younghusband was a connoisseur of risks rather than a gambler; on the 13th, the day after O'Connor's interview with the first lot of emissaries, he took the biggest risk of his life. In terms merely of physical danger he may have faced greater hazards elsewhere, but here there was much more than his life at stake. He was placing in jeopardy the whole enterprise with which he had been entrusted, courting a martyrdom of which the consequences, directly involving Imperial prestige, would have metamorphosed Britain's hesitant Tibetan policy in the harshest possible manner. And Younghusband did this by putting his head into the lion's mouth when the only thing he knew for certain about the lion was that it had a sufficiency of teeth. Early in the morning of 13 January, with two companions, he rode out of Tuna, headed for the Tibetan camp at Guru, about ten miles away.

O'Connor ('I merely remarked that it was a bit risky') went with him to interpret. The third member of the party was Lieutenant Sawyer, of the 23rd Pioneers; he was supposed to be studying Tibetan, but one doubts whether the educational benefits of this excursion were uppermost in his mind when he asked to be allowed to join it. Younghusband dispensed with an escort; he did not even take an orderly to hold their ponies, and the omission by so experienced a man of this small precaution, which might easily have had a decisive importance, heightens the impression that he was acting on impulse and relying on intuition. He had not forewarned the Tibetans of his arrival in their lines. He was behaving with great gallantry and a kind of Puckish folly.

Guru was a poor village at the foot of a little hill. All round it the plain was dotted with Tibetan soldiers collecting dung for their camp-fires. There were no sentries, no barricades. The three Englishmen rode straight into the village. Its garrison, which they estimated at six hundred, came tumbling out of their bivouacs to stare at the intruders, 'not with any scowls, but laughing to each other as if we were an excellent entertainment.' They were armed with spears, broadswords and matchlocks; no breech-loading rifles were to be seen.

O'Connor asked for their commander. They were directed to the principal house, dismounted and were received with marked cordiality by the Tibetan general, 'a polite, well-dressed and well-mannered man,' behind whom stood other senior officers, equally affable in their demeanour. They shook hands all round and were ushered into a large, ill-lit room, acrid with the smoke from yak-dung fires.

Here the temperature dropped sharply. At one end of the room sat three 'monks' from Lhasa.* Their faces were hostile and their greetings perfunctory; they did not rise from their cushions. Everyone sat down in a hollow square: the commander-in-chief, who came from Lhasa, opposite the monks, three lesser generals from Shigatse on his left, the three British officers on his right. Tea was served, and the Lhasa general opened the proceedings by enquiring after Younghusband's health.

The preliminary courtesies having been disposed of, Younghusband explained the purpose of his unheralded visit. He had not, he said, come to Guru in his official capacity; he had ridden across, without ceremony and without escort, to talk matters over in the hope that they might jointly discover a path leading through their difficulties to a peaceful solution.

The Lhasa general replied that the people of Tibet were bound by covenant to bar Europeans from their country; their purpose in doing so was to preserve their religion inviolate. Here the monks chimed in, repeating in acrimonious tones the gist of the general's remarks. The general added that, if the British really wanted an amicable settlement, they must go back to Yatung and negotiate there.

Younghusband then made what was almost certainly a tactical error; he mounted his hobby-horse and brought Russia into the debate. Why was Tibet so hostile to Great Britain when she was in close relations with Russia? Why did the Dalai Lama, who sent letters to the Tsar and to Russian officials by the hand

---

* These 'monks' must in fact have been senior members of the Tibetan hierarchy. Younghusband's use of a word which was then, in most English ears, a faintly sinister pejorative is typical of his attitude to an important element in Tibetan society for which he felt, on moral grounds, a strong repugnance. He was later to express in demi-official correspondence his desire to 'smash those selfish filthy lecherous Lamas' (letter to Lord Ampthill, 5 May 1904). The note of vindictiveness, so uncharacteristic of the writer, betrays a depth of disillusionment.

of Dorjieff, refuse to receive letters from the Viceroy of India? 'We could understand their being friendly with both the Russians and ourselves, or their wishing to have nothing to do with either; but when they were friendly to the Russians and unfriendly to us, they must not be surprised at our now paying closer attention to our treaty rights.'

Curzon was perturbed when Younghusband reported his use of this argument, and a letter which he wrote to him on 23 January draws a revealing distinction between the ostensible and the ulterior purposes of the expedition—between the Government's aims and the Viceroy's. 'Remember that in the eyes of His Majesty's Government we are advancing not because of Dorjieff or the Mission to Livadia or the Russian spies in Lhasa—but because of our Convention shamelessly violated, our frontiers trespassed upon, our subjects arrested, our representatives ignored. In your recent talk with the Tibetan General and the monks you seem to have forgotten this, and to have thought only of the bigger objective.'

The general from Lhasa rebutted Younghusband's charge; Tibet had no truck with Russia. The monks weighed in with similar but more heated denials. The Tibetans disliked the Russians as heartily as they disliked the British. They had nothing to do with them. There was no Russian anywhere near Lhasa. Dorjieff was a Mongol, not a Tibetan. 'They asked me not to be so suspicious.' The discussion veered away into an academic wrangle about religion. Younghusband argued that the British, who notoriously never interfered with the diverse religions of India, could not be said to represent a threat to Tibetan Buddhism; the monks' prevaricating replies revealed that it was the priesthood's dominant position in the country, rather than the sanctity of their faith, which they regarded as likely to be imperilled by intruders. The talk was getting nowhere; an ominous chill had begun to pervade the atmosphere.

'So far the conversation, in spite of occasional bursts from the monks, had been maintained with perfect good-humour; but when I made a sign of moving, and said that I must be returning to Tuna, the monks, looking as black as devils, shouted out: "No, you won't; you'll stop here." One of the Generals said, quite politely, that we had broken the rule of the road in coming into their country, and we were nothing but thieves and brigands in occupying Phari Fort. The monks, using forms of speech which Captain O'Connor told me were only used in addressing inferiors, loudly clamoured for us to name a date when we would retire from Tuna before they would let me leave the room. The atmosphere became electric. The faces of all were set. One of the Generals left the room; trumpets outside were sounded, and the attendants closed round behind us.

'A real crisis was on us, when any false step might be fatal. I told Captain O'Connor, though there was really no necessity to give such a warning to anyone so imperturbable, to keep his voice studiously calm, and to smile as much as he possibly could, and I then said that I had to obey the orders of my Government, just as much as they had to obey the orders of theirs; that I would ask them to report to their Government what I had said, and I would report to my Government what they had told me. That was all that could be done at present; but if the Viceroy, in reply to my reports, ordered me back to India I should personally be only too thankful, as theirs was a cold, barren and inhospitable country, and I had a wife and child at Darjeeling, whom I was anxious to see again as soon as I could.

'This eased matters a little. But the monks continued to clamour for me to name a date for withdrawal, and the situation was only relieved when a General suggested that a messenger should return with me to Tuna to receive there the answer from the Viceroy. The other Generals eagerly accepted the suggestion, and the tension was at once removed. Their faces became smiling again, and they conducted me to the outer door with the same geniality and politeness with which they had received us, though the monks remained seated and as surly and evil-looking as men well could look.

'We preserved our equanimity of demeanour and the smiles on our faces till we had mounted our ponies and were well outside the camp, and then we galloped off as hard as we could, lest the monks should get the upper hand again and send men after us. It had been a close shave, but it was worth it.'*

Younghusband telegraphed to the Viceroy a brief report of his adventure—he called it 'an unceremonial visit'—but only the officers with him at Tuna can have realised how recklessly he had acted. He claimed, and was justified in claiming, that by making contact with the Tibetan leaders on their own ground he had gained a clearer insight into their mentality than would have been possible by any other means; he now for the first time fully realised how implacable was the opposition of the priesthood, and how paramount their control over Tibetan policy. And he had, perhaps, advanced the British cause by making, in person and at hazard, a demonstration of frankness and goodwill. It had been a useful reconnaissance.

But what if things had gone wrong, as they so very nearly did? Without seeking the authority of his superiors or even the advice of his staff, without telling anyone at Tuna what he was doing or why he was doing it, the British Commissioner had wantonly exposed his person to the risk of capture and humiliation, perhaps of death. How would the Viceroy, how would the Cabinet, have viewed this outcome? What consequences would have flowed from it, and what would history have made of Younghusband's part in provoking them? It is impossible not to admire the serenity with which Younghusband made his intuitive decision to beard the Tibetan leaders at Guru; it is equally impossible to maintain that the escapade reflected a sound judgment.

It ended happily. Younghusband was not made prisoner or hostage at Guru, nor was he censured for going there. Whether, afterwards, his own conscience was entirely clear may be doubted. In his unashamedly autobiographical novel, *But In Our Lives*, published more than twenty years later, the hero, Evan Lee, embarks on a venture closely modelled on the Guru episode. It, too, is a close shave, and a comment by

* *India and Tibet.*

the narrator of the story can fairly be assumed to embody Younghusband's verdict on his own conduct on 13 January 1904.

It was a venturesome undertaking. I would not call it foolhardy, for Lee was too sensible to do anything actually foolish; but it was running pretty near in that direction.

CHAPTER ELEVEN

The Action at Guru

'THE Government of India,' the *Spectator* opined in November 1903, 'has a disagreeable expedition on hand.' In England the public's attitude to the Tibetan enterprise ranged from outright disapproval, to which the Liberal opposition intermittently gave expression in both Houses of Parliament, to a vague and slightly apprehensive curiosity. Interest, which might have been expected to languish during the period of three months' stagnation at Tuna, in fact quickened for two reasons.

One was the arrival at New Chumbi during January of four newspaper correspondents to whom the military authorities had, tardily and with extreme reluctance, granted permission to accompany the force. Their graphic descriptions of an unknown land were supplemented, in the illustrated magazines, by an assortment of sketches and photographs with which some of the officers had begun to bombard Fleet Street, hoping for fame and fortune but receiving, to their chagrin, only skinflint remuneration.

Another source of enlightenment was the appearance of the first of three Blue Books which the Government devoted to Tibetan affairs. This did not have a particularly good reception. Its publication in February coincided with the outbreak of the Russo-Japanese War, and, since British sympathies were on the whole with Russia, it was felt to be unfortunate, if nothing worse, that a collection of documents containing hostile criticism of Tsarist policy in Asia should have issued from His Majesty's Stationery Office at such a moment. Curzon's hand in the Tibetan business was clearly recognised and aroused

FORCED FAVOURS.

The Grand Lama of Thibet. "NOW THEN, WHAT'S YOUR BUSINESS?"
British Lion. "I'VE COME TO BRING YOU THE BLESSINGS OF FREE TRADE."
The Grand L. "I'M A PROTECTIONIST. DON'T WANT 'EM."
British Lion. "WELL, YOU'VE *GOT TO HAVE 'EM!*"

["The advisers of the Dalai Lama, having ignored their obligations to us under the Convention of 1890, have now ignored the British Mission;" . . . "an advance is to be made into the Chumbi Valley on the frontier of Thibet."—*Daily Paper.*]

uneasiness. A certain speciousness in the selection of evidence with which to buttress the Government's case for its Tibetan policy was also detected; 'the first hundred pages or something like that,' Lord Rosebery told the House of Lords, 'are devoted entirely to the desire and ambition of the Indian Government to impose the drinking of Indian tea on a people which prefers Chinese tea.' The Blue Book, nevertheless, provided a background of information which helped the editors of the more serious papers to interpret events in Tibet to their readers.

Meanwhile stockpiling for an advance to Gyantse in the spring went slowly on. It was still hampered by the Escort Commander's insistence that every convoy should be strongly guarded, although there had been no indication that the Tibetans were taking any interest, hostile or otherwise, in the British line of communication. Candler, the *Daily Mail* Correspondent, gave this account of a supply-column crossing the Tang La towards the end of the winter:

> In mid-March a convoy of the 12th Mule Corps, escorted by two companies of the 23rd Pioneers, were overtaken by a blizzard on their march between Phari and Tuna, and camped in two feet of snow with the thermometer 18° below zero. A driving hurricane made it impossible to light a fire or cook food. The officers were reduced to frozen bully beef and neat spirits, while the sepoys went without food for thirty-six hours. . . . The drivers arrived at Tuna frozen to the waist. Twenty men of the 12th Mule Corps were frost-bitten, and thirty men of the 23rd Pioneers were so incapacitated that they had to be carried in on mules. On the same day there were seventy cases of snow-blindness among the 8th Gurkhas.

The two companies of Pioneers, here mentioned as escorting the mule-train, were almost certainly below strength; but they cannot have mustered less than a hundred men between them, and a sizeable part of the convoy was diverted from its main purpose by the need to carry the kit, rations and spare ammunition of these *bouches inutiles*. 'Such a lot of transport runs to waste in the large escorts which Macdonald sends with every convoy,' Younghusband wrote to his father on 11 March.

Tuna was a god-forsaken place. The cold, the discomfort, the desolation were oppressive; it was however the consciousness of a steady accretion of delay that irked the officers most. 'The present idea,' Captain Ryder wrote to his wife when they had been there three weeks, 'is that we stop here all February and reach Gyantse on 14 March.' But the time-table lengthened inexorably. On 6 March Ryder recorded the dispatch of 'a pretty stiff letter' from Younghusband to Macdonald about the effect of over-caution on the supply-programme; on 12 March 'the General hopes to have things ready for an advance early in April.' Meanwhile the plain around Tuna had been totally denuded of yak-dung; fires were fed sparingly with charcoal brought over the Tang La. Somebody remarked that to light a fire for inessential purposes was as unthinkable as to light your pipe with a ten-pound-note.

The handful of seventeen machine-gunners from the Norfolk Regiment under Hadow, the only British other ranks at Tuna, maintained their health and spirits better than anyone else—except, perhaps, the British Commissioner. From his relish for the austere solitudes of High Tartary Younghusband derived benefits comparable to those which a camel derives from its hump; a manuscript note among his papers, dated 2 March, gives this sketch of his surroundings as the rearguards of the winter drew away:

The last two mornings have been absolutely perfect. The sun strikes our tents at 7 and I have got up soon after and walked over the plain. The sky is cloudless except for a long soft wisp of haze. But now in the early morning the mountains eastward under the sun are not sharp and clear as in the noon day. They are covered with some of that blue hazy indistinctness which makes the view of Kanchenjunga from Darjeeling so marvellously beautiful. From the river course and later in the lower part of the valley a soft mist is rising, adding to the dreamy haze, and the bare brown of the base of the mountains is toned into purples and pinks; while the snow summits become the most ethereal blue shading into the cerulean blue of the sky above.

On the plain plump little larks and finches are scurrying about, in short rapid runs, in search of food. Now and then a little vowl [*sic*] is seen basking in the sun at the mouth of his hole. Over all there is a sense of peace and quiet and coming joy and it is hard to think that for the last five days some of the highest lamas from Lhasa have been cursing us at the Tibetan camp only six miles off, and that tonight is fixed for a great attack on our camp.

The lamas' protracted commination worried Younghusband as little as the familiar rumours of a night-attack, although double sentries, who had to be relieved hourly because of the cold, were posted. But he had much on his mind. He fretted, as most men do, under inaction. He did indeed, while at Tuna, manage to exorcise one of the spectres which had always haunted the expedition: the threat of Bhutanese hostility. Bhutan's frontier, as can be seen from the map, ran parallel and very close to the British axis of advance; her people had ancient ties with Tibet and worshipped the same gods. Bhutan, whose people were more apt for war than the Tibetans, could have made things very awkward for the intruders; to ensure at least her neutrality was an essential precaution.

This Younghusband was able to achieve by winning wholly over to his side a Bhutanese envoy ('the first sensible man I have met on this frontier') who visited him at Tuna. This man, known as the Timpuk Jongpen, went out of his way to be helpful; he attempted mediation with the leaders at Guru and, when this failed, offered to send letters to Lhasa urging the Tibetan Government to negotiate. Later Bhutan readily allowed the British to by-pass the Jelap La by using a route over a less intractable pass—the Natu La—in Bhutanese territory.

(The more-than-benevolent neutrality of Bhutan and Nepal is worthy of remark. Though both received financial subsidies, the Government of India had no direct control over, nor could it indirectly menace, either kingdom; it maintained a Resident at Katmandu but had no representative in Bhutan. Both countries were well aware that the British forces launched into Tibet were numerically weak and strategically insecure. From the fact that in these circumstances Tibet's two closest neighbours actively sided with the invaders it would perhaps be too much to make copy-book deductions, to predicate that these remote mountain-communities thought that Britain's cause was just and found the conduct of the Tibetans unreasonable. But it was a fact, and it should not be overlooked.)

A minor diplomatic success was not, however, much to show for three months of immobility, over which there brooded *in absentia* (though he did pay one brief visit to Tuna) the figure of Brigadier-General Macdonald, that unaccommodating slow-coach. He annoyed Younghusband by his refusal to extend the telegraph-line from Phari to Tuna, although the requisite materials for the work (which would have to be carried out in any case when the advance was resumed) were lying idle at Phari. There was also a minor row—it led to a question being asked in the House of Commons—about the press censorship. This was supposed to be in the hands of the Mission, who were represented at Macdonald's headquarters by an official named Walsh, but the military insisted on taking a hand in it too, so that press telegrams underwent a double censorship; this was, inevitably, a cause of exasperation and delay—the more so since it was inconceivable that anything published in London or elsewhere could percolate to Lhasa in time to damage the interests (in so far as they existed) of military security.

These were small matters. What worried Younghusband was the future of his maladjusted, undefined relationship with his Escort Commander. He had now had enough experience of Macdonald to make him realise how unlikely it was that they would ever see eye to eye over anything. He sensed the other man's craving for supremacy within the expedition; he was all too well aware that their respective spheres of responsibility—even if they had been clearly demarcated, which they had not—were bound to overlap; and he saw with a terrible clarity how gravely their disharmony of outlook might damage the whole enterprise. 'Great Heavens,' the exasperated Lugard had written in his diary twelve years earlier, 'I shall be glad when I am quit of Macdonald.' Though he had not yet been as sorely tried as Lugard was, Younghusband was beginning to share his sentiments.

In an endeavour to clarify the division of their duties, Younghusband telegraphed on 19 March to enquire how matters would stand if the advance met opposition: 'Does present political Mission become military expedition by that fact alone, or must definite orders of Government on the point be awaited?'

The answer came eight days later; it was a bitter blow. 'As it seems likely that resistance will be encountered when Mission leaves Tuna, General Macdonald should have full control during the move to Gyantse . . . when conduct of affairs will revert to you as Head of Mission.'

On paper this was a sound ruling; five months earlier Younghusband had recognised the need for some such arrangement when he told Macdonald that 'he must regard me simply as a precious parcel of goods to be carted from one place to another.' But he now knew more about his Escort Commander than he had known then, and he reacted vigorously against the Government of India's decision; in it he smelt danger, perhaps ruin, for a project in which Younghusband believed speed of action and firmness of resolve to be—with tact—the prime essentials. All these attributes Macdonald had shown himself to lack.

Younghusband's reply was despatched on 28 March, the day on which Macdonald with his advance-guard arrived at Tuna to resume the forward movement. He asked the Government of India to reconsider their decision. He suggested that 'political risks of control being in the hands of a military officer are as great as military risks of control being in the hands of a political officer.' In support of this argument he revealed—for the first time officially—that on their arrival at Tuna Macdonald had 'wished Mission, and ordered Escort' to withdraw over the Tang La; and he mentioned the (in his view) ill-advised occupation of the Fort at Phari.

But it is the last part of his telegram which shows how strongly he felt. 'If Government maintain their present order, I would ask to be relieved of such a delicate political matter as the conduct of our relations with Tibet.' He recommended that Macdonald should assume full control of the enterprise, 'with my very able staff as political advisers,' and that 'I be permitted to return to India.'*

Younghusband was in no sense a prima donna; it cannot be doubted that he would have handed over the helm without demur to an officer—Brander of the 32nd Pioneers, for instance, or Hogge of the 23rd—in whom he had confidence. It was not the idea of being relegated to the status of a passenger that irked him; this was a long-foreseen contingency. He offered to resign because he was convinced that Macdonald—vacillating, dilatory and morbidly prudent—would make a hash of things.

His telegram elicited an immediate reply. In persuasive terms Dane, the Foreign Secretary, urged him to think again, pointing out that 'the military authorities consider the advance on Gyantse a military operation.' Younghusband's sense of duty prevailed. He replied on the following day (31 March) that he would 'loyally accept' the Government of India's decision; and that morning, in intense cold, the expedition formed up in three columns and began to move slowly across the snow-covered plain towards Guru. The Tibetans had been warned that they were coming. 'The crucial moment which was to decide upon peace or war was now approaching.'†

The soldiers were glad to be on the march. The main body had reached Tuna on the evening of the 29th and had had a miserable day on the 30th. 'From the earliest dawn till after sunset,' wrote *The Times* Correspondent, 'a piercing wind swept the camp from end to end with a hurricane of tingling grit, and

* This telegram, and the short correspondence of which it forms a part, are marked in the Foreign Office archives OMIT FROM PRINT, and do not appear in the relevant Blue Book (Cd. 2054). Younghusband did not mention the matter in *India and Tibet*, where all references to his Escort Commander are couched in generous and appreciative terms.

† *India and Tibet.*

the discomfort of the men was increased by the device which Brigadier-General Macdonald employed to deceive any Tibetan scouts who might be lurking among the hills. All tents were struck and the men received strict orders to conceal themselves.' This can hardly have been a profitable ruse. In so naked a place it was impossible for a thousand men, with their mules, ponies, guns and stores to melt into the landscape; nor does there seem much point in playing hide and seek with an enemy against whom you intend to march on the morrow, especially when he has been forewarned of your intention.

The advance to Guru was described in the Escort Commander's orders as a reconnaissance in force. The troops taking part were the two Pioneer regiments, the 8th Gurkhas, two companies of Mounted Infantry (each about a hundred strong), two ten-pounders of the 7th Mountain Battery (a British unit), the Gurkha-manned seven-pounders (Bubble and Squeak), the Norfolks' two Maxims and various ancillary units. Their total strength was just over a thousand; British personnel numbered between a hundred and two hundred. 'The Force looks quite imposing,' a Staff officer wrote in his diary, 'but as a matter of fact we can hardly put 800 rifles into action;' baggage-guards, mule-leaders, medical orderlies, clerks and so forth made up the inevitable tail.

The distance from Tuna to the village of Guru (the place Younghusband had visited) was about ten miles. Two or three miles south of the village there was an outcrop of small, rocky hills; the road or rather the caravan-trail to Gyantse ran between these and a salt lake called the Bham Tso. Once the passage between the lake and the escarpment had formed a narrow bottleneck; but down the centuries the waters of the Bham Tso—like those of the Mediterranean at Thermopylae—had receded, and the bottleneck was no longer a naturally defensible position.

This however was the light in which the traditionally-minded Tibetans still regarded it. From a ruined house (which had perhaps at some vanished epoch stood on the shore of the lake) they had built a stout, loopholed wall across the road to the foot of the spur; and on the steep slope overlooking the wall they had sited seven or eight of the stony emplacements known on the Indian frontier as sangars. They had chosen to disregard the fact that the soggy verges of the lake were now some three thousand yards distant from the ruined house which formed the left-hand extremity of their defences, and that this flank (which they made no further effort to defend) could be turned at will. It was surmised by the officers of the expedition that the authorities in Lhasa had based their plans on an obsolete map and, perhaps, on the hallowed recommendations of some long-defunct Maginot, and that protocol had prevented the commander-in-chief at Guru from pointing out their error. What the truth of this matter was we shall never know.

Cumbered by bulky clothing and hampered by shortness of breath, the force trudged methodically across the windswept plateau, with the Mounted Infantry fanning out ahead. Twice they were intercepted by emissaries from the Tibetan camp. The first of these delegations repeated the well-worn demand that the British should retire to Yatung. They were sent back with instructions to tell their General that the British were bound for Gyantse and would reach Guru that night; they had no wish for a fight; if he wanted to avoid one, the Lhasa General must withdraw his troops from their positions and leave the road clear. With this message the emissaries galloped back to Guru and the advance continued.

Slowly they drew nearer to the wall and the sangars on the bluff above it; it could be seen that these crude fortifications were strongly manned. Just over half a mile from them the force was halted and the guns (the ten-pounders were carried on mules, Bubble and Squeak by coolies) were assembled and made ready for action. The stage was set.

Into the centre of it rode the General from Lhasa at the head of a small retinue. They trotted briskly up to the centre of the British line where Younghusband and Macdonald sat their ponies side by side under a Union Jack that snapped and crackled in the savage wind. Rugs and sheepskins were spread on the ground, the leaders dismounted, and the last parley began.

The Tibetans made—on orders, they said, from Lhasa—their usual demand: go back to Yatung. Younghusband, courteous but firm, transmitted through O'Connor his usual reply. 'It was a curious incident,' Landon recorded, 'the impassive *non possumus* which Younghusband returned to the heated declamations of the two senior delegates; the gay yellow and green coats of the generals from Lhasa and Shigatse; the various head-dresses; the purple and blue of the robes; the strange forked guns embossed with turquoise and coral; the richly worked sword-hilts; the little grey and bay ponies, saddle-clothed with swastika-patterned stuffs and gay with filigree brass head-bands and wide moulded iron stirrups—all these things straight from the sacred and forbidden city possessed a new and intense interest for all of us.'

This wrangle at the eleventh hour was as bootless as all its predecessors had been. 'We might just as well have spoken to a stone wall,' wrote Younghusband; 'not the slightest effect was produced.' After twenty minutes he broke up the little conclave. He gave the Tibetans a quarter of an hour in which to clear the road; if they failed to do so, they would be dislodged by force. Shouting excitedly to each other, the General and his fellow-notables sprang into their saddles and set their small ponies in a headlong scurry back to the wall.

A quarter of an hour passed; no sign came from the Tibetans. Still Younghusband could not bring himself to cry havoc. 'Twice Macdonald asked me to be allowed to commence fighting,' he wrote to his father next day, 'but each time I refused.' Instead he prevailed on the Escort Commander to order an advance in which the troops were to hold their fire until they were fired on. Whistles blew, and the thin khaki line moved forward under an ash-grey sky.

These were quixotic tactics, testing in the severest possible way the steadiness of the British-led troops. They had forsworn the almost certainly decisive advantage which their artillery, meagre though it was, would have given them. They were now required to walk calmly towards a line of dominating barricades through the loopholes in which they could see perhaps a thousand muskets and rifles trained on them. They did this without flinching. Landon compared their discipline to that of the Old Guard at Fontenoy. But at Fontenoy both sides were equally exposed; neither was advancing against emplacements.

The strange ceremonial of a dumb-show attack went on, the danger growing as the distance lessened. Still no shot was fired by either side. At last the centre of the British line reached the wall and the sangars, while its right and left flanks, unopposed, curled round the Tibetan fortifications and took up positions in enfilade. Up on the escarpment the 8th Gurkhas and the 23rd Pioneers began to hustle the grey-clad musketeers out of their sangars; this was done in silence, and with something of the good-humoured severity that London policemen display on Boat Race Night. The men from the sangars drifted down to join the great bemused throng behind the wall, now covered at point-blank range by the rifles of the 32nd Pioneers. The Mounted Infantry were at this stage evicting a concentration of Tibetans from the shelter of a rocky spur which projected from the plain six hundred yards *behind* the wall, while the Lhasa General with his staff and bodyguard was *in front of* the wall, sitting sulkily on the ground amid the long legs of the Sikhs. He was a man of fine presence, but now, as he muttered to himself and gazed stonily about him, he seemed lost, shrunken, benighted; 'at the end of his tether' was how O'Connor described him.

At this point it looked as if the fantastic and perilous encounter had produced an absurd situation, but nothing worse. Officers were busy taking snapshots. Candler dismounted and, resting a notebook on his saddle, scribbled a short dispatch to the *Daily Mail* reporting a bloodless victory; Younghusband wrote a similar message to the Government of India and an orderly set off at full gallop for the end of the telegraph-line.

But the Tibetans, greatly outnumbering the British, were still behind the wall, and although they were surrounded they refused to budge. The expedition could not with safety by-pass

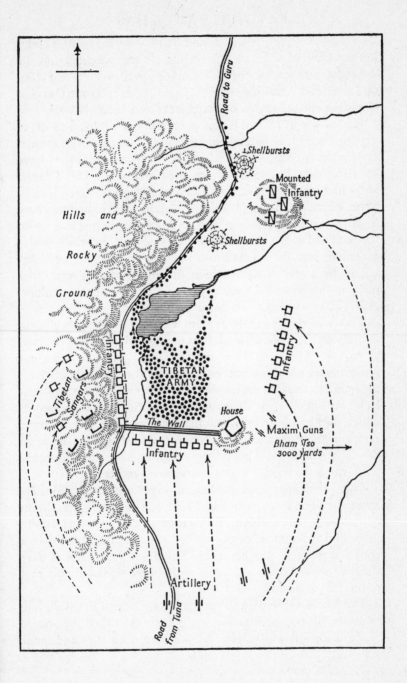

an army as though it was a puddle in the road; and Young-husband and Macdonald, after a consultation, decided that the Tibetans must be disarmed. The troops were ordered to do this, and a mêlée of wrestling-matches began, with Sikhs and Gurkhas disputing the possession of matchlocks and broad-swords.

It is, as the world has learnt to its cost since 1904, difficult to disarm by mutual agreement; to disarm men without mutual agreement is possible only when they recognise that they have no alternative but to lay down their weapons. The Tibetan army had no alternative but did not recognise that fact. It had never seen a machine-gun before; it understood only dimly how frightful was the menace of the Lee Metfords trained silently on the confined space, roughly an acre in extent, in which it was corralled; and the superstitious peasants in its ranks were sustained by a sort of half-faith in the charms, spells and other mumbo-jumbo which were supposed to render them invulnerable. They were in a death-trap, but they did not know it.

This was not the only reason why the attempt to disarm forcibly an amorphous, leaderless mob of Tibetans was doomed to failure. Many, perhaps most, of their weapons were not government property but belonged to the men themselves; they understandably resented efforts to wrest from them matchlocks on which they depended for hunting, or broadswords which they had inherited from their fathers. The point escaped notice at the time and is nowhere mentioned in *post mortems* on the Guru affair; yet it must have contributed to the vehemence with which the sepoys' importunities were resisted.

This vehemence bred confusion, anger and noise. Tension mounted. The scene, which had been one of anticlimax, almost of bathos, became suddenly full of urgency. With polyglot oaths more and more men, empty-bellied and irascible, tussled in a confined space for the control of lethal weapons. Stones were thrown, blows exchanged. The atmosphere was no longer that of Boat Race Night.

The Lhasa General, still on the wrong side of the wall, had mounted his pony. Shouting hysterically, he urged the animal forward towards the mêlée. A Sikh barred his way and made as if to seize his bridle. The General drew a pistol and shot the soldier through the jaw.

Firing broke out instantly. At one end of the wall Candler of the *Daily Mail* was cut down by Tibetan swordsmen; he received seventeen wounds, lost a hand, but was saved from death by his thick poshteen. An officer with him was also wounded. For a moment the situation in the centre of the British line, where both sides were closely intermingled, looked ugly.

But only for a moment. From the escarpment above the wall and from the plain to the left of it, volley after volley crashed into the solid grey mass of men; for one company of Gurkhas the range was only twenty yards. Across the wall itself the Sikhs were firing point-blank. Shrapnel was bursting on the Tibetans' line of retreat; Ottley's detachment of Mounted Infantry, already in the enemy's rear, was caught in this fire and lost three men wounded and two ponies killed. Out on the plain, to the left of the ruined house, the Maxims chattered vindictively

Under such fearful punishment no troops in the world could have stood their ground. It was not a battle but a massacre. Hadow, manning one of the Norfolks' Maxims, wrote to his mother that night: 'I got so sick of the slaughter that I ceased fire, though the General's order was to make as big a bag as possible.' The Tibetans broke.

They did not flee. They turned their backs on the wall and walked away, very slowly, through a hail of bullets that continued to mow many of them down until they reached the shelter of a spur half a mile distant. 'They walked,' Candler recorded, 'with bowed heads, as if they had been disillusioned in their gods.' 'I hope I shall never have to shoot down men *walking* away again,' young Hadow confided to his mother. 'It was an awful sight,' wrote Landon; 'the slowness of their escape was horrible and loathsome to us.'

The infantry engaged fired on the average only twelve rounds, or two magazines, per man. The Tibetan army, estimated at 1500, left between 600 and 700 dead on the field, among them the Lhasa General. One hundred and sixty-eight of their wounded—all of whom expected to be butchered—were treated by the British doctors; their cheerful stoicism was much admired. Only twenty died. The British force had about half a dozen casualties, none of them fatal.

The grisly action had lasted a matter of minutes; the Maxims expended 700 rounds each—enough only for ninety seconds of continuous firing. The British officers, sickened and shaken, debated endlessly whether, and if so how, it could have been avoided. Afterwards, in Lhasa, the Tibetans told Younghusband that he 'might have known their General did not mean to fight, for if he did he would not have been in the front as he was;' but, as Younghusband pointed out, it was not the General but the lamas who controlled affairs at Guru and brought on the catastrophe. There is much to be said for Candler's view that 'to send two dozen sepoys into that sullen mob to take away their arms was to invite disaster.' But something had to be done to clear the road. Given the Tibetan commander's refusal to do it, a clash was inevitable; given the British superiority in weapons, it was bound to be onesided.

By holding their fire during the final advance, the British courted disaster. Their force was small, its situation isolated and precarious. Chivalry is one of the luxuries of war; it was not a luxury they could afford. They chose nevertheless, on Younghusband's insistence, to trade the risk of heavy casualties, perhaps of a serious reverse, for the chance of a bloodless outcome; and the gamble came off. Then a single shot brought on a shambles; it was fired by the last man who should have fired it, by the one man who at that stage could have ensured that no blood was shed.

The officers of the expedition, looking back on what had happened with a mixture of compassion and repugnance, found comfort in the hope that the brisk slaughter of their army would teach the Tibetan authorities a lesson which they seemed incapable of assimilating from less drastic arguments. Lhasa, it was felt, would be brought to its senses; there would, with any luck, be no more of this embarrassingly futile resistance. These hopes were to prove vain.

The Lhasa General

Tibetan dead on the battlefield at Guru

CHAPTER TWELVE

Pressing On

To say that England was shocked by reports of the affair at Guru, which arrived over the Easter week-end, would perhaps be an overstatement; but the news aroused disquiet as well as remorse.

The Tibetan enterprise had been embarked upon over the heads of the British electorate, which has—like most electorates —a distaste for the *fait accompli*. Once launched, it had been presented as an almost ultra-legalistic undertaking; a diplomatic mission was being escorted into the interior to clear up certain mainly commercial questions which had been over-long in dispute. Now, suddenly, several hundred ill-armed Tibetans had been shot down and killed. The public's conscience was stirred.

Tibet was debated in the House of Commons on 13 April. An Act of 1858 stipulated that India's revenues might not be spent outside her statutory frontiers, except to repel aggression, without the sanction of Parliament; it was therefore needful that the House should be invited to give its consent to these revenues 'being applied to defray the expenses of any military operations which may become necessary beyond the frontiers of His Majesty's Indian possessions for the purpose of protecting the Political Mission which has been despatched to the Tibetan Government.'

The House, uneasily aware that this motion was, as someone put it, 'playing with words,' was restive and unhappy. 'A number of our [Conservative] Members,' Brodrick wrote to Curzon, who was due to sail home on leave at the end of the month, 'went to the Whips early in the afternoon, and told them that they intended to vote against the Government, unless it was made clear that we adhered to the policy laid down in the telegram of the 6th November, and did not intend to keep a permanent mission in Tibet. . . . The slaughter ten days before naturally barbed the contentions of those who urged that the Tibetans were an inoffensive people who only wanted to be left alone.' But in the end an able speech by the Prime Minister rallied his followers and spiked the guns of the Opposition. The motion was carried by a handsome majority.

The newspapers remained, at best, unenthusiastic about 'an expedition which has never been popular, if only because we are obviously crushing half-armed and very brave men with the irresistible weapons of science' (*Spectator*, 9 July 1904). *Punch* (in whose political cartoons Tibet was invariably personified as a llama, a quadruped indigenous to South America) expressed the general feeling in a sourly facetious paragraph: 'We are sorry to learn that the recent sudden and treacherous attack by the Tibetans on our men at Guru seriously injured the photographs that the officers were taking.'

It was at this stage that a reassessment of the British Government's foreign policy, envisaging a *rapprochement* with France and Russia, began to play a part, behind the scenes, in the destinies of the Tibetan expedition. One of the articles in an Anglo-French Agreement, which was concluded on 8 April 1904, had reference to an instrument known as the Khedivial Decree. This embodied certain financial arrangements, the effect of which was considerably to strengthen Britain's position in Egypt. To become fully effective, the Decree needed the assent of the other major European Powers, whom (since they had nothing to gain by giving, and nothing to lose by withholding, their approval) it was incumbent upon Britain to sweeten with minor inducements. It was felt in London that a suitable *quid pro quo* for Russia could be found in Tibet.

In hard fact it is difficult to see what, in regard to Tibet, the British had to offer the Russians that they had not given them

already. Balfour's Government, having nailed the telegram of
6 November to the mast, continued at intervals to promulgate
what Curzon called 'stupid and gratuitous pledges' that they
regarded themselves as bound by its terms; despite their textual
obscurity these, as we have seen, imposed definite restrictions
on Britain's freedom of action. Only on the assumption (which
may well have been made in St Petersburg) that these guaran-
tees meant little or nothing can their renewal, in the specific
context of the Egyptian negotiations, have acquired in the eyes
of the Russian Government a bargaining value.

Meanwhile the bogey of Russian intrigue in Tibet, though
nourished only on scraps of rumour and surmise, displayed
a yak's capacity for subsisting on next to nothing. No less
than three Russian rifles had been captured at Guru; the
barrels, which appeared to be of an obsolete service pattern,
bore the imprint of the Imperial arms factory at Tula, the
wooden stocks were of local manufacture. Landon sent one of
them to Curzon, with whom he was acquainted.

On 8 April *The Times* published a report from a correspondent in Moscow to the effect that 'few Russian military men
have any doubt that there does exist between Russia and Tibet
a more or less definite understanding whereby Tibet in certain
circumstances may safely count on Russian help if assailed from
outside.' The Russians, this report added, had presented the
Dalai Lama with a machine-gun. The Imperial Government
repeated, through its Ambassador in London, its previous
assurances that such reports were baseless.

On 24 May a patriotic citizen called Vickers transmitted to
the Foreign Office the information, obtained from a reliable
source in St Petersburg, that some ten thousand 'Tibetan
Cossacks,' serving in a number of different Russian regiments,
had been sent home on leave, taking with them their rifles and
five hundred rounds of ammunition each. 'This seems absolute
nonsense' was the first comment on the Foreign Office minute-
sheet; but Lord Lansdowne felt that there might be 'a foundation of truth' in the report, which 'should have gone *at once* to
the Intelligence Branch.' The comments of this Branch were

highly sceptical; but, as always happens, more people knew of the existence of the report than heard the verdict on it, and various versions of the story circulated with the port round politically-minded dinner-tables in London.

There never had been any valid evidence that Russia took a malevolent interest in Tibet, or indeed any active interest at all. Her Government had more than once formally disowned a Tibetan connexion. Nothing in recent British experience suggested that it was easy, or even possible, for an alien Power to establish any form of influence over the Tibetans. And now Russia was locked in a desperate struggle with Japan at the other end of Asia.

In all these circumstances it might have been expected that Lord Curzon's chimera would be turned out to grass, that the shadow of Dorjieff would shorten. This did not happen. The British outlook on Russia has seldom, in modern times, been dominated by *le sens du praticable*; and common sense failed to assert itself. The nebulous threat on which the Government's Tibetan policy had been largely based continued to assume, at will, the appearance of a stark though imprecise reality.

In Tibet the British advance continued. Behind the main body trailed one of the strangest supply-columns in the history of modern warfare. The pack-animals included mules, ponies, donkeys, bullocks, yaks and even sheep. The ranks of the various Coolie Corps were swollen by Tibetans who had been taken prisoner or lightly wounded, and whom nothing would induce to leave the society of their kindly and interesting captors. But easily the most efficient unit of transport was the ekka. This two-wheeled cart, in the words of an official report, 'practically saved the situation.' Dismantled, manhandled piecemeal up on to the plateau, and there reassembled, some two hundred of them plied to and fro between Phari and Kangma. They were drawn by a diversity of animals, of which—perhaps because their thick coats saved them from being irked by the harness— yaks proved the most satisfactory. Their value lay in their carrying capacity; at 400 lbs, one ekka-load was the equivalent of two and a half mule-loads, and there was only one beast to feed. Their wheels were the first specimens of this useful invention ever to be seen in Tibet.

Besides Hayden, the geologist, the force was accompanied by several officers whose specialist qualifications would, it was hoped, advance the cause of learning. A pseudonymous writer, in whose style it is possible to trace the influence of Jerome K. Jerome, left us this glimpse of them:

> There was a man who came with us armed only with a bicycle wheel and a cyclometer, with which he has corrected all preconceived notions of Tibetan distances. There was a man with a hammer who, if his pony stumbled over a stone, got off his pony and beat the stone with his hammer, not really vindictively but merely to find out what precious ore the stone might contain. There was a man with a butterfly net, who pickled the flies that got into his eyes, and chased those that did not with his butterfly net and pickled them too. There was a man with a trowel, who did a lot of useful weeding by the roadside.*

During the advance the most indispensable—and the most rewarding—role was played by the Mounted Infantry. Two companies (later increased to three) of these auxiliaries had been raised before the force left Sikkim; it was Macdonald's idea, and it was a good one. Each company was about a hundred strong. One was composed of Sikhs with no previous cavalry experience; the other of Gurkhas, possibly the least equestrian race in Asia. They were mounted initially on pack-animals from the pony-lines, wretched little brutes between twelve and thirteen hands, already exhausted by long marches. Mule-girths, the only ones available, were too long by eighteen inches. Bridles did not fit. Although delighted with their new status, the cavaliers were wholly inexperienced as such, and there were often empty saddles in the early days.

But during the long winter-lull rigorous training brought them up to the mark. Nose-bands, hoof-picks, head-ropes,

* 'Powell Millington': *To Lhasa at Last.*

brushes, curry-combs and other essentials arrived from India. The pack-ponies were replaced by a better stamp of animal. Riding-breeches were substituted for the loose serge trousers of the infantry, which chafed the riders' legs cruelly and wore out after one long march. When the advance on Gyantse started in April, the Mounted Infantry—a jolly, swashbuckling crew who regarded themselves as a *corps d'élite*—were to prove invaluable in reconnaissance and demoralising in pursuit. The expedition, groping its way at a foot's pace through inadequately mapped territory where sources of reliable intelligence were non-existent, relied heavily on its contingent of light horse, questing miles ahead of it and patrolling far out on its flanks. There can have been few occasions in the twentieth century when cavalry so fully discharged its traditional tasks on active service.

The column skirted, without incident, the desolate shores of the Bham Tso and the Kala Tso. Both salt lakes were partly frozen, but open stretches of water were dark with wildfowl— ruddy sheldrake, pintails, bar-headed geese, teal, mallard and many other varieties. Thanks to the tenets of Buddhism, the birds had no reason to regard man as a predator (though Bogle had offended local prejudices by shooting some in 1774) and they provided a welcome change of diet.

Seventeen miles beyond Kala Tso a Mounted Infantry patrol was fired on from the village of Samada, where Turner had spent the night in 1783; but the Tibetan garrison, without waiting for a fight, fell back on Kangma, where a wall four hundred yards long, flanked by sangars on the hill above it, had been built across the floor of the valley. Between Samada and Kangma the expedition saw, 'with a gratitude which can hardly be believed,' the first tree which many of them had set eyes on for three months.

Macdonald halted for the night of 8 April some distance short of the wall, and on the following day advanced cautiously against it, only to find that it had been abandoned. Beyond it the Nyang Chu, along whose banks the road to Gyantse ran, plunged into a defile, known—from the pigmented carvings of

Buddha on its cliff-like walls—as Red Idol Gorge. Here it was clear that the Tibetans meant to make a stand.

Although there is, strictly speaking, no such thing as an impregnable position, this looked very like one. The sides of the gorge, often precipitous and never more than barely climbable, rose to a height of three thousand feet; the boulder-strewn track, flanked by a raging torrent, narrowed to a width of six. Beyond this bottleneck a spur, covered by a scree of hugh rocks, dominated the defile. This spur was the centre of the Tibetan defences; but from the heights above it muskets and jingals—a kind of blunderbuss-cannon—opened fire on the British advance-guard when it rounded a sharp bend in the ravine. It was an ugly place for a fight.

Macdonald decided that no frontal assault was possible until the cliff-top positions on the Tibetan right were cleared. The Gurkhas, to whom this task was entrusted, began a painful ascent which was expected to take three hours. Then, from the north, a violent storm of sleet and snow swept down the gorge, reducing visibility to a few yards and numbing the waiting troops to a state approaching insensibility. As long as the storm lasted the gunners would be unable to support the Gurkhas, since nobody could see where they were; possibly for this reason, a message was sent recalling them.

But the message miscarried, and by noon the storm had blown itself out. The Mounted Infantry, sent forward to reconnoitre the main position, were driven back by a hot though ineffective fire. The long, cold lull went on until (in Landon's words) 'upon the representation of Colonel Brander of the 32nd Pioneers, that regiment was allowed to go forward and clear the gorge.' Their advance coincided with the Gurkhas' arrival on the heights, where no determined resistance was offered. The ten-pounders of the 7th Mountain Battery were in action. A stream of bullets from the Maxims whined down the defile. The Tibetans broke and fled. They lost about two hundred killed; the British had three sepoys wounded.

The defenders of the Red Idol Gorge were for the most part impressed peasants with no stomach for a fight; prisoners, of whom some seventy were taken, addressed themselves with relish to the task of converting into firewood the matchlocks with which they had been issued by the monks. Even brave and determined men could not have held the gorge for long with the weapons at the Tibetans' disposal. The jingals were hopelessly inaccurate; although some of the soldiers had breech-loading rifles of poor quality, most were armed with matchlocks from which, when aimed downhill, the bullet was apt to dribble prematurely, which took a long time to reload, and which could not fire at all if rain extinguished the fuses used to detonate the charge.

Next day, 11 April, Gyantse was sighted. The enormous Fort, built on an outcrop rising sharply out of the plain to a height of five hundred feet, reminded some officers of Gibraltar, others of Mont St Michel. Adjoining it, on the same spur, was a monastery of equally stout construction. The usual warren of a town—the third most important in Tibet—crouched at its foot. All round lay a fertile, tree-dotted plain through which flowed the Nyang Chu.

The Fort (*Jong* might in this instance have been better translated as 'Citadel') looked a formidable place; and it turned out afterwards that they were viewing its least minatory aspect, where the rock on which it stood had only a relatively gentle slope. It was difficult to see how such a stronghold could be stormed by a small force with nothing in the way of siege-artillery and no reinforcements in sight; and as the column crawled towards it across the plain the great Fort, barring the way to Lhasa, seemed likely to have a decisive influence on the expedition's prospects. They camped on the bank of the river, about two miles from the Fort, from which there presently emerged a decorative cavalcade of delegates.

They were led by the Jongpen, or Commandant, and by a Chinese general called Ma, an envoy of the Amban, with whom Younghusband had already had one brief meeting on the march from Tuna. They were in a submissive mood. The Jongpen, whom Landon described as 'a kindly heavy old man like

Gyantse Fort seen from Chang Lo

Ekkas drawn by yaks

Jingals in action

a saddened Falstaff,' explained that he could not surrender the Fort, or he would be executed by the Dalai Lama; on the other hand he could not defend it, as all his soldiers had run away. This placed him in a difficult position; and he suggested that, in the circumstances, the best course would be for the British to ignore the Fort's existence.

He was told, in a friendly manner, that this was not possible; and next day, under the rueful supervision of the Jongpen and his Chinese colleague, the Fort was entered and explored, due precautions having been taken against treachery. It was found to be deserted, and the Union Jack was hoisted alongside the gilt copper finial which crowned it. Many discoveries were made in its dark and labyrinthine chambers. The most valuable was a vast quantity of barley, estimated at thirty-six tons; the most gruesome (and also, since capital punishment had no place in the Tibetan penal code, the most inexplicable) was a store-room crammed with the severed heads of men, women and children.

The British did not remain in occupation of the Fort. Subsequent events were to call in question the wisdom of Macdonald's decision to leave it ungarrisoned, but Younghusband was not among his critics on this score. 'I think he was right,' he wrote to Dane on 4 June. 'Water was the difficulty. A numerous enemy could have cut off our water and we had not enough men to hold both the Jong and this hamlet which is by the river.'

'This hamlet' was Chang Lo, a cluster of buildings grouped round a nobleman's residence just over a thousand yards from the Fort. Here the Mission were installed while Macdonald ('Retiring Mac,' they had begun to call him) returned to New Chumbi, a hundred and fifty miles away, 'to arrange posts and communications and convoys.' He took with him, on 20 April, about half his force, including—typically—its only effective artillery, the two British-manned ten-pounders. To guard the Mission he left at Chang Lo, under Brander, four companies of the 32nd Pioneers, two companies of the 8th Gurkhas, fifty Mounted Infantry, the Maxims, Bubble and Squeak, part of a

Mule Corps and one section of an Indian Field Hospital; in all about five hundred men.

Gyantse, it will be recalled, was the Mission's official destination. No further advance had been authorised, or was under contemplation, by the British Government. It was now Younghusband's painfully familiar duty to await the arrival of competent negotiators.

Of these there was, as usual, no sign. It had been known for some time that the four Shapés, or State Councillors, had been thrown into prison in Lhasa. It was believed that their advocacy of a peaceful settlement had brought this fate upon them. It seemed probable that their successors, if appointed, would be extremists, sharing the supposedly intransigent views of the Dalai Lama; and it was doubted whether anybody below the rank of Shapé possessed the authority to negotiate on behalf of the Tibetan Government.

As for the Chinese, the new Amban, Yu-t'ai, had now been in Lhasa for two months after taking over a year to get there; he might as well have been in Liverpool for all the influence he was exerting on Tibetan policy. He was, he wrote to Younghusband on 27 March, 'anxious to hasten to the frontier and discuss with you all matters requiring settlement;' but the Dalai Lama had refused him transport. 'I think,' he said, 'that you will recognise my perplexities and my effort,' concerning which he was forwarding 'a succinct report' to Peking. Meanwhile, although 'ashamed even to mention to you the question of your retirement to Yatung,' he longed to hear 'whether you deem a retirement to Yatung feasible or not.' This missive held out few hopes that the Suzerain Power was taking a realistic view of the situation. At Gyantse China continued to be weakly represented by General Ma and Captain Parr, who (Landon wrote to Ampthill) 'accompanies us by his own invitation and to everyone's irritation.'

Younghusband by this time could smell stalemate a long way off; he was desperately anxious that the moral effect of the British advance should not be allowed to seep away during a long, thankless vigil at Gyantse. In a telegram dispatched on 22 April and received in London six days later he reported that 'our prestige is now at its height; Nepal and Bhutan are with us; the people are not against us; the soldiers do not want to fight; the Lamas are stunned;' and he recommended that 'at the earliest moment by which military preparations can be completed, the Mission should be moved straight to Lhasa. . . . This would be the most effectual and the only permanent way of clinching matters, besides being the cheapest and quickest.'

The suggestion did not appeal to the authorities in London, whence Brodrick was impressing on Curzon the importance, in view of the secret negotiations over Egypt, of 'disarming' Russian suspicions about Tibet, and where, early in May, Lansdowne told the Russian Ambassador that, if his Government would give its adherence to the Khedivial Decree, 'I felt no doubt that I should be able to give, in reference to Tibet, an assurance that we still adhered to the policy of the telegram [of 6 November].' The situation—of whose altered diplomatic background Younghusband had no inkling—could hardly have been less favourable to the adoption of his proposed course of action. His telegram was not answered.

Gyantse is two thousand feet lower than Tuna, and spring had come at last. For the Mission and its escort life was as placid as it had been at Khamba Jong. The demeanour of the Tibetans was friendly and respectful. From Shigatse the Tashi Lama, the second dignitary in the Tibetan church, sent an abbot to intercede for the monks of Gyantse, whom Younghusband proposed to fine for taking part in hostilities. A regular bazaar, presided over mainly by women, established itself outside the British lines. The peasants were ploughing the no longer frost-bound fields. The British officers rode out on sightseeing, shooting or fishing expeditions. Vague, temporising letters came intermittently from the Amban, who now hoped to arrive on 12 May if the Tibetans would allow him transport.

But nobody took the Amban's protestations seriously, and of

Tibetan delegates there was no news at all; the prospects of a negotiated settlement seemed for practical purposes as remote as they had been, ten months ago, at Khamba Jong. There is no evidence that the Mission thought wistfully of the two Lachung men, who had played so helpful a part in breaking the former deadlock; but they were, whether they realised it or not, in an *impasse* from which—failing a sudden change of heart by either the British or the Tibetan Government—only an Incident could offer the prospect of release.

In the last days of April rumours came in that a Tibetan army was being concentrated in the Karo La, a sixteen-thousand-foot pass forty-seven miles east of Gyantse on the road to Lhasa. A Mounted Infantry patrol, dispatched to investigate, found a wall built across a narrow defile. On approaching it they were greeted by a hail of bullets and a shower of boulders from the cliffs above, the latter proving the more dangerous type of missile. They put the Tibetan strength at three thousand and described them as better armed and better led than in previous engagements. Their report reached Chang Lo on 1 May.

Colonel Brander had dash and a sense of the dramatic;* he decided to march against the Karo La immediately. Additional pack-animals having been requisitioned from the Jongpen, he set off early on 3 May, taking with him about three hundred and thirty riflemen, forty-five Mounted Infantry, the two Maxims, and Bubble and Squeak. He went with the full concurrence of the British Commissioner; the Tibetans, Younghusband wired to India on 5 May, were recovering from the shock of their first encounter with the British and he foresaw trouble if gatherings such as that at the Karo La were not dispersed promptly. 'Colonel Brander is confident that he can defeat the Tibetan forces without difficulty, and that the Mission left at Gyantse will be safe.'

* Sir Arnold Wilson, writing a quarter of a century later, remembered Brander as 'one of the most stimulating and eager-hearted men it has been my privilege to know'. (*Loyalties.*)

Brander, naturally, reported the action he was taking to Macdonald (the telegram in which he did so is dated 1 May and reached New Chumbi on 3 May); but the telegraph-line extended, at this stage, only to Kala Tso, sixty miles from Gyantse. However expeditiously the despatch-riders of the Mounted Infantry scurried between Gyantse and Kala Tso, and back again from Kala Tso to Gyantse, it was impossible for Macdonald to countermand Brander's expedition before it started. Brander and Younghusband were well aware of this; and both must have been equally well aware that Macdonald would be horrified when he heard of the Karo La sortie and might, if he was able, recall it.

This last statement, which is supported by no documentary evidence, needs amplification.

If Brander received any written orders from Macdonald concerning his duties at Chang Lo, they have not survived; but much internal evidence makes it clear that he had been forbidden to take offensive action except

(a) to protect the Mission, or
(b) to safeguard its communications.

Even if his freedom of action had not been thus specifically limited, a detachment-commander of Brander's experience must have realised that the foray to Karo La was bound to strike his superiors as over-audacious.

He had in all some five hundred men guarding the Mission at Chang Lo. He was now taking more than two-thirds of these into the blue, with both his guns, both his machine-guns and almost all his cavalry; his purpose was to attack, in a narrow defile nearly fifty miles away, an enemy outnumbering him by ten to one. At the best of times this would have been a difficult decision to justify; and in view of Brander's orders, summarised above, he would appear to have been courting a charge of insubordination.

Against this charge Brander and Younghusband had concerted a bland defence. The Karo La column, they asserted, was carrying out one of the two main duties assigned to Colonel

Brander by Brigadier-General Macdonald; it was safeguarding the Mission's communications. Here the reader should consult the map, from which it will be seen that from the Karo La a route, by-passing Gyantse, runs south-west, via Ralung and Nyeru, through the mountains to Kangma. Since this route was neither guarded nor patrolled by the British, there was nothing to prevent the Tibetans at Karo La from using it. If they had used it—and there were no grounds for assuming that they had not this intention—they would have severed the Mission's communications at Kangma. It was (the Brander–Young-husband argument ran) to avert a perilous contingency in their rear that the bulk of the Mission's escort found it necessary to make an advance of nearly fifty miles towards Lhasa.

There was a strong element of casuistry in this reasoning. To the Government of India Younghusband reported only that he had 'raised no objections on political grounds to proposed movement;' but a few days later he wrote to Curzon: 'I was delighted when he [Brander] made the proposal,' and he well knew that he would be suspected as the instigator of a deliberate act of provocation. He knew, too, that public opinion in England would not be behind him; Landon, writing to Curzon from Chang Lo on 11 May, cited as an instance of Younghusband's 'wariness' the fact that 'when discussing beforehand the Karo La movement by Brander, he voluntarily asked me not to hesitate for a moment if I wished to condemn the operation at home!' Landon, who was in Younghusband's confidence, cannot have left him in any doubt of what the reactions to Karo La would be in England. 'Speaking of the home conscience,' he wrote to Ampthill on the eve of Brander's departure, 'I confess that I think our forty-six-mile expedition towards Lhasa tomorrow to attack the Tibetans during the period of time which was to elapse before the Amban's visit is injudicious, and quite out of keeping with the studious way in which we have hitherto kept ourselves in the right.'

When Brander marched away eastwards on the morning of 3 May, Younghusband must have known that in letting the column go he was placing his own career in jeopardy; he risked, with open eyes, recall and disgrace. But he was courting, too, another risk: a risk so obvious and so easily acceptable that he chose to disregard it. In the event, by a strange twist of fate, these two risks were to cancel each other out; the danger on his doorstep stole the thunder of Whitehall.

CHAPTER THIRTEEN

The Danger on his Doorstep

THE news that two-thirds of the Mission's escort had gone off along the Lhasa road to fight a battle caused consternation in New Chumbi, in Simla and in London. Immediate efforts were made to recall the force.

The only message which stood any chance of achieving this was telegraphed from New Chumbi, on his own initiative, by Brigadier-General Macdonald. It was dispatched at 1736 hours on 3 May and franked CLEAR THE LINE (the equivalent in those days of MOST IMMEDIATE). It reached Chang Lo some time on the following day. It read:

> From Gen. Macdonald, Chumbi.
> To Lt. Col. Brander, Gyantse.
> CLEAR THE LINE. 318T. Your No. 12.
> The Moveable Column should not have gone as far as the Karo La without reference to me. If you are not committed return at once to Gyantse. Fear your action will be considered as attempt to force hand of Government. Younghusband's concurrence does not relieve you of responsibility. You may clear out any Tibetans threatening communications between Ralung and Kangma and this piece of road should be reconnoitred. Please acknowledge.

This urgent signal was delivered to Major Murray of the 8th Gurkhas, whom Brander had left in command at Chang Lo. Since it was a military message Murray should, strictly speaking, have arranged for its onward transmission himself; instead, he handed it to Younghusband.

Asia had schooled the British Commissioner, to whom this

168

development was far from unexpected, in the uses of delay. He sat down and wrote—on a leaf taken, one might almost say, from the Amban's book—a covering note:

> My dear Brander,
> I am sending you an urgent letter, which Murray has handed me to send on to you. My Jemadar will take it, but he is rather nervous of the Tibetans, and his pony is slow, so perhaps he will not reach [you] very quickly. . . .

(The implications, obvious enough, of this opening are made still clearer in a letter which Younghusband wrote to his father five days later: 'If I had sent that message on at once Brander would have got it a march before he reached the Karo La and before he was actually committed. But I knew that the effect of his returning without fighting when all the Tibetans knew that he had gone out *to* fight would have been absolutely disastrous. So as it had been left with me to procure a messenger I took my time about it and I told the messenger he was to go along very cautiously and not hurry and I hoped he would reach Brander *after* his fight. . . . Unfortunately the messenger showed too much zeal and did arrive at Brander's camp before the fight [this, according to a note by Younghusband on the original document, was at 0600 hours on 6 May] and he was greatly unnerved by Macdonald's message. But he wrote me a line from the field of battle thanking me for my "strong and cheering letter" which he had acted on.')

The 'strong and cheering letter' went on:

> . . . I need hardly assure you that we are perfectly safe here, or that any turning back now on your part would have a disastrous effect. On political grounds I would have the strongest objection to your returning, unless the enemy have so increased in strength that the result of a conflict would be doubtful. You have my warmest wishes for success.
>
> Yours sincerely
F. E. YOUNGHUSBAND.

Having written this message and instructed the jemadar in the manner of its delivery, Younghusband, after supping in a much-depleted mess, went to bed. The jemadar's orders—he could not in any case have ridden by night—were to leave early on the following day (5 May). Before dawn the need to add a postscript arose.

During the past days there had been several small indications that Younghusband's diagnosis of the situation was correct in at least one respect, and that the Tibetan will to resist was hardening; the evacuation of the Fort, followed by Macdonald's departure from Gyantse with half his force, had probably contributed to this. Besides the concentration in the Karo La, reports came in of a gathering of four thousand armed men at Shigatse; some of these were said to be moving up to Dongtse, only twelve miles away. On 2 May, in an attempt to insure against an outbreak of hostilities in the Gyantse area, the old Jongpen was brought into the British camp as a hostage. But nobody was seriously worried. 'If they were not such hopeless soldiers,' Landon wrote to Curzon, 'they would of course attack this place during the seven days' absence of more than half the garrison. However, they will do nothing of the sort.'

Relations between the invaders and the citizens of Gyantse had from the first been close; 'the friendliness of the inhabitants,' Landon recorded, 'is almost excessive.' Apart from the open-air bazaar outside the fortified perimeter there was a constant *va-et-vient* of curio-sellers, carpenters and other craftsmen. Although it was against orders, many of the officers' Tibetan servants spent their nights in Gyantse, drinking and whoring and boasting about the marvels among which they lived. A garden —never very productive; mustard and cress was the only crop that flourished—was started in the main compound, and for this a masterful Tibetan woman provided a labour force in the persons of her two husbands, whom she bullied mercilessly; she was known as Mrs Wiggs, after the eponymous heroine of *Mrs Wiggs of the Cabbage Patch* by Alice Hegan Rice, a best-seller of the period. The Mission's medical officer, Captain Walton, ran a small hospital in a shrine which was always crowded with patients.

On the morning of 4 May Walton noticed a sudden slackening in the demand for medical attention, and in the course of the day almost all the inmates of his sickroom picked themselves up, or were picked up by their relatives, and disappeared. The Tibetans were always shy and unaccountable, but nothing like this had happened before. That evening Walton thought it worth mentioning the matter to Younghusband. Afterwards it was remembered as the only portent which the Mission had received of what impended.

At 0430 hours on 5 May a force of eight hundred Tibetans attacked the post at Chang Lo. They had crept up to its walls under cover of darkness while another force, of similar strength, occupied the abandoned Fort; both parties had come from Dongtse.

The onslaught was heralded by war-cries which reminded some of the defenders of hyenas or jackals.* Thrusting their muskets through the loopholes, the Tibetans poured an indiscriminate fire into the British position, where for a time confusion reigned. Chang Lo was completely surrounded. The reduced garrison mustered barely a hundred and twenty riflemen. For a moment—as generally happens when a surprise attack is delivered at night—all seemed lost.

But in fact the ill-aimed muskets caused no casualties; in sectors allotted to the Sikhs, who are taller than most Tibetans, the loopholes were too high for the latter's fire to be effective. It was generally agreed afterwards that the assailants would have done better to discard their firearms, which, like their war-cries, did little more than sound the alarm; if they had swarmed silently over the defences with their broadswords, the outcome might have been different.

As it was, the garrison suffered nothing worse than a rude awakening. Stumbling to their posts, they turned their Lee Metfords on the Tibetans who, massed round the perimeter, were

---

* Sven Hedin described the noisy prelude to an attack on his camp by Tibetan brigands in 1896 as a 'hyena concert.' (*Central Asia and Tibet*.)

now betrayed by the dawn. Some fled to a grove of poplars, some to the shelter of the river-bank; but for most there was no cover at hand, and terrible execution was done. After two hours the attack had been beaten off. 'It was a lovely peaceful morning,' Younghusband wrote to Curzon two days later, 'with sky-larks singing and sparrows chirping unconcernedly away. . . . But all round the post were the dead bodies of Tibetans—140 is, I think, the exact number—and away over the plain the remainder were flying, pursued by half our garrison and by my Parsi clerk, who with a revolver in his hand had been my constant fear all through the attack!' The British had two sepoys wounded; revised figures of the Tibetan casualties put them at two hundred and fifty killed and seriously wounded.

The letter to Curzon quoted above began: 'The Tibetans as usual have played into our hands.' This was to prove true. The Tibetan attack on Chang Lo preceded by twenty-four hours the British attack on the Karo La. The latter, in isolation, must have proved a grave embarrassment to the British Government. It would have aroused the misgivings of the electorate, the moral indignation of the Opposition, and the suspicions—if nothing worse—of St Petersburg. It cannot be said for certain that these repercussions would have led to further restraints being placed on the Tibetan enterprise, already hobbled by the telegram of 6 November. What can be fairly assumed is that, if in early May the British had attacked the Karo La and the Tibetans had not attacked Chang Lo, the Cabinet would have become even more reluctant than they already were to sanction an advance to Lhasa.

Younghusband was a perfectionist; in his own mind the slightest suspicion—even if nobody else could have shared it—that his conduct had fallen below the highest standards was apt to rankle. Reading between the lines of his brief account of the Chang Lo incident, published six years later in *India and Tibet*, it is difficult not to feel that he was dissatisfied with his immediate reactions to a nightmare experience. 'Personally, I did not deserve to get through the attack unscathed, for directly I was out of my tent I made straight for the Mission rendezvous. I was in my pyjamas, and only half awake, and the first thought that struck me was to go to the rendezvous . . . in what we called the Citadel. But I ought, as I did on other occasions—and as I think should always be done in cases of any sudden attack—to have made straight for the wall with whatever weapon came to hand, and joined in repelling the attack during the first few crucial moments.'

Whether or not a sense of personal failure—almost certainly misplaced—coloured his feelings about the attempt on Chang Lo, his report of the affair was marked by an acerbity and a sense of affront not previously noticeable in his official telegrams. 'Attack confirms impression I had formed that Lhasa Government are irreconcilable, and I trust His Majesty's Government, in deciding future attitude towards them, will remember that I have now been ten months in Tibet, that I have met with nothing but insults the whole time in spite of the extreme forbearance I have shown, and that I have now been deliberately attacked. . . . Now that Tibetans have . . . thrown down the gauntlet, I trust that Government will take such action as will prevent the Tibetans ever again treating British representative as I have been treated.' Since it was telegraphed from Kala Tso on the same day, this ruffled message must have been written immediately after the fight.

Besides justifying—or appearing to justify—Brander's assault on the Karo La, which was delivered on the following day (6 May), the Tibetan attack on Chang Lo enabled if it did not oblige the authorities in India and in London to reappraise their policy. The attack was an outrage. It was unprovoked; it was carried out by stealth; it had—since the Chinese General Ma, who was in Gyantse and must have known about it, sent no warning to the British—a distinct flavour of treachery; and it was accompanied by atrocities, for those of the Mission's servants who were sleeping in the town were hacked to pieces in a peculiarly barbarous manner. It was moreover an event which seemed likely to have dangerous sequels. It called for stern action.

This, at any rate, was the view taken by the Government of India. On 6 May, after the matter had been discussed in Council, the Viceroy (Ampthill was by now deputising for the home-bound Curzon) wired to the Secretary of State that his Government 'could not but fear' that Younghusband was right, and that the Chang Lo incident must be taken as conclusive proof of Lhasa's intransigence. They suggested that 'some definite limit of time should now be imposed, and that a further advance should at once be made, unless within that time proper representatives of both Chinese and Tibetan Governments, invested with full powers, reach Gyantse. A month [Ampthill added] would be required for the necessary military preparations.'

Brodrick replied six days later. His Majesty's Government, he told the Viceroy, 'agree that recent events make it inevitable that the Mission must advance to Lhasa unless the Tibetans consent to open negotiations at Gyantse.' They should therefore be given, through the Amban, a month's grace. The Government of India should however 'clearly understand' that no departure from the policy laid down in the telegram of 6 November was contemplated by the Cabinet. 'So the die is cast in Tibet,' Sir Arthur Godley, Permanent Under-Secretary at the India Office, wrote to Lord Ampthill a few days later. 'The telegram of the 12th, authorizing the advance, was drafted not in this office but in the Cabinet, and the reference to the telegram of 6 November was exactly what I expected.' The bit was still in the horse's mouth; but the reins had broken.

Twenty-four hours after the attack on Chang Lo had been beaten off, and nearly fifty miles to the eastward, Colonel Brander confronted an enormous wall, six feet high, four feet thick and eight hundred yards long. It was more strongly built and ingeniously loopholed than any of the fortifications hitherto encountered; it was flanked by sangars and stone-shoots on the semi-precipitous slopes above it; and it blocked, just beyond its narrowest point, the defile of the Karo La, nearly 17,000 feet above sea-level and the highest point on the road to Lhasa. The cold was intense, the place forbidding. 'On either side,' wrote Landon, 'the cliffs rise so steeply that one hardly catches a sight of the eternal snows that slope back from these frowning heights.' It was like Red Idol Gorge, only worse. The British force was smaller, the Tibetan force was larger, the wall was stronger and the altitude was more than two thousand feet greater.

For a commander in the field a difficult battle is not made easier if he has in his pocket a reprimand for fighting it at all; and Younghusband's postscript told Brander that only a swift victory would serve, for his first duty was to protect the Mission and he must get back to Gyantse as quickly as he could. The composure with which he addressed himself to the task of defeating, in a matter of hours, three thousand men holding a position of immense strength was admirable; his own force numbered less than four hundred.

The floor of the defile at this point was roughly funnel-shaped; the British, debouching from the narrow end, had to attack the Tibetan fortifications which blocked the wide end, and from which almost the whole of the funnel could be swept by fire. As at Red Idol Gorge, flanking parties were sent up against the sangars; but the shale-covered slopes which offered the most direct approach were prohibitively steep and soon both detachments were pinned down by fire, spreadeagled on the valley walls like a trapper's pelts pegged out to dry. A frontal advance by the 32nd Pioneers and the Mounted Infantry (on foot) against the Tibetan centre accomplished nothing and was driven back; Captain Bethune of the 32nd, who had been with the Escort ever since Khamba Jong and was much liked, lost— or threw away—his life in an almost single-handed attempt to storm the wall.

By the middle of the morning the outlook was bleak. Bubble and Squeak (those 'irresistible weapons of science') made their veteran voices heard, but the range was beyond them, and of seventy rounds expended only one reached its target. The Norfolks' Maxims, though accurate, were impotent against the wall. The Tibetans' fire was brisker and better directed than it had ever been before. The noise, magnified by the acoustics of the gorge, was deafening. But a deadlock had been reached. Brander, whose supply of ammunition was limited, ordered his riflemen to cease fire; he told Younghusband afterwards that he was 'on the point of despairing.'

For the next two hours the main British effort was devoted to mountaineering. On the left the Gurkhas, on the right the Sikhs, detached a handful of men to inch their way upwards until they overlooked the commanding sangars from the rear; both were led by native officers. Burdened by their arms and ammunition, devoid of training in or equipment for rock-climbing, pinched by the terrible cold, these two small parties, numbering about a dozen each, went doggedly to work. 'What the hardship must have been of climbing up to an altitude which could not have been less than 18,500 feet it is difficult for the ordinary reader to conceive,' wrote Landon. His 'ordinary reader' knew nothing of the aids to mountain-warfare without which, in the present day, soldiers would never be called on to perform feats of this kind. The cheapness of the British victories in the Tibetan gorges should not be allowed to obscure the hardihood and the virtuosity which won them.

'Still, in spite of everything, the little figures crept upwards,' Landon went on, 'and at last reached the line of perpetual snow, where they could be seen clambering and crawling against the dazzling surface of white.' At about one o'clock a cheer, heard faintly but with curious distinctness in the bottom of the defile, came from the heights on Brander's left. It was followed by the rattle of Lee Metfords, and soon about fifty Tibetans were seen to be withdrawing from the most troublesome of the sangars across a steep face where they were caught in a cross-fire. A few were taken prisoner by the Gurkhas; all the rest were shot down or, losing their footing, fell to their death over the precipice on which their emplacement stood.

An hour's lull ensued and was ended by a similar engagement on the cliff-tops opposite, where the Sikhs had had an even harder climb. From the captured sangars fire could be brought

Troopers of the Mounted Infantry

Camp in the Karo La Defile

Ekkas in the plain below Chomolhari

to bear (though only from a couple of dozen rifles) on the Tibetans massed behind the wall. So far they had shown themselves more resolute and soldierly than usual; but now, although their main position was not seriously weakened, they lost heart, and a general retreat down the defile began.

The Mounted Infantry under Ottley, a flamboyant, red-haired Irishman,* were launched in pursuit. It took them ten minutes to make a breach in the wall. Through it they poured at full gallop, fifty men on the heels of three thousand. Here and there a herd of Tibetans tried to make a stand, but the horsemen tore into them, firing from the saddle, and the soggy phalanxes broke up. A reinforcement of five hundred men, on its way to the wall, abandoned its purpose and its cohesion. Singly or in small parties the disintegrating army took to the side-valleys or the hills. Ottley's men captured and burnt two well-stocked camps and did not draw rein until they were twelve miles beyond the wall and had secured several of the enemy's ponies—prizes in quest of which the Mounted Infantry were always apt to disregard the strictly operational requirements of their forays.

Their own mounts, which had been on half-rations since they left Gyantse, were by now exhausted. A blizzard raged as the men trudged back to camp through the icy darkness, leading their ponies. Two of these died, and several of the sepoys were in a state of collapse before they got in at 2130 hours. 'It was most decidedly unpleasant, to say the least,' Ottley recorded; and he felt intensely grateful for 'a glass from Colonel Younghusband's bottle of green chartreuse kindly kept for me by Colonel Brander.' In the whole action—fought at a greater altitude than any other in the history of war—the British lost four killed and thirteen wounded.

Brander was naturally anxious about the situation at Gyantse, and next day the Mounted Infantry were called upon to perform another feat of endurance. After riding forty-seven miles

---

* 'About the most dashing man on the show, steeped in gore for months, must have killed his hundred men, quite unscrupulous in war.' (Candler, in a letter.)

in eight hours, they slipped into Chang Lo under cover of darkness. Younghusband wrote afterwards that he was 'indeed relieved' to hear the news they brought him. Considering how heavily he had gambled on a victory at the Karo La, and how much he stood to lose by any of the possible alternatives, he can hardly be suspected of exaggeration.

CHAPTER FOURTEEN

The Mission Besieged

To Younghusband it seemed that luck was with him. 'I think after the attack on us this morning,' he had written to Ampthill on 5 May, 'His Majesty's Government must see that the necessity for going to Lhasa has now been proved beyond all doubt.' He knew that Brander, with his force intact and a dashing victory to his credit, was on the heels of the Mounted Infantry and that his arrival would guarantee the Mission's safety, which in any case nobody at Chang Lo regarded as seriously threatened. His hopes were high. In a letter to Curzon on 7 May he urged the unwisdom of withdrawing the expedition from Lhasa when it got there; to do so would play into the Russians' hands, 'and we shall have to return to Lhasa ten years hence as we had to return to Kabul and to Chitral.' The future was still uncertain, but events were moulding Imperial policy into the pattern which Younghusband had known, all along, it must assume if it was to be fruitful.

Younghusband, though straightforward, was astute; it was perhaps this quality which Landon had in mind when he mentioned his 'wariness.' Yet he was never very good at gauging the effect on higher authority of his telegrams and reports. In some ways he was like a child dealing with grown-ups; he failed to realise how transparently, at times, his purposes showed through the arguments with which he buttressed his recommendations or justified his actions. To telegraph, for instance, as he did on 8 May, 'Brander has most effectually carried out his object of removing threats to our line of communication' was to enhance rather than to diminish the impression that the British Commissioner had sponsored, in the Karo La venture, a course of action which he had no business to sponsor; and his excuse for doing so, here gratuitously repeated, was not made more convincing by the fact that, whether or not the Mission's rearward communications could justly be said to have been menaced by a force fifty miles in front of it, it was now entirely surrounded by hostile bands of Tibetans in the suburbs of Gyantse. Small points of this kind consistently eluded Younghusband's attention.

But not the attention of his superiors. In a telegram to London Ampthill revealed (in a passage omitted from the Blue Book) that GHQ, on hearing of Brander's departure for the Karo La, had sent an urgent signal ordering his recall; 'we at once telegraphed to the same effect, and at the same time asked for an explanation from Colonel Younghusband.' It is clear that the incident gave the Indian authorities a shock, and that their disquiet was further increased by news (received less than forty-eight hours later) of the unexpected attack on the Mission and its dangerously depleted escort.

Their reaction was prompt, and almost inevitable; on 8 May a telegram from Dane relegated Younghusband once more to the status of a passenger. 'Owing to attack on Gyantse and serious opposition at Karo La, Government of India consider that preponderance for the present must be given to military considerations, and General Macdonald has been authorized to take all measures necessary to secure safety of Mission and communications short of permanent advance on Lhasa.* He will also exercise same control of military operations and press censorship as during advance on Tuna. As soon as active opposition ceases, and you are able to open negotiations with proper Chinese and Tibetan delegates, the former arrangement will be restored.'

This telegram, almost certainly inspired by Kitchener, threw Younghusband into a state of despondency. Curzon, his patron and friend, had sailed from Bombay on the last day of

---

* It will be remembered that an advance on Lhasa was not sanctioned by the British Government until four days later.

April, and Younghusband had just received his first letter from the Acting Viceroy. Lord Ampthill wrote, on 2 May, in friendly and appreciative terms, promising him 'the same sympathy and support' as he had had from Curzon. But he reminded Younghusband that, because of their pledges to Russia, the Home Government were strongly averse to an advance on Lhasa, and he revealed that he had been directed by the Secretary of State to give the British Commissioner 'a hint against undue precipitancy.' Brodrick had 'noted throughout your telegrams, all of which have been repeated to him verbatim, a distinct eagerness for a further advance which, I gather, has caused the Cabinet some apprehension.'

Younghusband could not fail to read the news of his demotion in the light of this warning. He wrote to Curzon on 15 May that it had depressed him; he found it 'a little unfair,' which perhaps it was. The Government, he reasoned, 'may take my view or not as they like, but surely it is my business to express one.' He was saddened, too, by his superiors' reaction to the Karo La episode. 'If it were not for the personal devotion I have for Your Excellency . . . I would resign at once, and try in other ways than as the tool of a supine Government to help my country.'

There was no blinking the fact that he was under a cloud. Macdonald was a hundred and fifty miles from Gyantse; to charge him with 'securing the safety of the Mission,' for which he was in any case already responsible, was mere pedantry. The reassertion of his control over the expedition might have been no more than the formal outcome of one of those joustingmatches between the military and the civil power for which Simla so often provided the lists. But Brodrick's veiled rebuke, tactfully passed on by Ampthill, revealed that there was something more than a storm in this teacup behind Younghusband's demotion. 'I am afraid,' he had written to his father three months earlier, 'that Lord Curzon is right, that Home Government have to be treated like a pack of children.' But now it was Younghusband who was being treated like a child, and a wayward one at that; he was being stood in the corner. He asked for permission to pay a brief visit to Simla, to discuss matters. His request was not granted; 'although,' Ampthill told him, 'the chances of proper negotiators presenting themselves at Gyantse seem to be hopelessly improbable it would not do for you to be away if they did come after all.'

An extraordinary situation was meanwhile developing at Gyantse. Strong—or at least large—Tibetan forces were converging on the town. The hamlets surrounding Chang Lo were held by the enemy, and the Mission was under continual bombardment by jingals and snipers in the Fort, 1350 yards away. Macdonald reported on 10 May that the British Commissioner and his escort were 'loosely invested.' 'Mission is perfectly safe, but is besieged as far as enemy dare besiege us' was how Younghusband put it five days later. Landon, in a letter to Curzon written at the end of the month, described their situation as 'one of security tempered by ignominy.' The siege went on for seven weeks.

It ought to have been a grim affair. The Tibetans outnumbered the British garrison by at least ten to one. The Fort completely dominated Chang Lo and its improvised defences. The British were a hundred and fifty miles from their most advanced supply-base. They had no early prospect of reinforcements. Yet no one in Chang Lo seems to have felt the slightest anxiety. Reuter's Correspondent, Henry Newman, even went so far as to call the siege 'almost a delightful episode.' Younghusband's telegrams reflected a serene confidence in the Mission's safety.

To the reader his reiterated assurances that a situation which was on paper perilous held no real dangers may sound over-complacent or unrealistic; but although Whitehall worried about his predicament, Simla did not. It was an axiom of Frontier warfare that, provided supplies were adequate, a well-disciplined force armed with modern weapons could hold out against overwhelming odds, no matter how isolated it was or how remote the prospects of relief. In 1879 Roberts withdrew his hard-pressed Afghan expedition into the fortified cantonments of Sherpur, which stood in much the same relation to

Kabul as Chang Lo did to Gyantse. A warlike nation was in arms against him; he had seven thousand fighting men to hold a perimeter of four and a half miles; he could not expect, nor did he ask for, reinforcements. 'The moment the gates were closed' he reported the main facts of the situation to India before the Afghans could cut the telegraph-line. 'It was a satisfaction to me,' he wrote afterwards, 'to be able to assure the authorities in these, to me, otherwise painful telegrams that there was no cause for anxiety as to the safety of the troops.' * The British in India were accustomed to skating on thin ice; experience had made them fair judges of just how thin it could be.

At Gyantse it was a good deal thicker than it looked from London, where there was considerable alarm. 'The Tibetans,' the Permanent Under-Secretary at the India Office wrote to Ampthill, 'have quite suddenly assumed a character of which we never thought them capable. They are no longer stupid defenceless sheep, but ferocious determined fanatics with a steadily increasing perception of the military advantages at their command.' For the first fortnight, however, the fanatics made no serious attempt to sever the British communications. Despatch-riders maintained a daily mail-service with Kangma, thirty-two miles away, to which the telegraph-line now reached.

Perhaps nothing was more typical of the situation in the Gyantse plain than the fact that the Post Office engineers were allowed to continue the extension of this line, of which Chang Lo became the new terminus at the end of June. Legend attributes the line's immunity from interference to the resource of Mr Truninger, the official in charge of its construction. One day two lamas, after watching his men at work for some time, asked what the wire was for. To the British, Truninger explained, Tibet was an unknown land and they had only poor maps. They were constantly getting lost, and feared that it might prove as difficult to find their way out of the country as it was to find their way in. They were extremely anxious to leave Tibet as soon as they had settled their business there, and

* *Forty-One Years in India.*

the sole purpose of the wire was to mark their homeward route and thus facilitate a speedy withdrawal when the time came.

How firmly this story is rooted in truth it is no longer possible to say; but it is a fact that a telegraph-line, which eventually reached a length of over three hundred miles and carried 300,476 messages, was only interrupted on 173 occasions. Most of these interruptions were from climatic or other natural causes, only fourteen being caused by the Tibetans. Their average duration was sixteen hours.*

The bombardment to which Chang Lo was subjected was irritating but ineffective. Looking down, afterwards, on his scarred but intact headquarters from the battlements of the Fort, Younghusband compared its position to 'a house and garden in the fields about Eton' seen from the Round Tower of Windsor Castle; to the Tibetans, 'in a lofty and seemingly impregnable fortress in the heart of their own country, we were a little dot in the plain below. The idea of making a treaty with us, if they did not want to, must have appeared ridiculous.'

By the end of the siege about twenty cannon and jingals, some of them specially brought from Lhasa, were firing into the tiny British post. The biggest of them discharged a projectile the size of an orange, weighing four and a half pounds. As time went on the Tibetans ran short of lead, and used stones coated with this metal; these were later replaced by glittering red-gold cannon-balls of copper. A howitzer-like trajectory was needed to give them the necessary range; this meant that the report arrived before the missile, and the defenders found that this warning gave them time to get under cover if the cover was not more than four yards away (or three yards in the case of 'William,' the Big Bertha of Tibet). In seven weeks only about a dozen sepoys were killed or wounded by the guns. But nobody likes living under an intermittent hail of roundshot; the bombardment caused resentment and frayed nerves.

The garrison were irked by their inability to make any adequate reply. It was useless for Bubble and Squeak to throw shrapnel at the Fort, and doubtful whether it would get there

* *Report on Field Telegraph Work with the Sikkim–Tibet Mission 1903–04.*

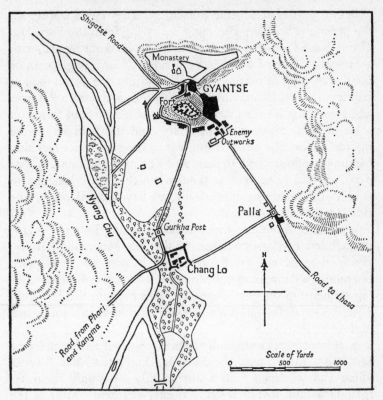

if they did. Snipers pecked at the loopholes, and Hadow, ensconced on a roof-top known as the Crow's Nest, trained his Maxim on rare targets of opportunity; but, ammunition being scarce and its expenditure apt to invite reprisals, Hadow often contented himself with using the heliograph to dazzle the Tibetan gunners, in whose superstitious minds it was hoped that this form of psychological warfare might breed dark fears.

Convoys as well as mail continued to come in, under escort, from Kangma, and the Mounted Infantry scoured the country-side, bringing in livestock and fodder, burning recalcitrant villages, and on one occasion fighting a successful cavalry action with two parties of Tibetan horsemen. They could not regain the perimeter without attracting heavy fire from the Fort, and Ottley made them gallop across no-man's-land one by one, with a fifty-yard interval between each rider. 'Not a single man or pony was hit,' he wrote, 'notwithstanding the jingal bullets falling all round them, which cut down branches from the trees and sometimes hit the ground in front of a pony and threw up a lot of dust, making the pony shy and the man sit all the tighter. It was the best training-school imaginable for teaching Mounted Infantry how to ride. . . . The men said one day that if bullets had been fired at them when they were learning to ride at Lingmathang they would all have passed out of the riding-school in three days.'

A column of reinforcements reached Chang Lo on 24 May; it included two ten-pounders of the 7th Mountain Battery, eighty men of the 1st Sappers and Miners under Captain Sheppard, a detachment of Mounted Infantry and the remaining elements of the 32nd Pioneers. This brought the garrison's effective strength up to about eight hundred, excluding sick and wounded.

Reinforcements were badly needed. Since it had been left at Gyantse a month ago, the Mission's Escort had had fifty-six killed and wounded, and a further fifty were unfit for duty, making a total loss of roughly twenty per cent. Most of the battle-casualties were sustained in vigorous sorties, undertaken to clear the enemy out of buildings uncomfortably close to the British position. One of these buildings—a white house six hundred yards away, known, after its captors, as the Gurkha Post—was allotted a permanent garrison of fifty men, thus reducing Brander's main force by a further ten per cent.

The arrival of reinforcements made possible a more ambitious offensive operation. Before dawn on 26 May a village called Palla, 1100 yards from Chang Lo, was attacked and—after six hours of desperate fighting, much of it hand-to-hand—carried. The storming-parties had to blast their way with gun-cotton into the stout-walled houses, in which a bloody hide-and-seek ensued. One of these parties was led by O'Connor, never one to take a narrow view of the duties pertaining to his appointment, which was that of Secretary to the Tibet Frontier Commission; he was shot through the shoulder. Garstin, a newly-arrived subaltern of the Sappers and Miners, was killed outright, two other British officers were wounded, and three sepoys killed. Of the Tibetans, fighting in their burrows of masonry with the clumsy tenacity of badgers, three or four hundred were loosely estimated to have lost their lives.

Although it lay, like Chang Lo, in the shadow of the great Fort, Palla bestrode the main road leading from Gyantse to Lhasa; Chang Lo itself commanded the bridge over the Nyang Chu, which offered the only convenient southward communication. After 26 May, therefore, a curious situation arose, in which each side was half-besieging the other. The British were impotent to assault the Fort; the Tibetans, despite a ten-to-one superiority in numbers, were incapable of overcoming the defences of Chang Lo. Abortive diplomacy had given place to a lame, lopsided warfare. In both, it seemed, deadlock was quick to supervene in Tibet.

On 14 May Kitchener wired to Macdonald at New Chumbi: 'If all troops, guns and transport asked for by you are sent can you begin advance towards Lhasa in a month from now? Reply urgent.' Macdonald answered on the following day: 'Reply is yes, unless unexpected complications arise.' Younghusband was simultaneously instructed to give the Amban the ultimatum envisaged in the Secretary of State's telegram of 12 May; 'the day on which Macdonald says he can advance should be specified, in your communication to the Amban, as the date on which you will decline negotiations at Gyantse.'

This directive elicited a somewhat curt rejoinder. 'I have no means of communicating with Amban,' Younghusband telegraphed on the 16th. 'We are bombarded from Fort all day long, and any messenger sent to town would undoubtedly be murdered as were the servants of even Parr, the Chinese Joint Commissioner.' Dane, replying four days later, pointed out that 'No advance can be commenced until formality of giving notice has been complied with.' Could not a prisoner or a friendly peasant be used as a go-between? Younghusband was told that he should write to the Dalai Lama as well as to the Amban. The British Commissioner left this message unanswered for a fortnight.

This was an injudicious lapse. In London, and to a less extent in Simla, Younghusband had forfeited confidence. 'Now what I want to tell you is this,' Ampthill felt obliged to write on 13 June. 'Your latest proposals and the manner in which they were made will certainly give the Home Government the impression that you do not wish or intend to act in accordance with the present policy; and that you are bent on forcing on operations which will ultimately commit us to the occupation or annexation of Tibet.' What these 'latest proposals' were we shall see in a moment; but it is clear from the tone of Ampthill's long and carefully considered letter—the first he had written to Younghusband for four weeks—that, even before the proposals were made, the authorities in India and in England had come to regard the British Commissioner as a person on whom complete reliance could no longer be placed.

In a letter to Ampthill, on 21 May, Younghusband had recommended that the Government of India should 'make up their minds to conduct a regular campaign against the Lamas and to give up all idea of being able to effect anything by merely advancing the Mission to negotiate, as it was advanced here.' Ever since reaching Gyantse he had been trailing Russia's coat for all, or more than, it was worth. There were a thousand Russians ten marches north of Phari: a Tibetan reported the presence of four white men in the Fort: officers who had fought at Karo La believed that the Tibetans had been 'aided, and probably led, by men versed in warfare according to European methods:' Dorjieff was said to be in charge of the arsenal at Lhasa, where it was probable that 'skilled mechanicians and expert military advice' had been obtained 'from Russia or elsewhere.'

Younghusband never suggested that any of these reports—few of which found their way into the Blue Book—was wholly or even partly true; but in a letter to Ampthill on 3 June he revealed the depth of his conviction that there was something, indeed a great deal, behind them. 'I have been trying not to let myself degenerate into rabidness about Russian action in Tibet, but we are accumulating so much evidence that it is impossible to shut our eyes to the fact that the Tibetans are relying most absolutely on Russian support and receiving a very substantial amount of it. They could not possibly defy us like this if they were not.'

Throughout May and June Younghusband's conduct was headstrong and erratic; 'he seems to have been rather "jumpy" lately,' Brodrick wrote to Ampthill on 17 June, and Younghusband himself had afterwards to 'confess that during all this Gyantse period I was not so steady and imperturbable as an Agent should be.'* Few of his armchair critics made any allowance, and none made enough allowance, for the stresses to which he was being subjected; these, and the conditions under which he worked, were scarcely conducive to the preservation of an impassive objectivity.

He was virtually a prisoner in Chang Lo. At intervals a cannon-ball, striking the stout building which housed the Mission, brought a shower of dust down on his papers; more dust fell when the Maxim rattled into action on the roof above his head. Save for his Parsi clerk, Mitter, he had no trained secretarial staff; he had to do much of his cyphering himself. His brother-in-law, Vernon Magniac, was on his way to join the Mission in an honorary capacity as a sort of personal assistant; but Macdonald, glad of a chance to assert his authority at Younghusband's expense, was detaining Magniac at New Chumbi. 'As we have received no orders about him,' a staff officer wrote in his diary on 14 May, 'the General has refused permission for him to proceed until they arrive from the Government of India.'

Like all servants of that Government, Younghusband was burdened by its cumbrous machinery with a mass of pettifogging administrative detail. In the last week of May he had to

* *India and Tibet.*

write a long report accounting for the loss in transit of soldiers' pay amounting to 4290 rupees. Before they left Darjeeling the bank-notes had been cut in half and the halves put into separate bags, so that if only one bag fell into the enemy's hands he would be none the richer. But somewhere on the empty uplands both bags had disappeared, and until the Indian Treasury had received from the British Commissioner a full report on the circumstances in which this loss had been sustained, no one had the authority to write the money off.

Next there was the complex matter of Wilton's expenses on the voyage from Shanghai to Calcutta. If (and it was a doubtful point, which would be resolved in further correspondence) Wilton was to be regarded as having been transferred from the pay-roll of the Foreign Office to that of the Government of India from the moment he left Chinese soil, he was entitled to a 'wine-allowance and Government table-money' while at sea. But to qualify for these benefits he must produce 'a certificate from the commander of the vessel showing the number of days on which you messed.' Wilton, ignorant of the regulations, had failed to do this; while the guns boomed outside, Younghusband set patiently about explaining to the Government of India that this particular claim for their table-money had an unusual background and deserved especially sympathetic consideration.

Few officers knew better than he did how, in a side-show on the Frontier, such domesticities were apt to claim their attention —like seagulls squawking in the wake of an outward-bound ship—long after they had become an irrelevant distraction. It is not suggested that the burden of these small cares helped to upset the balance of Younghusband's judgment; but the importunities of far-off babus did nothing to lessen the tension (and it needed to be lessened) of the life which Younghusband had been leading, without rest and at high altitudes, for the best part of a year.

His failure to answer, or even to acknowledge, the Government of India's telegram of 20 May, which confirmed and amplified his orders about the delivery of the ultimatum, brought the growing distrust of Younghusband to a head. From Simla he appeared to be in an incalculable, perhaps even a dangerous mood. The British Government's policy could not be given effect until the ultimatum had been delivered; if Younghusband was determined to stultify that policy—and there was plenty of evidence that he vehemently disagreed with it—he could do so by pleading the physical impossibility of complying with his orders. His first reaction to them (the telegram of 16 May) and the silence that had followed suggested that he might be taking this line.

The Government of India cracked the whip. 'You have not acknowledged our telegram of 20 May,' they wired on 3 June. 'Please report immediately what action you have taken to communicate wishes of His Majesty's Government to Tibetan Government and to Amban, and what you have arranged with General Macdonald as regards date of advance. . . . Government of India consider it essential that you should be in direct communication with them and with General Macdonald. You will therefore return to Chumbi at once. If you have not already despatched messages to Chinese and Tibetan authorities, you should do so before leaving Gyantse.' It is perhaps hardly necessary to say that this message was not printed in the Blue Book.

This stinging reprimand was all the more hurtful for having been, by a narrow margin, undeserved. It crossed a telegram, dated 1 June, in which Younghusband had reported to Simla the despatch of a brief, double-barrelled ultimatum to the Chinese and Tibetan authorities. The latter, after refusing to receive his messages, thought better of the matter; by 7 June the Government of India were proposing to London that 1 June should be treated as the date on which the ultimatum had been delivered, and 25 June as the date on which it would expire.

They tried to make amends for their peremptory language with a havering telegram dated 5 June. 'It is left to you whether to meet Macdonald on his way up or to remain at Gyantse.' ('On his way up' was, whether Simla realised it or not, a euphemism; Macdonald had no intention of leaving his base before 13 June.) 'It will perhaps,' this unhelpful message ended, 'be better for you to remain where you are.' Before he received it Younghusband had begun his long ride south.

It is typical of the man that he rode alone, save for a body-guard of forty Mounted Infantry under Major Murray,* and that none of those who shared the intimate siege-life of Chang Lo knew the full reasons for his going. 'On the orders of Government' was all the explanation that the Mission's Political Diary gave for his sudden departure; the diaries and letters of his companions are equally noncommittal about an unexpected event which must have loomed large in their lives.

In the perfectionist—as for instance in Wavell of Cyrenaica—pride and humility are often blended. Younghusband was too proud to complain or lament, too humble (and perhaps, partly, too considerate) to invite others to share the burden of his personal troubles. But no one is self-sufficient; in the illusion that he is lies danger. Younghusband needed a confidant, somebody with whom he could talk over the cares which increasingly beset him: not an adviser, for the mainsprings of his action were intuitive and his was not the sort of mind which waits for a second opinion to confirm, to modify or to embellish its decisions. He wanted, as he saw it, no outside help in solving his problems; what he failed to see was that his problems needed airing.

Younghusband confided, at long range, in his old father; but these frank letters, compiled in solitude, served rather to lapidarise than to dissipate his troubles. A kind of chivalry, commoner in his day than it is now, prevented him from criticising his superiors in the presence of his subordinates; as a result, they became at times the target for emotions which, had they been sublimated over a mug of rum in a mess-tent, might have made a less uncompromising impact.

When he left Chang Lo before dawn on 6 June, Younghusband faced a ride of a hundred and fifty miles through semi-hostile country. At his destination he would find his Escort Commander, now once again vested with control over the ex-

* Murray with half the bodyguard returned to Chang Lo on the next day.

pedition. Although Younghusband did not dislike Macdonald personally, he distrusted his methods and deplored his pusillanimity; he was not looking forward to their reunion. The peremptory terms of the unmerited rebuke he had just received from Simla were hardly congruous to correspondence between the Government of India and its Special Commissioner in Tibet; the orders recalling him to Chumbi could not have been more stiffly worded if he had been an insubordinate subaltern.

All in all, Younghusband had much to brood on as he went southward through a desolate land. His natural reserve and his great self-control had become handicaps, preventing the relief of inner tensions to which he had been too long subject and which the latest developments had served to increase. A weaker or a less withdrawn man—almost anybody else, indeed, but Younghusband—would have taken a companion with him on this thankless and embittered journey: somebody to talk to, somebody to share his burdens with. Younghusband, incapable of recognising or anyhow of admitting his need, rode. to his detriment, alone.

CHAPTER FIFTEEN

The Storming of a Stronghold

YOUNGHUSBAND spent his first night in the little fort at Kangma, held by a hundred men of the 23rd Pioneers under Captain Pearson. Next morning (7 June) he was up and dressed before dawn, ready for an early start, when he heard 'a peculiar jackal-like yell' and three hundred Tibetans, emerging from a gully only a bowshot away, hurled themselves on the south-east bastions. Another, larger force was seen approaching from the opposite direction. The British Commissioner seized a rifle and began to fight (as it momentarily seemed) for his life.

The attackers came from the distant province of Kham, whose people have always been noted for their warrior-like qualities. Many of them had slung their rifles, leaving both hands free to scale the stonework. 'They came on undismayed, like men flushed with victory. The sepoys said they must be drunk or drugged. They rushed to the bottom of the wall, tore out stones, and flung them up at our sepoys; they leapt up to seize the muzzles of our rifles, and scrambled to gain a foothold and lift themselves on to the parapet; they fell bullet-pierced, and some turned on the wall again.'* For a few minutes it seemed as if their numbers and their dash might tell.

But the crudity of their tactics, and their sacrifice of stealth at the very moment when stealth was most needed, cost them such meagre chances as they had. Soon discipline and the Lee Metfords gained dominance over the battlefield. The attack

* Edmund Candler: *The Unveiling of Lhasa.* Candler, convalescing from his wounds at Darjeeling, was not present at Kangma; but his account of the action, based on eye-witness reports, is clear and circumstantial.

wilted and broke, leaving more than a hundred dead under the walls. The Mounted Infantry were unleashed in pursuit, and the British Commissioner sat down to an only slightly belated breakfast.

That day he rode another twenty-eight miles to Kala Tso; its garrison included the regimental headquarters of the 23rd Pioneers under Colonel Hogge, who had looked after him through the bleak winter months at Tuna. Younghusband was touched by the warmth of his welcome, but he could not relax in its glow. That morning, before leaving Kangma, he had received a telegram instructing him, after consulting Macdonald, to 'communicate your views on general situation. . . . The Government of India wish to have these as soon as possible.' He had pondered this telegram throughout a long day in the saddle, and had decided to communicate his views forthwith.

Younghusband had been under fire for a month; he had ridden sixty miles in thirty-six hours; he had fought a battle before breakfast. It is not surprising that his telegram to the Government of India from Kala Tso was lacking in urbanity; 'its tone I do not now in cold blood seek to defend,' he wrote six years later.

It was essential, he urged, that the expedition should winter in Lhasa. Macdonald had told him that this was impossible, but from what had been seen of the Gyantse valley and heard of the country round the capital, Younghusband was confident that both localities could support a thousand men. 'If,' he went on, 'it is [really]* the case that troops cannot be maintained in Lhasa next winter, I had better not go to Lhasa [at all],* for there is little use in my commencing negotiations with two such obstructive peoples as the Tibetans and Chinese in any place where I cannot stay for a full year if necessary. I have been eleven months trying even to begin negotiations. I should be quite unable to complete them in two or three months, especially if Chinese and Tibetans knew we intended to leave before winter.'

* These words do not appear in the telegram as printed in the Blue Book.

There was much to be said for this view, nothing for the tone in which it was put forward. 'I got back,' Younghusband wrote to his father ten days later, 'a very God-Almighty-to-a-blackbeetle style of telegram.' It was dated 14 June and began: 'Your telegram of the 7th June has been considered in Council. The Government of India find it necessary to remind you that any definite proposals which you make for their consideration should be, as far as possible, in conformity with the orders and present policy of His Majesty's Government.' After the inevitable reference to the telegram of 6 November, he was told that 'the Government of India, therefore, expect you to do your utmost to carry out the present plans until there is unquestionable proof that they are impracticable. It is impossible to argue the political necessity of remaining at Lhasa during the winter until you have arrived there and gauged the situation. The military objections are great and obvious.'

By now neither party to this correspondence was being wholly fair to the other. If Younghusband's tone was over-shrill, the Government of India's strictures were too sweeping. If the British Commissioner foresaw (as he had every reason to foresee) that it might prove impossible to negotiate a treaty without wintering in the capital, it would have been the height of irresponsibility to keep his forebodings to himself; it was as much part of Younghusband's duty to call attention to the political risks of withdrawing from Lhasa as it was part of Macdonald's duty to point out the military risks of staying there.

But to be reasonable was not, at this juncture, the main concern of the Government of India. The truth of the matter was that Lord Ampthill had been attacked by defeatism; he was in a mood (which Kitchener shared, and may have inspired) to cut Britain's losses in Tibet. On 16 June, just after the 'God-Almighty-to-a-blackbeetle' telegram was sent off, he wrote two letters to England. One was to Brodrick. 'Are we to purchase the success of the Tibet Mission at the cost of implacable Russian hostility or are we to sacrifice the objects of the Mission for the purpose of maintaining friendly relations with Russia?' The Acting Viceroy revealed that he favoured the latter course, though 'there is only Lord Kitchener who sees eye to eye with me in this matter;' it was, he felt, 'unquestionably the better course to risk the failure of the Mission and to pocket the humiliation than to lay up for ourselves a harvest of infinitely greater trouble in the future.' In a letter to King Edward VII, written on the same day, he expressed similar views; only, he feared, by putting the forward policy into reverse could a way be found out of 'this seemingly hopeless dilemma.' *

If, as Ampthill now half-hoped, the Mission was to be allowed to peter out, Younghusband was expendable. He was already in Kitchener's black books; Ampthill had written to Curzon on 2 June: 'The Commander-in-Chief and Elles [Military Member of Council] are both indignant with Younghusband and want to make him entirely subordinate to Macdonald as merely the political officer on the latter's staff.' If all that impended in Tibet was an anticlimax *de convenance*, Younghusband's exceptional qualifications were no longer needed; it would indeed be preferable in every way to replace the stormy petrel by a 'safe man,' for Younghusband, who had been troublesome enough when the Mission was advancing, was unlikely to preside with a good grace over its disengagement. The telegram of 14 June was drafted with a view to provoking his resignation.

Four months after he received it, Younghusband found this out while going through the files at Simla. 'What has saddened me much,' he wrote to his father on 18 October, 'is to find from

---

* Royal Archives. Curzon got wind of these letters. From Bexhill on 8 July he wrote a short, furious note to Ampthill. The Government of India, he gathered, retained the views on Tibet which they had held unanimously when he left India, and for which he had been 'battling' in London; 'yet it appears from things that you have written in other quarters that you are only in partial sympathy with them yourself, and that you contemplate with equanimity the retirement or failure of the expedition before it has accomplished the objects for which it was sent. . . . I now anticipate that our efforts and sacrifices will have been thrown away, and if this be the consequence I shall have no other consolation than that I was completely devoid of responsibility.'

the [Indian] Foreign Office records that there was a regular set against me. That telegram which provoked me into resigning in June was sent with the greatest deliberation. Lord Ampthill drafted it and sent it round the Council for each member to re-mark on. The idea was that I was much too forward—that I was bent on landing Government in trouble and that I must be brought up short. Kitchener was more severe than anyone—though he is most cordial and appreciative *now*. He said I had wrong ideas in my head and the sooner and more thoroughly they were eradicated the better. One member complained of the "tone" of my telegram [of 7 June]—a telegram, mark you, which was written on the very day I was attacked at Kangma and had to personally assist in the defence using a rifle myself, and to ride another thirty miles afterwards on guard against another attack the whole way. Two members [the Viceroy's Council numbered six in all] did however stand up for me. One said that even if my views were not right it was better for Government to have them instead of checking me. And another said he did not see any harm in them.'

The telegram in which, for the second time, Younghusband offered his resignation has not survived. 'My reply is not published [in the Blue Book], so I will not quote it,' he wrote in *India and Tibet*. No reader of that book will doubt that old loyalties, good manners and a sense of the proprieties were chiefly responsible for his decision to suppress the text; but Landon's 'wariness' may have played a secondary part.

Ampthill, writing to Brodrick on 22 June, described it as 'a very petulant telegram, saying that, as he did not know what he was expected to do and as the Government did not support him and give him advice, he had no alternative but to resign.' Ampthill replied at once that he could not consider Young-husband's resignation until after the ultimatum—which bore Younghusband's signature—had expired on 25 June; mean-while he proposed to treat the telegram as though it had not been sent.

He told Brodrick, however, that 'my first inclination was to accept his resignation and have done with him, but I was loath to bring to an ignominious end the career of a man who has really done extraordinarily well and whose only failing is occasional bursts of self-opinionated ill-temper. I also thought of all the undesirable speculation and comment which would arise in the press and in Parliament, and I therefore decided that it was best to make an effort to retain Colonel Younghusband, at any rate until the time for negotiations was over. If he does go when the advance to Lhasa commences it will not make much difference. The expedition will be more military than ever and General Macdonald will be able to manage quite well with one of the young officers [of the Mission] as his Political Adviser.'

What in effect had happened was this. The Government of India had set a trap for Younghusband; Younghusband, by resigning, appeared to have fallen into it. But his resignation was in its turn a ruse or bluff, designed, as he told his father, to teach the Government of India 'that this is not the way to treat me.' In the same letter (17 June) he revealed that it was the worldly-wise Landon who had put into his mind the idea of resigning 'as the only means of inducing Government to make up their minds.' He foresaw what Lord Ampthill failed to foresee—that however ready his superiors were to 'have done with him,' they would not dare to face the political and public consequences of his recall. This time it was Younghusband who cracked the whip; and thereafter his fortunes, which from a 'pinnacle of trust' had fallen so low, began, very slowly, to rise.

From Kala Tso he continued his journey to New Chumbi without mishap, and at the end of it met a man who was to play an important and auspicious part in the destinies of the expedition. This was the Tongsa Penlop of Bhutan, a jolly, astute individual who was the *de facto* (and later became the *de jure*) ruler of his country.

He possessed a golden crown of great splendour, but (Landon wrote) 'he is a small man with a powerful but plebeian cast of countenance, and his habit of perpetually wearing a grey uncloven Homburg hat pressed down all round his head to his eyebrows, instead of his official crown, does not increase his dignity.' The British soldiers called him 'the Tonsil,' as they later called the Amban 'the Hambone;' but what with his *embonpoint*, his vivacity and his little imperial beard there was something vaguely Gallic about him, and to the officers he was known as 'Alphonse.' He brought with him a numerous and predatory retinue, whose looting caused distress to the Tibetans and embarrassment to the British. Landon summed him up as 'a cheerful but not a particularly distinguished adjunct to the Mission.' Younghusband liked the Tongsa Penlop; he found him straight and possessed of a natural authority.

His mission was to mediate, but he made no pretence of impartiality and can only have been regarded by the Tibetans and Chinese as a puppet or collaborator of the British. He was however much respected by the Tibetans, and Bhutan's good offices—like those of Nepal, whose Maharajah had just renewed his attempts to make the Tibetans see reason—were of great value to the Mission, because both states possessed that rare amenity, a well-established, two-way channel of communication with Lhasa.

Younghusband reached New Chumbi on 10 June and left for Gyantse again, with Macdonald and the much-reinforced Escort, on the 13th. Short though it was, his stay was 'refreshing in the extreme, a softening and welcome relaxation.' Four thousand feet lower than Gyantse and surrounded by pine forests, rhododendrons and a wealth of flowers, Macdonald's headquarters provided an idyllic, an almost voluptuous contrast with Younghusband's surroundings during the past months. He found several old friends among the newly arrived officers; he was gratified by the size of the reinforcements; he relished hearing news and gossip of the great world. He was lionised. He relaxed.

The force which was to relieve Chang Lo, with its garrison of about eight hundred, moved off in two columns. The first comprised 125 Mounted Infantry, eight guns, 1450 infantry (including half a battalion of the Royal Fusiliers), 950 followers and 2200 animals; in the second, which included the supply-train, there were 500 infantry, 1200 followers and 1800 animals. It was still not a very formidable expedition—the staff estimated that some 15,000 Tibetans were arrayed against it between Dongtse and the Karo La—but in six months it had more than doubled in size.

Moving with Macdonald's customary deliberation, the leading column reached Kangma without incident on 22 June. Here Younghusband received an unexpected telegram from the Tongsa Penlop, temporarily left behind at Phari. He reported that an important Lama and one of the four State Councillors were on their way from Lhasa to Gyantse to meet the British Commissioner, to whom a present of silk was being sent. This unprecedented development revived long-discarded hopes that the Tibetans might consent, at the eleventh hour, to negotiate; but if they did they were cutting it fine—the ultimatum, it will be remembered, was due to expire on 25 June—and Young-husband immediately telegraphed to India a recommendation that the time-limit should be extended by five days. His proposal was accepted with alacrity.

The advance was resumed on 25 June, when, to everyone's relief, the potential death-trap in Red Idol Gorge was found unmanned. Beyond it the fortified monastery at Naini was captured after a four-hour fight, in which Brander, leading a vigorous sortie from Chang Lo, joined with good effect; and on the evening of the 26th the tents of the relief-force made a spiky pattern on the plain before Gyantse Fort, just out of range of the jingals.

On 28 June, after a day and night of heavy rain, the Tsechen monastery was captured and the villages round it cleared. The monastery, emplaced on a hill, commanded the Gyantse–Shigatse road, and the reduction of this strong position not only cut Gyantse's communications with Western Tibet but opened the fertile Shigatse valley to foraging parties. The cannon in Gyantse Fort continued to hurl copper at the invaders, but there were reports of desertions from the garrison.

On the 29th a white flag of ample dimensions was seen approaching Chang Lo from Gyantse. Its bearer asked for an armistice pending the arrival of the Ta Lama from Shigatse; the other emissary from Lhasa, coming from the opposite direction, had already arrived. Younghusband gave the Tibetans until sunset on the following day, but said that meanwhile they must evacuate the Fort.

Throughout the next few days the behaviour of the Tibetan delegates was characteristically exasperating. None of them had put in an appearance by sunset on the 30th, but as the Ta Lama was said to be due next day and the Tongsa Penlop was also on his way, the armistice was tacitly prolonged. The Tongsa Penlop, who had twice as far to travel as the Ta Lama, arrived first. He bore a letter which he had received from the Dalai Lama; it solicited his help in making a peaceful settlement, 'as fighting is bad for men and animals.' He also produced, allegedly from the same source, a gift of silks, which the British Commissioner refused to accept unless it was accompanied by a letter from the Dalai Lama or presented by one of his own officials.

The Ta Lama reached Gyantse in the afternoon. Younghusband sent him a message pointing out that he was a day late and inviting his attendance at Chang Lo without further delay. The Ta Lama replied that he proposed to visit the Tongsa Penlop on the morrow, and would look in on the British Commissioner after he had done so. Younghusband gave him until nine o'clock in the morning to present himself, failing which military operations would be resumed.

The next day, 2 July, the Ta Lama was observed, shortly after nine o'clock, making leisurely progress towards the Tongsa Penlop's camp. O'Connor intercepted him with a stern warning that, although he was at liberty to discuss matters with the Tongsa Penlop before paying his respects to the British Commissioner, a serious view would be taken of any further delays. At eleven o'clock the Ta Lama, like a child who realises that there is a limit beyond which its bed-time cannot be unilaterally postponed, turned up; he was a grave, courteous, foolish old man dressed from head to foot in figured gold silk. With him, similarly attired, came the Grand Secretary, a man whom Younghusband had dealt with, and disliked, at Khamba Jong. The Tongsa Penlop's grey Homburg, crammed down over his ears like a candle-snuffer, slightly lowered the sartorial standards of this embassage, but could not prevent its voluminous finery from outshining the trim, proconsular dark blue of the Mission's full-dress uniforms.

The usual long-drawn-out exchanges took place. Younghusband once said that negotiating with Tibetans was 'like throwing butter at a granite rock,' and all that needs to be recorded about this particular parley is that it ended inconclusively. The Tibetans, before withdrawing, expressed a wish to talk matters over with the Tongsa Penlop on the following day; they would revisit the British Commissioner on the day after that. Younghusband said that they were welcome to employ the Tongsa Penlop as a mediator, but that they must come back in one day, not in two. They undertook to return at noon on the morrow, 3 July.

The preparation of a Durbar, as even the humblest of such ceremonial conclaves was known in India, was no light matter for a political mission living under active service conditions. The mounting of a guard of honour involved preliminary spit and polish; the cookhouse was called on to provide the men involved with either an early or a belated meal; the officers' quarters had to be denuded of chairs, tables and carpets; orderlies stood by with tea, biscuits and cigarettes; Younghusband and his staff put on their full-dress uniforms. On the Frontier the need for the King-Emperor's representative, however austerely circumstanced, to present an impeccable and as far as possible imposing front to official visitors formed part of the traditions of the Indian service.

When therefore by midday only the Tongsa Penlop had arrived, the British (Macdonald and many of his officers were present, as well as the members of the Mission) were understandably annoyed. The Durbar was disbanded. The Tibetan delegates, appearing at half-past one, were put in an empty tent

and kept waiting until four o'clock, when the Durbar reassembled.

Younghusband, grave in demeanour, took his seat in the
centre. The Tibetans were brought in by O'Connor and shown
their places. Younghusband looked them over and said nothing.
He was a small man, but there was something compelling about
him. His penetrating blue eyes, his stillness, the impression he
gave of having hidden depths—these attributes endowed him
with the power (which had often before stood him in good
stead) to discountenance outlandish adversaries; and now the
golden-robed envoys began to fidget and look sideways until at
last the Ta Lama broke a painful silence by offering an apology
for their late arrival. The proceedings began.

They were unfruitful. Younghusband's immediate object
was to secure the evacuation of the Fort, whose walls the
garrison had been busily strengthening during the armistice.
But the Tibetans, of whom the Grand Secretary was the most
obdurate, were unable to see the force of Younghusband's
arguments, let alone agree to his demands; the granite rock
proved, once again, impervious to butter, and Younghusband
brought the Durbar to a close with yet another ultimatum.
Unless the Fort was evacuated by noon on 5 July, the British
would take it by force.

Despite intense diplomatic activity by the Tongsa Penlop,
the 4th passed without any useful developments. On the
morning of the 5th Younghusband sent various last-minute
warnings into Gyantse, urging the authorities to get the women
and children out of the place. At midday a short admonitory
burst of fire came from one of the Norfolks' Maxims. Nothing
happened for half an hour. Then, from the Crow's Nest in
Chang Lo, Younghusband heliographed to Macdonald's headquarters in the village of Palla the signal for operations to
begin.

Still nothing happened. 'General Macdonald,' Landon
recorded, 'was slow to begin the work of assault, and . . . it
was not till two o'clock that the first gun was actually fired.'
From a note which Macdonald sent to Younghusband on

1 July it is clear that the Escort Commander had no stomach for ultimatums, or anyhow for ultimatums whose enforcement would commit him to attacking a large fortress. 'A little more patience,' he wrote, 'and I think you have a fair chance of having the game in your hands and reaping the reward of your efforts.'

'Macdonald's letter may be the very essence of wisdom and prudence,' Younghusband wrote to Dane a week later. 'But it is such a letter as you or the Viceroy would address me, not the letter which I would expect from the commander of the force upon which I have to rely to enforce my word.' And he revealed that Macdonald, after receiving from Chang Lo the prearranged signal to open fire, had heliographed back two irrelevant enquiries about the diplomatic situation before ordering his troops and guns into action. 'Little,' Landon told his readers, 'was done that day;' and it is difficult to blame Younghusband for confiding to Dane 'I feel like going up to Lhasa with a pistol which is liable not to go off when it is wanted to.'

In the same letter he made generous allowances for his Escort Commander's poor state of health. 'Macdonald is thoroughly ill and not his proper self. He had to be carried in a *dhoolie* [litter] for four marches. He has had gastritis for some weeks now. He has to live on a poor diet, mostly of slops. He suffers from insomnia. So, though he is exceedingly plucky in bearing up, he naturally has not his normal amount of "go" in him, takes a gloomy view of the outlook and hesitates to act.' There is much other evidence that Macdonald was handicapped by ill-health. Although only forty-one, he is often referred to as 'old;' Candler, for instance, after their first meeting described him in a letter as 'a dear old chap.' Several other sources suggest that he did not improve matters by smoking too much. One officer wrote: 'He smokes cigarettes till he is sick. They say that he never has a cigarette out of his mouth and certainly I have never seen him without one.' Another diarist recorded: 'He suffers continually from the trots [diarrhoea] which have completely shattered his nerves.'

It is beyond doubt that the uncertain health of one officer delayed, hampered and in the end came near to frustrating Britain's purposes in Tibet. Macdonald's physical disabilities were a contributory, not a primal cause of his edginess as a colleague and his failure as a commander. No mention is made of them in official documents dealing with the campaign; references in private correspondence are sparse and belated. Yet the Escort Commander's ailing condition was an important factor in the whole affair, a pebble which deserves its place upon the cairn of truth.

Macdonald's intention was to put in his assault from the south-east. During the afternoon of 5 July six companies of infantry, one of Mounted Infantry and two guns made a demonstration against the north-west bastions, facing the Shigatse valley; a village within three hundred yards of the outworks was captured, and when the diversionary force withdrew under cover of darkness camp-fires were left ostentatiously burning. Meanwhile the artillery, emplaced opposite the true objective, kept silent save for a few ranging shots. This feint seems to have produced the desired effect on the garrison's dispositions.

At 0400 hours on 6 July the main assault was launched by three columns of infantry feeling their way in the darkness through the fringe of gardens and mean suburbs round the base of the great rock on which the Fort stood. Though they were greeted only by a ragged, ineffective fire, there was what Landon called an 'unfortunate incident' involving (as other sources make clear) the only British regiment present; after some delay the three columns were reorganised into two. Demolition-squads formed the spearheads of both. With Bubble, the antique seven-pounder, doing for the first time useful work (a point-blank range was well within her capabilities) the storming-parties gradually blasted their way through a labyrinth of stonework until, soon after sunrise, the whole built-up area lying along the southern flank of the rock was in British hands. Lieutenant Gurdon of the 32nd

Pioneers, an officer of promise, was killed by flying masonry during this phase, but otherwise casualties were negligible.

A lull ensued. The sun blazed down oppressively on the tired assailants, who had been on the move since soon after midnight. The Tibetan fire, which had been brisk though promiscuous, gradually died away. Silence fell. The Fort was inviolate. It looked as though an impasse had been reached.

This was not the sort of situation in which Brigadier-General Macdonald's powers of leadership showed to advantage. It was left, as it had been in Red Idol Gorge, to one of his subordinates to take the initiative. At two o'clock Colonel Campbell of the 40th Pathans, in command of the storming parties, put up with some urgency a plan for an assault on the eastern corner of the Fort, below which it appeared that the rock, slightly less precipitous than elsewhere, might prove scaleable. Macdonald havered but at length sanctioned the operation.

Soon after 1500 hours the ten-pounders went into action against the thick walls of the Fort where they overlooked this daunting approach-route. Hitherto the Escort's artillery had been equipped only with shrapnel, which was useless against strong fortifications; but latterly supplies of 'common shell'— solid projectiles containing an explosive charge—had come up from India. Now round after round shrieked through the sunlight to burst with admired precision on the target, and soon, through the cloud of dust made by their impact, the fascinated onlookers could see a black and steadily widening hole appear in the great stone bastion above them.

Presently a dull explosion was heard from inside the Fort as a powder-magazine went up. The Tibetan fire, which had been furious, immediately slackened off, and two companies— one from the 8th Gurkhas, the other from the Royal Fusiliers— debouched from Palla, charged across open ground to the base of the rock and began to climb.

The Gurkhas, much apter for this sort of work than the Fusiliers, led the way. As they clambered painfully upwards the guns still pounded at their objective, dislodging masses of masonry which crashed and slithered down the semi-precipice, taking some of the climbers with them. More rocks were hurled by the defenders. Muskets enfiladed them from out-jutting turrets.

But the Gurkhas went on, and at last their commander, Lieutenant Grant, his havildar and a handful of men reached a point immediately below the breach. Further progress could be made only by one man at a time, crawling on hands and knees. From the plain bugles sounded the cease-fire; the guns fell silent, and Grant went up. In the mouth of the breach he was hit by a bullet. So was the havildar, close behind him. Both men glissaded down the rock for a distance of thirty feet. They picked themselves up and went at it again. The watchers below saw them disappear into the reeking cavern, followed by the riflemen at their heels. Almost immediately there were signs that Tibetan resistance was at an end. Bent figures were seen dodging away along the battlements; the jingals ceased to boom; here and there ropes were dangled from embrasures and men slid down them, seeking shelter in the warren of buildings to the north of the rock, as yet untouched by war. There was no more fighting.

Grant was awarded the Victoria Cross for his gallantry and determination; 'the havildar really led,' he modestly recalled fifty-five years later,* but it was not until 1911 that native officers and men became eligible for the supreme reward of valour, and Karbir Pun received a lesser honour, the Indian Order of Merit. Between them the two men, powerfully assisted by the ten-pounders, had seen to it that Colonel Campbell's flair and enterprise did not go unrewarded. Gyantse Fort, traditionally the key to Tibet, had fallen to the British; the road to Lhasa was open.

* Private interview.

The truce delegation entering Chang Lo

A Kham warrior who became an officer's servant after capture

CHAPTER SIXTEEN

The Fount of Policy

IT was now exactly a year since the Tibet Frontier Commission had established itself at Khamba Jong. In principle Britain's Tibetan policy was still trussed by the telegram of 6 November 1903, the restraints imposed by which had been reinforced by subsequent pledges to Russia. In practice, however, the Government was committed to a course of action in which the adventurism of Curzon's original conception was not very happily combined with the obsessive caution of a weak Cabinet; for, while an advance to Lhasa was now accepted as unavoidable, it was to be followed—whatever happened—by a prompt withdrawal. On the Frontier, where it had often proved misguided, this was known as the policy of 'butcher and bolt'.

In India it had been assumed that Curzon's presence in England would serve to clarify and stiffen the Government's attitude towards Tibet. The Viceroy shared this expectation, but it was not fulfilled. The country he had served in India for five arduous and fruitful years gave him a resounding welcome; the newspapers, Godley told Ampthill, greeted him with 'a *feu de joie*,' and he was 'met at the station by everyone whose name is worth mentioning; the only important person who was absent on the occasion was the King, and he was represented by two of his principal officers.' The City of London and the Borough of Derby offered him their Freedom, Oxford an Honorary Degree; his speeches, at the Guildhall and elsewhere, were hailed as memorable. Yet towards the end of his leave, in October, he wrote to Ampthill: 'Little did I think when I left India in May that five months of so much suffering and misery were to lie before me.'

Within a month of his arrival neuralgia in his right leg laid him low, 'in constant and almost unendurable pain.' This affliction put a stop to his private pleasures and curtailed his public activities; 'my holiday,' he wrote in September, 'has been one of almost continuous pain and depression, relieved only by struggles to push forward some of the things that seem to be important.' But worse was in store for him, for towards the end of that month Lady Curzon, who had been seriously ill for some time, lay at death's door. Hope for her life was abandoned, and she said farewell to her husband. Then she rallied, and a slow recovery began: but not before Curzon, who loved her devotedly, had suffered the extremes of mental anguish.

To his domestic troubles were added public worries and frustrations. The full scope of Kitchener's tortuous antagonism was for the first time revealed to him. The Cabinet sought, and then rejected, his advice about Afghanistan. His relations with the Secretary of State for India were strained; Brodrick, who wrote to him in August: 'I have not had one conversation with you in the last eleven weeks except on business,' reproached him three months later for 'the withdrawal of your friendship which you made clear in the summer.' Crippled by pain and bowed by grief, Curzon continued to urge upon Ministers views about Indian problems which were based on wide experience and detailed knowledge. The Ministers, who shared none of his experience and very little of his knowledge, received his advice with constrained deference; but they never acted on it. It is small wonder that Curzon became increasingly bearish and intractable, or that, according to his biographer, 'his holiday came to a close amid a storm of bitter controversy.'

Tibet stood high among 'the things that seem important,' yet the Viceroy proved impotent to shake the Cabinet's ill-founded conviction that, despite appearances to the contrary, they knew best what to do there. Lansdowne—the only one of them who knew India; he had been Viceroy from 1888 to 1894—blocked Curzon's argument that 'we ought to have our man [in Lhasa]

as the Russians have theirs already in the shape of Dorjieff'
by replying 'We have no evidence that he is a bona fide Russian
agent.'* In August, just before Parliament rose, Lord Hard-
wicke wrote to Younghusband: 'The rooted objection to
departing from that telegram of 6 November has possessed the
Government to an extent I for one would hardly have believed
and even Curzon's influence has utterly failed to have any effect.'

On 30 June Curzon attended a meeting of the Cabinet and
took part in 'a long and not very fruitful discussion about
Tibet.' There were, he wrote to Ampthill on the following day,
three schools of thought:

    1. The extreme—Younghusband.

    2. The less extreme like myself who think that the
treaty ought to be concluded, that it ought to provide for
an Agent somewhere, that we ought not to leave Tibet
and possibly Lhasa until it is concluded, and who want to
exercise some sort of influence in Tibet in the future.

    3. Those who think that any treaty, even if we can
conclude it, will be a farce, and who argue that after
inflicting as much damage as we can we ought to retire
from Lhasa and Tibet, doing nothing more. This is the
'reparation' school; and they want the expedition to be
merely retributive.

    No decision was arrived at. . . . The Cabinet are, as you
know, anxious to get out of the whole thing. They are
naturally ignorant of anything but large and frequently
incorrect generalizations; and the discussion wanders
about under imperfect control.†

The Cabinet met again on 6 July—Curzon was too ill to
attend—to decide what terms Younghusband should be
authorised to offer the Tibetans if, as seemed possible from the

---

* Letter from Curzon to Younghusband, 26 May 1904.

† The Prime Minister, as always, summarised the results of his Cabinet's
deliberations in a note written in his own hand to the King. It is possibly
symptomatic that, in the first three references which Balfour made in this
correspondence to the capital of Tibet, he spelt it in three different ways—
Lassa, Lhahsa, Lhassa. None was correct. (Royal Archives.)

latest reports, they were at last prepared to negotiate. The Government of India had already telegraphed, on 26 June, a seven-point summary of its recommendations, which were amplified in a written despatch. This able and closely reasoned document had not yet reached London (when it did, Curzon told Younghusband, 'it produced no more impression in Downing Street than it would have done if it had been read in the streets of Lhasa'). The first, the most important and the most contentious condition proposed was that the Government of India should demand the right to station an Agent at Lhasa or, failing that, that the Agent should be placed at Gyantse with the right of access to Lhasa for the purpose of official discussions with the Tibetan authorities and the Chinese Amban.

The question of an Agent at Lhasa was to assume great significance, and the pros and cons of the matter need to be briefly reviewed. The Government of India, relying in part on arguments put forward by Younghusband over the past year, maintained that 'the best guarantee for the observance of the new Convention, and for the adequate protection of our rights as the only European Power limitrophe [i.e. sharing a frontier] with Tibet, must be that, in addition to the appointment of officers to watch over our commercial interests at the marts to be established in Tibet, we should demand the acceptance of an accredited British Agent in Tibet.' They felt strongly that the best place for this Agent was at Lhasa, 'the pivot of the religious and political life of Tibet.'

There had, they pointed out, been a British Agent at Kat-mandu, the capital of Nepal, for eighty years. In 1860 a campaign, on a far larger scale than that now being conducted in Tibet, had been fought to instal a British Minister in Peking. China and Nepal had long maintained official representatives in the Tibetan capital. The difficulties of keeping open communications with an Agent in Lhasa had, judging by the successful advance of the Mission at the height of a severe winter, been exaggerated. Finally, if His Majesty's Government were unable to sanction the demand for an Agent at Lhasa, it was essential, if he was to carry out his duties effectively, that he should be stationed at Gyantse with the right of access to Lhasa; 'we cannot, however, conceal from ourselves that this alternative, the least which can be contemplated, is not calculated, in the same degree, to afford a guarantee of satisfactory results.'

The despatch made other suggestions as to the terms to be imposed on the Tibetans—the occupation of the Chumbi Valley, a sizeable indemnity, facilities for trade and so on. But, stripped of its circumspect verbiage, the message which the Government of India was trying to convey to His Majesty's Government was this: Unless you allow us an Agent at Lhasa, we shall be unable to ensure that the Tibetans observe their treaty obligations, we shall be unable to counteract Russian influence, and, what is more, we shall be unable to implement your present or any future policies in Tibet.

These arguments seem unanswerable. Ever since 1890 the British in India had been trying, and failing, to settle a series of petty disputes with Tibet; the main cause of their failure had been the lack of the normal channels of intercourse between neighbouring states—channels which from time immemorial have been established by an exchange of envoys. The experience of the past year had proved that a display of might was powerless to achieve political ends, or even to bring about the discussion of such ends, anywhere outside the capital. If the British had learnt anything about Tibet it was surely that whatever they wanted to do there—whether it was to reassert Sikkimese grazing-rights or to frustrate Tsarist ambitions—could not be done short of Lhasa. Even there it might, indeed, prove impossible; but it was at least worth trying.

The Cabinet thought otherwise. The list of 'terms to be named to Tibetans by Younghusband' which they telegraphed to Simla after their meeting on 6 July began:

> 1. Neither at Lhasa nor elsewhere is Resident to be demanded.

This uncompromising veto was based on the telegram of 6 November 1903, in which His Majesty's Government affirmed that they were 'not prepared to establish a permanent Mission in Tibet' and which, the Russian Government had been repeatedly assured, defined the limits of their Tibetan aspirations. But in eight months many things had changed. 'The fatal telegram,' as Curzon called it, had sanctioned an advance only as far as Gyantse; now the expedition was bound for Lhasa. The last occasion on which the British pledges to Russia had been renewed was on 2 June, when Lansdowne transmitted a written note to the Russian Ambassador. Count Benckendorff had more than once 'expressed a hope that our policy toward Tibet would not be altered by recent events,' of which at that date the most likely to provoke an alteration was the attack on the Mission at Chang Lo.

The Foreign Secretary chose his words with care, as he was bound to do in a communication of this kind. 'I am now,' he wrote, 'able to tell you that His Majesty's Government still adhere to the policy [outlined in the telegram of 6 November], though it is obvious that their action must to some extent depend upon the conduct of the Tibetans themselves, and that His Majesty's Government cannot undertake that they will not depart in any eventuality from the policy which now commends itself to them.' If this escape-clause could justify (as it was later required to) an advance to Lhasa, it could also have covered the less controversial issue of an Agent in Tibet.

It appears, moreover, from a letter written by Brodrick to Curzon after the Cabinet meeting of 6 July, that the British Government did contemplate, in a characteristically imprecise way, the posting of a representative in Tibet. 'The Cabinet view is most clearly in favour of having the power to send an Agent to Gyantse or any mart which may be finally arranged, rather than to lay down an intention of appointing one to which we should be bound to adhere;' and the Secretary of State referred vaguely to the possibility of subsidising the provision of intelligence by the Nepalese envoy in Lhasa. But neither Brodrick nor any of his colleagues placed on record an explanation of their emphatic refusal to accept the advice tendered, in the light of local knowledge and in almost obsequious terms, by the Government of India.

It would be wrong to leave this question without observing that an unhappy precedent was partly responsible for the Government's reluctance to station an agent at Lhasa; the ghost of Cavagnari stalked the corridors of Whitehall. In 1879 Major Cavagnari, a man of forceful character, was sent as Political Agent to Afghanistan, with whom Britain had fought a war mainly in order to assert her right to diplomatic representation in Kabul, where a Russian envoy had been welcomed in the previous year. Two months after their arrival in the Afghan capital, Cavagnari and his small escort were massacred, allegedly by mutinous troops, and another war had to be fought to avenge them.

It was widely feared that this disaster would be repeated if, once again, a political agent were to be posted, against the wishes of the native population, in a remote Central Asian city, and few discussions of Tibetan policy in Parliament or elsewhere ended without some reference, direct or indirect, to Cavagnari's fate. 'The association connected with the name of Cavagnari,' Sir Henry Campbell-Bannerman told the House of Commons in April, 'does not seem to invite us to undertake a similar policy again.' 'I feel sure if we do [leave an Agent at Lhasa] he will be murdered,' Kitchener wrote to Lady Salisbury on 16 June 1904;* and a fortnight later, in a memorandum submitted to the Cabinet, Curzon concluded his arguments in favour of an Agent at Lhasa with the words: 'I am well aware of the reasons which have influenced His Majesty's Government in the opposite direction, and I recognise their force, though I regard them as depending to a large extent upon an incorrect analogy between Lhasa and Kabul, and between the Tibetans and the Afghans.' Curzon had been in London for several weeks when he wrote this, and knew what was in Ministers' minds; it is clear that among opponents of his policy Cavagnari's was a name to conjure with.

* Salisbury MSS.

The handling of Tibetan affairs by Balfour's administration leaves one with two impressions. One is of men playing a card-game of whose rules, although they have played other games resembling it, they are uncertain. Anxious not to betray this uncertainty, they make their bids with an air of confidence, but with no real comprehension of how many tricks they are likely to win or lose. The British Government showed at no time any awareness that, as the game went on, the strength of their opponents' hands might and indeed did fluctuate. They took no heart from the disclosure (made to Sir Ernest Satow by Prince Ch'ing on 15 June 1904) that the Chinese Government regarded with indifference, and by implication welcomed, the British intervention in Tibet; nor were they influenced by the fact that Russia, whose supposed machinations were a main cause of that intervention, became, if not crippled by her war with Japan, at least sufficiently preoccupied to be deterred from peripheral activities in a remote part of Central Asia. They simply (like, in a way, the Tibetans) went on playing the same cards over and over again, hoping for the best. 'It is curious,' Younghusband reflected in a letter to his father on 19 August 1904, 'how we never will realise when we have a good hand. We pride ourselves on never knowing when we are beaten. It strikes me that we know still less when we have won.'

The other impression of British policy is that it was affected, to its detriment, by the interplay of personalities. The Tibetan project was Curzon's. It was more than half matured when, at the end of October 1903, Brodrick took office as Secretary of State for India. He was Curzon's oldest friend. His letters to Curzon, full of solicitous admiration, reflect a kind of hero-worship untarnished by envy; they seem by implication to acknowledge Curzon's innate superiority over the writer, there is no hint of rivalry or jealousy. It would be slightly unfair to Brodrick to suggest that theirs was a jackal–lion relationship, but the world saw a marked difference in their statures, and both were tacitly aware of it.

At the end of October 1903, unexpectedly, Brodrick found himself set in authority over his paragon; and it is difficult not to suspect that his first official action in his new appointment was prompted by a strong though perhaps subconscious impulse to assert his newly-won dominance. How otherwise is it possible to account for his decision, taken 'on his very first appearance' at the India Office, to call a halt to Curzon's Tibetan plans? Brodrick knew next to nothing about the problems which those plans were designed to solve and of which, when he had had time to study them, he never betrayed a lively understanding. There had been no fresh developments since the Government, a month earlier, had sanctioned an advance to Gyantse. None of the circumstances existed in which a newly appointed Minister may be required, almost before he has sat down at his desk, to deal with some matter of high policy on which, because of the exigencies of a change of Government or a Cabinet re-shuffle, a decision is overdue. Yet Brodrick lost no time in firing a warning shot across the Viceroy's bows (the telegram which served this purpose showed how infirm was his grasp of the situation) and thereafter set about procuring the annulment of a month-old Cabinet decision. His efforts were successful, and it was as a result of them that the telegram of 6 November was drafted and despatched.

It cannot be proved that Brodrick's precipitate and, on the face of it, uncalled-for action was prompted by the desire to thwart and humiliate his oldest friend, but his conduct throughout the Tibetan affair was, as will appear, disfigured at times by a kind of spite for which it is hard to account save on psychological grounds. The truth of the matter will never be known, but two facts cannot be gainsaid. Within a year the intimate friendship between Brodrick and Curzon was at an end; within two years Curzon, who had many enemies, regarded Brodrick as pre-eminent among them—'the man who brought about my downfall.' And Tibet was the battleground on which they first crossed swords.

CHAPTER SEVENTEEN

A River to Cross

LHASA is just under a hundred and fifty miles from Gyantse, and soon after the capture of the Fort on 6 July Macdonald reported that he would be ready to march on the 14th.

Younghusband's stock was rising; Ampthill told Brodrick that 'he has, I am thankful to say, cheered up completely. His latest communications, both by post and telegraph, have been cheerful, sanguine and full of enthusiastic zeal.' There was even a brief interlude (overlooked by the Blue Book) during which the British Commissioner and the Government of India exchanged roles, and the thruster needed, or pretended to need, prodding from behind. 'Until you hear further from us,' the Government of India wired on 7 July, 'on any account do not commit yourself to abandonment of advance on Lhasa.' To this Younghusband replied that he understood the objections to wintering in Lhasa were 'overwhelming;' Macdonald claimed that even a temporary advance would be attended by serious dangers. 'In these circumstances, therefore, the military risks being represented as so great, the demands to be made of the Tibetans being so small, and the punishment already inflicted on them being so severe, it does not seem either necessary or desirable that the Mission should proceed to Lhasa until it has been conclusively shown that the Tibetans will not negotiate here, at Gyantse.' But these arguments, of which the main purpose may have been to advertise Younghusband's capacity for prudence, did not prevail, and the force marched on 14 July.

A RIVER TO CROSS

Or rather, most of the force marched.* Not only was a garrison needed at Gyantse, but Macdonald's staff imposed what many regarded as an unnecessarily strict embargo on individual officers who, having for one reason or another no duties to perform at Gyantse, sought permission to accompany the advance. 'It would be hard,' one of these wrote, 'to find an occasion on any expedition when, to the individual soldier, going on seemed to mean so much, and staying behind so little.' The lure of the Forbidden City was strong, and much sympathy was felt for Colonel Hogge and the 23rd Pioneers, who were left at Gyantse. Of the three original infantry regiments they were the most closely associated with the Mission, with whom they had shared the winter ordeals of Tuna. It was recognised that for reasons of white prestige the Royal Fusiliers (who were not held in high esteem by the other units) must be included in the Lhasa force; but the second newly arrived regiment, the 40th Pathans, had no claim to precedence over the 23rd, who were not alone in resenting Macdonald's decision to deny them their due of glory. It seems likely that this decision was based partly on a desire to annoy Younghusband (who had to telegraph to India to get sanction for Hayden, the geologist, to go to Lhasa) and partly on an obscure incident at Phari, as a result of which the Escort-Commander had threatened Hogge with court-martial.

* The troops concerned were:

Headquarters Staff	
7th Mountain Battery	(6 guns)
30th Mountain Battery	(2 guns)
3rd Sappers and Miners	(half company)
Mounted Infantry	(2 companies)
Royal Fusiliers	(4 companies)
Norfolk Regiment	(Maxim gun section)
Royal Irish Rifles	(Maxim gun section)
32nd Pioneers	(4 companies)
40th Pathans	(6 companies)
8th Gurkhas	(6 companies)
British Field Hospital	(1 section)
Indian Field Hospital	(2½ sections)

Transport from the 7th, 9th, 10th and 12th Mule Corps.

Rain fell heavily as they retraced Brander's route towards the Karo La; the caravan-trail, winding between fields of barley and small, brilliant plots of mustard, became a quagmire. The worst effect of the rain was to make the tentage sodden, so that some of the pack-animals' loads became too heavy and had to be redistributed; but morale was high and grazing plentiful.

On 16 July the Mounted Infantry, reconnoitring the Karo La, found that the Tibetans had strengthened their old position; a second wall had been built behind the first, and fresh sangars, sited in greater depth on even dizzier eminences, protected both flanks. But a convoy of a hundred and thirty loaded yaks was captured, together with several prisoners, and Ottley's rough-riders returned to camp in their usual ebullient spirits.

Macdonald moved into the defile on the following day and on the 18th advanced against the wall while the Gurkhas climbed up (it was claimed) to a height of 19,000 feet to deal with the sangars. Round these there was a little fighting, but the Tibetans abandoned their main position at the walls without firing a shot. Throughout the campaign it was, in the main, the raw troops who showed the most courage: as in the assaults on Chang Lo and Kangma. Those who had had experience of battle with the British were not anxious to renew it. A Nepalese report summed up the characteristics of an unwarlike race as follows: 'The Tibetan sepoys, so long as they do not come in contact with the British, seem uncertain and wavering; but those who have once confronted them lose their presence of mind and through fear become as it were senseless.'

On 19 July, emerging from the Karo La, the invaders found themselves looking down into a great remote basin, the centre of which was filled by the Yamdok Tso or Turquoise Lake. Its waters were sweet or at any rate potable, not salt; by one of the more learned officers its shape was described—'happily,' according to Landon—as 'scorpionoid;' its boggy shores were dotted by half-ruined castles and loud with the cries of redshanks. Its colour was exquisite; 'near inshore the innumerable ripples are indeed blown in over the white-sanded floor as colourlessly as wavelets on a South Pacific strand of white coral, but twenty yards out the bottom drops suddenly, and the lake glows deeply with the colour from which it takes its name.' * Since the days of the Jesuits Manning was, as far as anybody knew, the only European who had seen this lake before.

Immediately in their path and not far from the lake-shore stood Nagartse, dominated by the usual fort. Here Young-husband was met by a delegation consisting of the Ta Lama and the Grand Secretary (with whom he had attempted nego-tiations at Gyantse), reinforced by the Yutok Shapé, one of the four State Councillors, a courteous and relatively sensible man. The parley, which it was clear from the first would be barren of results, lasted for almost seven hours.

These interviews, brief accounts of which recur throughout my narrative, imposed a severe strain on Younghusband; 'they exhausted everyone's patience except the Commissioner's,' Candler recorded. Logic was a concept wholly alien to the Tibetan mind. A small child, ordered to do something which it does not want to do, will enquire, over and over again, 'But why must I?' The Tibetans' power of reasoning did not extend even thus far. They did not evade issues, they declined to recognise their existence. The interplay of cause and effect was beyond their ken; they were incapable of realising, let alone of admitting, that circumstances had changed since they first advanced their arguments. They were for practical purposes impervious to the arts of diplomacy.

Their procedure in debate, or what passed for debate, was unvarying. Each delegate repeated, sometimes with small amendments, the observations of his colleagues. He did so in what O'Connor, who for more than a year interpreted these futile and inconsequent utterances, described as 'a low mono-tonous gabble,' accompanied by formal gestures. In the Tibetan language the negative particle is pronounced without emphasis; it was apt, O'Connor found, to be almost inaudible. Younghusband was a poor linguist. He could not seek a vicarious distraction in mastering the rudiments of the language.

* Landon.

His duty was to sit, impassive but alert, and to listen, hour after hour, while one man talked gibberish and two or more others, waiting their turn to repeat the burden of his discourse, watched the British Commissioner intently. It was an exacting task; but it cannot be called altogether thankless, for there were many in the expedition who shared Candler's opinion that 'it would be impossible to find another man in the British Empire with a personality so calculated to impress the Tibetans.'

At Nagartse Younghusband had more trouble with Macdonald. The Escort Commander did not want to go to Lhasa if it could be helped; 'I really believe he funks, he is so cautious,' one officer wrote to his wife. It was Macdonald's hope that, if a treaty was concluded on the way to the capital, honour would be satisfied, the Government of India would call off the advance and the expedition would turn about and withdraw to India. Whenever, therefore, negotiators presented themselves along the line of march he did everything in his power to prolong the jejune palavers and to delay the resumption of a forward move.

This policy did not commend itself to the men under his command, let alone to the Mission; and one source* suggests that something akin to a *pronunciamiento* was canvassed (without Younghusband's knowledge) by the senior British officers present, who contemplated deposing the Escort Commander in a discreet and gentlemanlike manner and pressing on to Lhasa without him. The only sponsor of this story was a subaltern himself at the time, and could have had no first-hand knowledge of a conspiracy half-hatched by colonels. Whether or not, in the mounting impatience with Macdonald's leadership, extreme measures were discussed, nothing came of them.

Nothing came, either, of the negotiations at Nagartse. While they were in progress, the Mounted Infantry intercepted and captured (allegedly after being fired on) a well-appointed convoy of eighty mules and ponies carrying the personal effects of the plenipotentiaries, who indignantly demanded their restitu-

* Letter written by Lt.-Colonel L. A. Bethell to Younghusband's biographer, the Very Reverend George Seaver, in 1950.

tion; when this was refused, they disappeared under cover of darkness, taking with them Macdonald's pretexts for delay. On the morning of 21 July the expedition resumed its progress along the shores of the Yamdok Tso, which, it had been discovered in the interim, teemed with unsuspecting fish; these, though handsome in appearance, proved of greater interest to the ichthyologist than to the epicure.

Pehte Jong, a romantic but dilapidated lakeside fortress, was reached on the 22nd, the force having covered only eighteen miles in two days. Thence their route led them up to the Kamba La (15,400 feet); this was the last pass on the road to Lhasa, and from it some of the officers claimed to be able to descry, through field-glasses, the distant roofs of the Potala, the holy citadel which dominates the capital of Tibet (these claims were rejected by the surveyors). Below them the Tsangpo— later identified by Lieutenant-Colonel F. M. Bailey, then serving as a young subaltern with the Mounted Infantry, as the upper reaches of the Brahmaputra—flowed, swift and yellow, through a valley far lusher than anything they had looked for in Tibet; 'we had come through the desert to Arcady,' wrote Candler. They dropped down into Arcady by a zigzag track which descended three thousand feet in five miles.

In the planning of the expedition curiously little account seems to have been taken of the Tsangpo. In the reports made by native spies of the Survey of India its width had been greatly exaggerated—Ottley said that it was expected to measure up to a thousand yards across—but even at its true span of roughly a hundred and fifty yards it was a most formidable obstacle. The expedition had with it a few collapsible Berthon boats, of which Macdonald had had experience in Africa, and some resourceful boatmen from Attock on the Indus to man them; otherwise it was wholly unequipped to make (let alone to force) the crossing of an unbridged, uncharted river with a fast current. The planners seem to have relied largely on luck to get the expedition over the strongest of all the natural barriers protecting Lhasa.

And luck was with them. On 24 July the whole of the Mounted Infantry, with Macdonald's Chief of Staff, Major Iggulden, in command, led their ponies down the mountain-side—it was too steep to ride—towards the village of Chaksam, from which it was known that some kind of ferry-service operated. Reaching the valley-floor, they mounted, and almost immediately Ottley's company flushed a badger from a field of barley. Bayonets were fixed by the leading files, and the new equestrian sport of badger-sticking briefly (and characteristic-ally) enlivened the advance; the unlucky badger was possibly the first and last of his species to succumb to the *arme blanche*.

They rode on, to find Chaksam looted by the retreating enemy and deserted by its inhabitants. The river here was spanned by four huge chains, the durable and strangely rust-free remains of a suspension bridge erected in the fifteenth century. The two barges serving the ferry could be seen on the further bank; with typical fecklessness the Tibetan army had omitted to scupper them.

The Mounted Infantry found some skin coracles hidden on the foreshore. Threats and bribery induced the local boatmen to cross the river and bring the ferries back. They proved to be clumsy lighters, forty feet long by twelve feet wide, their bows decorated with a quaintly carved horse's head. Of the many services which the Mounted Infantry rendered to the expedi-tion, their prompt seizure of these indispensable hulks was probably the most important; in them were transported across the great river 3500 men, 3500 animals and 350 tons of supplies.*

It took five and a half days. On the first of these a tragedy occurred. A raft, made by lashing two Berthon boats together, overturned, and two Gurkhas and a British officer were

---

* In one of these ferries the dotty Manning had crossed the Tsangpo nearly a century before. 'Its motion . . . brought on a fit of European activity. I could not sit still, but must climb about, seat myself in various postures on the parapet, and lean over. The master of the boat was alarmed, and sent a steady man to hold me tight. I pointed to the ornamented prow of the boat, and assured them that I could sit there with perfect safety, and

Ampthill

Macdonald and his staff

drowned. The officer was Major Bretherton, who had been responsible for the supply and transport arrangements ever since the early days in Sikkim. The expedition owed much to him, and his loss was deeply felt. During campaigns on the Indian Frontier it was the custom—wryly described by Sir Winston Churchill in his account of the Malakand Field Force —to auction the kit, apart from intimate personal belongings, of officers who lost their lives, so as to make the pack-animal which had carried it available for a more essential load. 'I found,' wrote the officer who conducted the sale of Bretherton's effects, 'that the adoption of the correct, breezy, business-like auctioneer's manner was uphill work.' Some idea of the standards of living within the expedition may be gained from the fact that a cake of soap which had cost 4½d. fetched 4s. 6d.

The current in the Tsangpo ran at seven knots, and at first the crossings proceeded at a painfully slow rate; at the end of the second day (26 July) the staff estimated that a fortnight would be needed to get the whole force on to the further bank. But Captain Sheppard of the Royal Engineers threw a steel hawser across the river and by hitching the barges on to this cut out the severe delays involved in hauling them two miles upstream from the point to which they had been swept in transit. From a village fifteen miles away the Mounted Infantry procured (and paid for) a flotilla of twenty-seven small skin boats, and by the third day the speed of the whole operation had been more than trebled. The last boatloads were landed on 31 July, and on the same day the final stage of the advance on Lhasa, now only forty-three miles away, began.

Before they crossed the river the British Commissioner received a letter addressed to 'the all-wise Sahib sent by the English Government to settle affairs, from the Tibetan National

---

to prove to them how commodiously I was seated, bent my head and body down the outside of the boat to the water's edge; but finding, by their renewed instances to me to desist, that I made them uneasy, I went back to my place and seated myself quietly. As the boat drew near shore I meditated jumping over, but was pulled back by the immense weight of my clothes and the clumsiness of my boots.'

Assembly.' The Tsongdu, as this body was known, had almost five hundred members; some of them came from outlying parts of the country but most were monks from the three great monasteries grouped about the capital. Theoretically the Tsongdu had the final say in national affairs, but since it had no chairman to preside over its deliberations (which neither the Dalai Lama nor the Shapés attended) and no votes were taken, it formed a somewhat cumbrous part of the machinery of state; its members, the Ta Lama told Younghusband, 'arrived at a decision by discussing till they were all of one mind.'

In their letter the Tsongdu acknowledged the receipt of a communication, sent by the Tongsa Penlop on Younghusband's behalf, setting forth the terms demanded by the British, and announced that delegates, headed by the Lord Chamberlain, had been despatched to Chusul, near the east bank of the river, to discuss them. 'Please,' urged the writers, 'do not press forward hastily to Lhasa. . . . Even if the Sahibs should come to Lhasa and meet the Dalai Lama, this will not advantage the cause of friendship. Should a fresh cause of dispute arise, we greatly fear that a disturbance, contrary to the interests of friendship, may follow.'

This message marked a great step forward, for it suggested that the Tibetan authorities had woken up to realities and were at last prepared to enter into serious negotiations. But it confronted Younghusband with a difficult decision. It now seemed possible that the mere threat of an advance to Lhasa might procure him his treaty, while if he did push on to the capital the outraged Tibetans might be driven to desperate measures and, even if a military disaster was avoided, no political results would be achieved.

Macdonald's health was deteriorating. On 25 July he wrote three letters to Younghusband, whose tent was no further from his own than Lugard's had been in Uganda. In the first he referred to a conversation on the previous day, in which 'you informed me that the primary object of the Mission and the Force escorting it was to reach Lhasa, and that the effecting [of] a satisfactory settlement was secondary. As this does not appear to be in accordance with such official communications as I have received, I would be much obliged if you would kindly let me have a copy of the order you referred to, or, if this is not possible, would let me see the order.'

Later in the day, news having come in that the Tibetans were offering to negotiate at Chusul, he exchanged a legalistic for an emotional standpoint: 'In these circumstances, I would be glad to know whether you propose to grant their prayer for peace, or if I am to continue military operations and force my way to Lhasa.'

Younghusband's reply was expository but ended on a firm note: 'The Mission will, therefore, advance to Lhasa, and, if any opposition is offered to its passage, I would rely on you to overcome it.' As at Tuna, 'Retiring Mac,' irresolute even in defeatism, abandoned his position. That evening his third letter was borne to Younghusband's tent. It contained regrets that his 'well-meant suggestion' had been misunderstood: denials that he was anxious to go no further than Chusul: warnings that the Escort was weakened by sickness and shortage of ammunition: and pleas for an early settlement when they got to Lhasa. The British Commissioner was acutely aware that, if it came to a showdown, he was armed only with 'a pistol which is liable not to go off;' and this strengthened the arguments in favour of abandoning the advance and settling down to roadside negotiations.

Instinct, backed by the experience of the past year, told Younghusband that these arguments were unsound. He wrote to the Dalai Lama that he must carry out his orders, which were to go to Lhasa; he would withdraw as soon as a treaty had been concluded; his troops would not fire unless fired on; no holy places would be occupied unless they were being used for war-like purposes, and all supplies would be paid for. If resistance was offered it would be overcome, as it had been at Gyantse, and the terms of the treaty would be made more severe.

The reply which this letter evoked, and the long, monotonous discussions which recurred throughout the river-crossing operations, are of small interest. The Tibetans merely re-stated their objections against the British going to Lhasa, and the only new development was the attendance of a Chinese official deputed by the Amban. Younghusband listened courteously to their representations, 'a monument of patience and inflexibility, impassive as one of their own Buddhas;'* but he declined to modify his plans, and on the last day of July, amid the jubilant war-cries of the Sikhs and Gurkhas, the force moved off along the Lhasa road.

The country was rich, the weather fine, the forts abandoned. The column, seven miles long, clanked its way forward under a pall of fine dust—the Mounted Infantry in front, followed by a caterpillar of bobbing turbans or topees or forage-caps, the advance-guard of Sikhs or Fusiliers, Pathans or Gurkhas: behind them the main body, a long stretch of it taken up by the fine upstanding mules of the mountain batteries. In the middle of the column rode the Escort Commander, 'jogging along with bent shoulders—a mile away you could tell that he was a sick man:'† the only soldier in the whole force who wished he was going in the opposite direction.

They debouched into the fertile valley of the Kyi Chu, the river on which Lhasa stands. There was keen competition to be the first to set eyes on the Forbidden City, but it was masked by a tantalising series of spurs and ridges; it was not until they were within twelve miles of their objective that the leading horsemen, dismounting, scrambled in a mad race up a steep bluff and beheld, flickering slightly in the heat-haze, the golden roofs of the Potala, set like a jewel in an embrasure of the hills. Captain Ottley, as might perhaps have been foretold, was the first to sight it.

* Candler.   † Landon.

CHAPTER EIGHTEEN

Enter the Amban

THE expedition halted seven miles short of Lhasa on the evening of 2 August. The inevitable deputation approached to make a last plea that they should come no further; its members 'enjoyed,' as Landon put it, 'what must have been to them unexpected support from the General.' But they got no change out of Younghusband, and next morning the force moved forward across the waterish plain towards the massive yet fairy-like buildings of the Dalai Lama's capital.

At first the Tongsa Penlop (who put on his crown for the occasion) led the way, with trumpeters in his retinue sounding erratic fanfares; but he was not a valorous man, and the Bhutanese soon saw to it that they lay a bad second to the Mounted Infantry. They passed the huge Drebung monastery, of which Dorjieff had been an alumnus. The pessimists had prophesied that its eight thousand fanatical inmates, armed with Russian rifles, would hurl themselves on the intruders, but those who were visible did nothing worse than scowl. Beyond it stood the Ne-chung, the residence and temple of the State Oracle, a building of greater luxury and refinement than they had yet seen in Tibet. Further on, surrounded by an appalling stench, was a place corresponding to the municipal *abattoir*. Buddhism strictly forbids the taking of life in any form, and the butchers, catering for an appetite common to all laymen and most ecclesiastics, were low-caste Mohammedans from India; they lived in huts walled and roofed with the horns of their victims. Thence the road, now a causeway running through a marsh, led on to the outskirts of the capital, and the force camped on a stretch of greensward near the Dalai Lama's Summer Palace, less than a mile from the sky-scraping Potala but still out of sight of the city crouched at its foot behind an intervening spur.

There now appeared upon the stage a figure who during the coming weeks was destined to play an unobtrusive but exceedingly important part in the affairs of the Mission; the Chinese Amban paid an official call on the British Commissioner.

Yu-t'ai, a Manchu, was a brother of Sheng-t'ai, who had negotiated the original Convention of 1890, breaches of which by the Tibetans were the ultimate cause of Younghusband's presence at the gates of Lhasa; he had a clever face, an ingratiating manner and few if any principles. In a document which appears to be an impeachment of Yu-t'ai he is described as 'a cowardly and incompetent poltroon,'* and a modern Chinese historian ascribes to timidity rather than to insuperable transport difficulties his failure to do his duty by going to meet the Mission at Gyantse.†

Yu-t'ai may well have been a coward, but he was not a negligible person. China's power and prestige in Tibet were at a low ebb, and Yu decided that his Government's interests would be better served if the British successfully overawed the Tibetans (for whom, like all Chinese officials, he entertained a cold contempt) than if they reached a compromise half-way to the capital. In at least one telegram to Peking, despatched after a Tibetan reverse, he expressed the hope that another British victory would bring about 'a favourable turn in the situation;' and one of the charges brought against him afterwards was that 'he proposed to avail himself of the British occupation of Lhasa as a means of asserting Chinese authority over Tibet.'

This policy, though unbecoming, was shrewd; and it absolved

* An undated translation of this document, entitled 'Flakes from Memory,' was found among the late Sir Ernest Wilton's papers. Its author styles himself 'Po t'i,' but a note suggests that he may have been Lo Tun-jui, a writer with some reputation at the Imperial Court.

† Tieh-tseng Li.

Yu-t'ai from disagreeable exertions during the British advance.
In this time of crisis, according to his pseudonymous critic, he
displayed somewhat too flagrantly his indifference to the fate of
the country whose Suzerain he represented, 'the fact being that
his favourite gate-keeper had purchased and brought into Tibet
five or six fair damsels whom he had presented to his patron. . . .
In broad daylight Yu, attended by his staff, proceeded to the
Willow Garden, where branches were plucked from the trees
[for masquerading purposes] and the wine cup was pressed
upon the guests, whilst that sequestered shade witnessed the
revelry of song and dance.' Grave offence was given to the
Tibetans by this *fête galante*, which took place on hallowed
ground.

Apart from the Dalai Lama, the Amban was the only person
in Tibet with the right to use a sedan chair. Yu-t'ai's, borne
into the British camp by ten men, was 'preceded by ten unarmed servants clad in lavender-blue, edged and patterned
with black velvet. Immediately behind them came forty men-
at-arms similarly dressed in cardinal and black, bearing lances,
scythe-headed poles, tridents and banners; after them came the
secretaries and their servants.'* The mere fact that Yu-t'ai
felt it incumbent upon himself to visit Younghusband before
Younghusband visited him acknowledged a loss of face; the
Amban had signally failed either to control his Emperor's
vassals or to comply with the British Commissioner's requests
to come and meet him. Younghusband, whose far-flung Chinese
experience was now of service, recognised his embarrassment;
'but he kept up appearances and made a brave show with all the
aplomb of his race, and I had a real feeling of relief in talking
to a man of affairs.'

The man of affairs presented the British Commissioner with
a number of sheep and cattle and a quantity of flour. These, it
was later computed by his accusers, might have cost between
15,000 and 16,000 taels; in the account of expenditure which
Yu-t'ai rendered to Peking they were valued at 40,000 taels.
The Chinese Empire, his impeachment observed, 'is mainly

* Landon.

served in Tibet by officials with bad marks against their names who have been cashiered or reduced in rank and who owe their reinstatement to skilful intrigue. . . . Since to them their reputation is a matter of no consequence, they hesitate at no enormity, batten on the Tibetans, and embezzle Treasury funds.' 'It is a very bad policy,' Manning had concluded in 1811, 'thus perpetually to send men of bad character to govern Tibet.'

The Amban's residence was on the far side of the city, into which the expedition had not yet penetrated; Younghusband was to return his call on the following day. The British Commissioner realised that there was a considerable risk in riding through Lhasa, and that he could easily reach his destination by a detour. But 'all this trouble had arisen through the Tibetans being so inaccessible and keeping themselves so much apart; and now I meant to close in with them, to break through their seclusion.' Overruling the agitated protests of his Escort Commander, he set off with a small bodyguard of Royal Fusiliers and Mounted Infantry, and some of the Amban's pikemen to act as guides. A stronger force, with two guns, stood by, ready to attempt a rescue if the British Commissioner was threatened by the fate of Cavagnari.

Unarmed, save for the elegant but far from lethal sword which is worn with full-dress diplomatic uniform, Younghusband rode at the head of his Mission through the city-gates. Above them, now for the first time in full view, towered the fabulous bulk of the Potala, golden-roofed, white-walled, taller than St Paul's Cathedral. Its central building, the private quarters of the Dalai Lama, was painted a deep crimson. Sanctuaries were shrouded by yak-hair curtains, eighty feet long and twenty-five feet wide, which cascaded down the precipice-like walls. Upon its terraces and stairways hundreds of monks, dwarfed by the height, perambulated or lounged, scratching themselves, in the sun. The Potala was an edifice much bigger, and much stranger, than any of the invaders had seen before.

It was surrounded by a nauseous squalor. 'If,' wrote Candler, 'one approached within a league of Lhasa, saw the glittering domes of the Potala, and turned back without entering the precincts, one might still imagine it an enchanted city.' It was in fact an insanitary slum. In the pitted streets pools of rainwater and piles of refuse disrupted the march-discipline of the Fusiliers. The houses were mean and filthy, the stench pervasive. Pigs and ravens competed for nameless delicacies in open sewers. There were no riders to add to Manning's verdict, delivered ninety-odd years earlier:

> There is nothing striking, nothing pleasing, in Lhasa's appearance. The habitations are begrimed with smut and dirt. The avenues are full of dogs, some growling and gnawing bits of hide that lie about in profusion, and emit a charnel-house smell; others limping and looking livid; others ulcerated; others starved and dying, and pecked at by ravens; some dead and preyed upon. In short, everything seems mean and gloomy, and excites the idea of something unreal.

There was something slightly unreal about the demeanour of the inhabitants as their conquerors tramped and jingled through the Forbidden City. Perhaps by order of the authorities, not many people were abroad. The monks, who struck Younghusband as 'lazy and sensual and effete,' gave them surly glances; but the commonalty, whom one diarist found 'very low, underbred, idiotic-looking people,' watched them pass with an almost total lack of curiosity.

There were no untoward incidents; although when, on arriving at the Amban's residence, they were welcomed by a discharge of fireworks, some feared that the sound of the explosions would be misconstrued and that Macdonald would order the ten-pounders, already trained on the Potala, to open fire. Nothing of the sort, however, happened and soon, to the strains of an invisible but all too audible Chinese band, the Mission were being regaled with tea, small cigars and Huntley & Palmer biscuits while Yu-t'ai explained to Younghusband, as one civilised being to another, what impossible people the Tibetans were. He appeared sincerely desirous of inducing them to reach a settlement with the British.

The news that Lhasa had been 'unveiled' was received with acclaim in England; it made a considerable impression throughout Europe, and even the Russian newspapers admitted, with a surprisingly good grace, that it was a striking achievement—'a gain to civilisation,' as the *St Petersburg Gazette* put it. The expedition had lost less than forty officers and men killed. Not everybody would have agreed with Lionel Cust, who wrote to his 'dearest Francisco' that the latter's entry into Lhasa was 'certainly the most interesting thing that has happened for the last two hundred years;' but there was a general feeling that the Tibetan enterprise, after promising very ill, had suddenly managed to crown itself with triumph.

This was far from being so. As long as Lhasa remained inviolate, there had always existed some possibility, however remote, that the central authority of Tibet would, in the end, enter into negotiations with the Mission; but upon the arrival of the expedition at Lhasa, the central authority disintegrated and this possibility appeared to have vanished. Younghusband summed it up in a telegram dated 8 August and received in Simla (for the telegraph-line had not kept up with the advance) five days later:

> Tibetan authorities all in confusion. Ta Lama disgraced, Yutok Shapé gone sick, and of remaining two Shapés one is inimical and other useless. National Assembly sits permanently now, but only criticises, and is afraid to act without reference Dalai Lama, who is three days distant, and will not in his turn act without sanction of Assembly. Everyone is in fear, not of us, but of each other. . . . No attempt commence negotiations been made. . . . General attitude of Tibetans, though exasperating, is probably more futile and inept than intentionally hostile.

In this bad situation Younghusband had three valuable allies, and it was mainly through them that he went patiently to work. The opportunist Amban could hardly have been more accommodating or shown more anxiety to help. When the British arrived in Lhasa he carried little weight with the Tibetans in his official capacity, and his personal standing was low; the first handicap was due largely to his predecessors' failings, the second entirely to his own. Very astutely he made no attempt to conceal the weakness of his position, but he invented new and more seemly reasons for it. 'We found him,' wrote Younghusband, 'to be practically a prisoner and almost without enough to eat, as the Tibetans had prevented supplies of money from reaching him, and he had actually to borrow money from us.' History, though full of improbable events, does not record the repayment of this loan; one of the charges in Yu-t'ai's impeachment is that he was always trying to borrow money from the Tibetan Government.

Although it helped, in the end, to get him cashiered, the Amban's espousal of the British cause swiftly enhanced his prestige in Lhasa. The unsuccessful suppliant for ponies was transfigured into a man of destiny, a bearer of state secrets, a writer of exigent letters to the absconding Dalai Lama. It may be suspected that the relief, which many travellers have known, of coming into contact with the Chinese mind—so darting, so percipient, so gay—after wrestling over-long with duller, more barbarian intellects went slightly to Younghusband's head; he never, at any rate, saw through the Amban.

His other two allies were the Tongsa Penlop, who was much respected by the Tibetans, and Captain Jit Bahadur, the Nepalese representative, a plump, courteous, quick-witted man, whose many years' service in Lhasa gave him a keener insight into affairs than either the newly-arrived Amban or the visitor from Bhutan possessed. It was through the good offices of Captain Jit that, after several frustrating and almost hopeless days, the first faint gleam of light revealed itself at the end of the tunnel.

In a letter which Younghusband received at Chaksam during the river-crossing, the Dalai Lama had announced that he was —in the religious sense of the phrase—'in retreat.' For a time he was believed to be in a monastery somewhere to the north-east of Lhasa, but by mid-August it became known that, accompanied by Dorjieff, he was fleeing towards the Kokonor, making (as it later transpired) for Outer Mongolia. He had however left his seals of office behind him with a benevolent and much-respected old lama called the Ti Rimpoche, who was thus vested with the powers of a Regent. The Nepalese representative got in touch with this dignitary and with the Dalai Lama's brother, and on 9 August reported that both were anxious to reach a settlement. Younghusband had his toe in the door; a week later the Tibetans complied with one of the nine conditions (of which more later) demanded by His Majesty's Government.

This was the release of the two men from Lachung. It was a year since they had been captured while spying for the Mission at Khamba Jong, ten months since Curzon had cited their alleged execution after torture as proof of the Tibetan Government's 'contemptuous disregard for the usages of civilisation.' So completely had they been forgotten in the interim that no mention was made of them in the proposed terms for a treaty put forward by the Government of India in June; but in Whitehall some clerk, full of zeal and perhaps also of compassion, had rediscovered their spoor in the files and tracked them back to the point at which, ephemerally, they had formed the spearhead of a weak *casus belli*. Now their release ranked third among the nine demands which Younghusband had been instructed to make of the Tibetans.

It was effected in full Durbar on 16 August. Blinking (they had been kept in solitary confinement a long way underground for a year) and still as anonymous as the yaks which Brander impounded in retaliation for their capture, the two humble instruments of destiny were led into Younghusband's presence by Tibetan notables. They deposed that they had been well fed and, save for a mild preliminary beating, not ill-treated (in their rough world a year's incarceration in a dungeon hardly counted as ill-treatment, provided the rations were adequate; they only mentioned it during subsequent interrogations). A medical officer examined them and reported them in good condition. Younghusband made an admonitory speech but waived the reparation which he had been authorized to demand. The Tibetans promised that they would never arrest British subjects again; everyone expressed their pleasure that a first step had been made toward the conclusion of a treaty; and the Amban, who got the credit for arranging this transaction, preened himself discreetly. The ice in Lhasa was breaking.

News of these quietly auspicious developments was however slow in reaching London, for there was by now a six-day delay on telegraphic communications between Lhasa and Simla. Hopes of a treaty had been virtually abandoned in Whitehall. There were, it was felt, few if any chestnuts to be pulled out of the fire which Curzon had kindled. It was up to Younghusband to retrieve what he could of the nation's honour. 'We must now trust,' Brodrick wrote to Ampthill on 18 August, 'to Younghusband's doing the right thing, and making himself felt in some way. If he could bring away a substantial indemnity in some form or another, it would go a long way to ease off matters.' A week earlier Kitchener had written to Lady Salisbury: 'Younghusband will have, I think, to be a little sterner with these absurd people if he intends to get the Convention signed without inordinate delay.'* There had been a see-saw of responsibility. The puppet-strings with which an Empire controlled the man on the spot had somehow been spliced into a life-line, with which the puppet was now required to pull his masters out of a hole. It was all up to Younghusband.

The bankruptcy of Britain's Tibetan policy at this stage is vividly revealed in a letter which the Prime Minister wrote to his Sovereign on the day on which—unbeknown as yet to him—the Lachung men were set free. Balfour briefly rehearsed the difficulties which had confronted his Cabinet during their meeting that afternoon: 'The position is not an easy one. The troops ought to return for climatic reasons in a few weeks. The Dalai Lama has fled, leaving no representative to treat with us. Yet we cannot retire without striking some blow at an enemy,

* Salisbury MSS.

which will neither keep its old engagements nor discuss new ones. The Cabinet decided that, if the Lama refuses even to consider our very reasonable and moderate offers, we have no choice but to turn the expedition from a peaceful into a punitive one: and with every regard to the religious feelings of the Tibetans, to destroy such buildings as the walls and the gates of the city, and to carry [off] some of the leading citizens as hostages. This course is painful; but apparently inevitable.' *

The men who took this decision were not at their best. Parliament was to have risen at the end of July, but Britain's relations with Russia were dangerously strained and the session had been prolonged. No landmark in the Edwardian calendar was more sacrosanct than the Twelfth of August; it was a social solecism to be found in London after the start of the grouse-shooting season, and a blend of self-pity with impatience may well have clouded judgments when the Cabinet met in Downing Street on 15 August. 'The Government is stale to a man,' Lionel Cust had written to Younghusband five days earlier; 'the PM is worried and utterly tired out.'

These circumstances may help to explain the Cabinet's decision, but cannot condone it. The course of action they proposed was petulant, barbarous and sterile; it was fortunate for Balfour that no record of it survived outside the archives at Windsor. The massive acts of vandalism which they advocated were ethically unjustifiable and politically inexpedient; they were also quite impracticable. The destruction of 'such buildings as the walls and the gates of the city' called for a programme of demolitions which were (as they ought to have guessed if they did not know) far beyond the resources of the expedition; before Gyantse was reached 'it was discovered,' Landon recorded, 'that the whole stock of explosives in Calcutta had been exhausted. From Karachi and elsewhere a little could still be obtained.' It is the business of staff officers, not of statesmen, to work out how many mules are needed to carry one ton of gun-cotton and how many tons of gun-cotton are needed to make a lasting mark on a Central Asian capital;

* Royal Archives.

but statesmen, when laying down a policy to which such calculations are basic, ought to be sufficiently agile-minded to suspect that both figures are likely to be high.

This victory for the 'reparation school of thought' marked the nadir of British policy. The Government fatalistically accepted the fact that its purposes in Tibet were unattainable. Only a miracle could avert what would amount, politically at least, to a fiasco. They were resigned to withdrawing from Lhasa without a treaty; and without a treaty they would be back where they had started—back with the Convention of 1890, which the Tibetans did not recognise, back with their fourteen-year-old grievances about transgressed grazing-rights, overthrown boundary-pillars, obstructed trade-facilities and unanswered letters. As for the wider implications of the enterprise—the scotching of Russian intrigue, the erection of a countervailing bastion of British influence—these things, which once loomed so large, had been forgotten. No evidence whatever of Russian machinations had come to light in the Tibetan capital; even Curzon, who six months earlier had written to the Lieutenant-Governor of Burma 'I have the best authority for saying that had we delayed much longer the Russians would have been securely installed,'* forbore from suggesting that the expedition had reached Lhasa only in the nick of time.

When in mid-August the members of Mr Balfour's Government dispersed to the Scottish grouse-moors and the European spas, the best they hoped for in Tibet was that Colonel Younghusband, besides blowing up the more secular parts of the Forbidden City, might be able to extort from its tiresome inhabitants some minor but face-saving political concession—a large indemnity, or something like that. Tibet, each hastened to make plain when the occasion arose, was not a subject on which he personally could speak as an expert; it was George Curzon's chickens that were coming home to roost.

* Barnes MSS.

CHAPTER NINETEEN

Exit The Times *Correspondent*

To the troops, and especially to the officers, Lhasa had seemed the most desirable of goals; but no sooner had they arrived than boredom and disillusionment set in, and they longed for nothing so much as orders to march back to India. 'For myself,' one of them wrote in his diary on the day they arrived, 'barring the fact that we are the first force to have ever come to Lhasa, there is nothing very wonderful about it;' a month later he was referring to the Forbidden City as 'such a smelly, nasty place.' Similar sentiments are reflected in other private sources; 'not a white man's country,' one of them observed severely.

There was little to do. At first the Tibetans were backward in producing the supplies, mainly of barley, for which requisition had been made, and a military demonstration was staged, without incident, against the great monastery of Sera; this had the desired effect, but the luxuries of life—whisky, jam, soap and so on—were still scarce, for Siliguri was now some four hundred miles away.

Relations with the populace, who, as at Gyantse, established a thriving bazaar outside the gates of the British camp, were cordial, but in mid-August a fanatical lama, wearing a shirt of chain-mail under his robe, attacked and wounded two British officers with a sword before being knocked senseless by a Pathan cook wielding a frying-pan. A gallows was erected and the lama was executed next day—'truculent to the last. He kicked a Tommy in the face as he was going up the ladder, and spat in another's face; but hanged he was, dangling like a blot against the sunset.'*

Time hung heavy on their hands. Gymkhanas,† race-meetings, rifle-meetings and football matches were organised (the football sailed to unnatural heights in the thin air). Armed parties of soldiers were conducted on 'school treats' round the city. Shooting was forbidden in deference to Buddhist suscepti-bilities, but fishing was a popular sport. Ugyen Kazi's surviving elephant was much photographed. Two *kyangs*, or wild asses, were ridden down in the plain by British gunners of the 7th Mountain Battery and lassoed; tethered alongside quiet old mules, they became quite tame. On the way back to India one died of heart-failure while swimming the Tsangpo, but the other eventually reached the London Zoo; its captors were later mortified to hear that, without reference to them, it had been borrowed by the Royal Fusiliers and paraded as a sort of trophy-cum-mascot when the Regiment exercised its tradi-tional right to march with fixed bayonets through the City of London.

Younghusband was groping his way, little by little, towards his objective. On 11 August the National Assembly returned, via the Amban, their first reply to the British proposals for a treaty; they refused each of the nine demands and contended that it was England who ought to pay an indemnity to Tibet, not the other way round. Younghusband declined to receive so preposterous a communication; the Amban supported his attitude and censured the Tibetans for their impudence. After

---

* Officer's diary.

† The principal events in the final gymkhana are recorded in a letter from a British NCO. They comprised:

(1) Bareback mule race for British troops over four flights of hurdles. No one finished.

(2) Wrestling. The winner, a Pathan, was disqualified for biting through the tendons of his opponent's knee.

(3) 440 yards race for Indian stretcher-bearers. Ended in a free fight.

(4) Wheelbarrow race. Won by two Gurkhas. 'The wheelbarrow lost a part of his nose and two teeth through the eagerness of his pusher.'

this the Regent's moderating influence began to make itself felt, and five days later the two Lachung men were released.

But progress was erratic and dangerously slow. Dangerously, because Younghusband had only a few weeks to work in. This question of time haunted him. It was a matter of vital importance in which he was largely at the mercy of his Escort Commander, for in a telegram which reached him towards the end of August the Secretary of State decreed that 'date on which return of force from Lhasa is to begin should be fixed by military authorities in communication with Younghusband.' This ruling gave rise to a bitter controversy.

Macdonald, who had gone to Lhasa against his will, was determined not to stay there a day longer than was, in his own view, necessary. In representing to GHQ that an early withdrawal was imperative, he was doubtless actuated mainly by a prudent concern for the men under his command; but he cannot escape all suspicion of rigging the evidence in favour of the policy he recommended, and it is clear—it even at this stage became clear to his superiors—that he was working against Younghusband and placing almost wantonly in jeopardy the slender but slowly improving prospects of the Mission's success.

His telegrams to India were loaded with ominous meteorological data; on 30 August he reported 'heavy rain every night for last three weeks. Severe snowstorm on night of 23rd at Ralung and low temperature in the Karo La,' and a week later 'very heavy rain with snow low down on surrounding mountains.' He impressed on GHQ that if he left his departure too late the passes would be blocked, and the expedition would be able to extricate itself only at the cost of heavy casualties from exposure.

Younghusband, who knew that these arguments were specious, did his best to counter them. 'Government,' he wired on 10 September, 'may rely on my experience of Himalayan passes, extending over many years, not to involve troops in undue hardships. . . . Snow, which falls on passes during rains, does not lie at all, clears away at end September, and passes between here and India are never closed even in depth of winter. . . . Mission was at 15,000 feet [at Khamba Jong] till December 6th last year, and then crossed pass one thousand feet higher than any we have to cross on way back from here.'

Macdonald's second line of defence was that his troops were short of warm clothing. Younghusband pointed out the flimsiness of this pretext in a clear-the-line telegram to India on 31 August. 'As whole population wears warm local-made cloth, it is obvious clothing must be obtainable.' White had ascertained that the bazaar was capable of producing 150 blankets and 150 jerseys a day. Samples of these had been shown to Macdonald as long ago as 21 August; he had been asked to state his total requirements but had failed to do so. It was not, Younghusband pointed out, the 'proper work' of a political mission to act as military outfitters; a matter of this kind could and should be handled by Macdonald's staff, who ought to have taken it in hand a month ago. Three days later he reported that White had had 515 blankets and 100 'vests' made in two and a half days; 90,000 yards of cloth had been promised within a week. Macdonald's contribution to this absurd correspondence (which was omitted from the Blue Book) was a statement that 'efforts on part of Mission for 8 days have produced nothing, while through Tibetans in 5 days we have got 1 jersey and 1 [pair of] trousers made up.'

He had yet a third line of defence: the health of his troops would be endangered by their inadequate attire. Younghusband described the manner in which he played this card in a letter to his father on 30 August:

Macdonald has done the most mean-spirited and almost traitorous act I have heard of for many a long day. He first told a committee of doctors to say the latest day we could stay here on the *existing* scale of clothing. Then he called together Commanding Officers and made the boss doctor—a miserable old woman whom he had tutored to say what he wanted*—tell them his opinion that September 1st was the latest date. Then he asked CO's their opinion and they, knowing nothing about conditions here in October or of the vital importance of staying here *as long as possible*, said September 15th. Then Macdonald comes to me and tells me it is the opinion of the medical officers and the CO's and his own opinion as well that we cannot stay here after September 15th and that he is telegraphing this to Government.

I then fairly let drive at him. I asked him if he had made any attempt to get warm clothing here. He had made none. I said I would undertake to get warm clothing for the whole force. I asked him if he had taken the opinion of officers of the Mission who were at Khamba Jong 15,000 feet through October and November last year. He had done nothing of the sort. I told him I was not going to allow an Imperial affair of extreme importance [to] depend on the opinion of a doctor and allow all the results of the sacrifices made by the troops and of their bravery and endurance to be thrown away because they could not stay two or three weeks longer to secure those results. . . . All my staff are with me tooth and nail, but if Macdonald is not cashiered before I have done with him I will eat that best top hat of mine. . . . I have never felt such contempt for any man as I did for him when he came up whining to me about the cold.

There are two sides to every quarrel, but it is difficult to feel that Younghusband was being unduly hard on his Escort Commander; in private sources the chorus of dispraise is unanimous. 'No one in this show has the slightest confidence in Macdonald, he is cursed day and night by great and small,' Candler wrote in a letter from Lhasa; 'Younghusband is as

* This must have been Lt.-Col. L. A. Waddell, author of *Lhasa and its Mysteries*. He was not much liked by his brother-officers, one of whom described him as 'a silly forgetful old man who never takes any care of his hospital or duties.' Waddell was something of a Tibetologist, and his principal concern was the collection of material for the British Museum.

sound as can be, and military and civil have complete confidence in him.' 'I've never known a General who is more universally disliked and looked down on by his officers,' one of them told his wife. A subaltern dismissed him as 'a worm' but found Younghusband 'a grand chap, we all like him, he's human, companionable and friendly with us all.'

It was not until he had suffered from them for nine months that Younghusband began to make guarded references to Macdonald's shortcomings in letters to Dane and to Curzon (who told Ampthill in mid-September that Younghusband had shown 'great reserve, forbearance and loyalty' in this matter); in official correspondence he had scrupulously refrained from direct criticism of his Escort Commander. By September, however, the authorities in India and in England had become aware that the military leadership of the expedition left much to be desired, that throughout the march to Lhasa Macdonald had been timorous and obstructive, and that—as Ampthill wrote in a memorandum to Kitchener and Elles on 4 September—he was 'at present the most serious obstacle to the successful conclusion of the negotiations, as his nervousness and fretful desire to return are a fearful drag on Younghusband.'

A main source of first Simla's and then London's enlightenment as to the true state of affairs within the expedition was *The Times* Correspondent, Perceval Landon, a spruce, gifted, slightly self-important man of thirty-five. 'The officers of the expedition,' he wrote to the Manager of *The Times* in March 1904 from New Chumbi, 'both political and military, seem to regard me as the only Correspondent worth consideration' (in the same letter he prophesied that 'the division of authority and responsibility between Younghusband and Macdonald will almost inevitably cause trouble in the future').* At least one young officer bore out Landon's self-appraisal by describing him in his diary as 'in a different class' to his three colleagues; and, unlike them, *The Times* Correspondent was made a regular member of the Mission mess.

Little more than a week after the expedition reached Lhasa

* *The Times* Archives.

Landon decided to return post-haste to England. From a journalistic point of view this was an indefensible decision. Landon's duty was to stay with the Mission and report the outcome, successful or otherwise, of the negotiations; in forsaking it when negotiations had scarcely begun he was acting as unprofessionally as a dramatic critic who leaves the theatre before the third act.

It was assumed by most of the officers that his action was opportunist and self-centred—that he was hurrying home ahead of everyone else to corner the limelight. But he himself took a very different view of his journey. 'Starting tomorrow dawn, probably Simla 30th, two nights,' he wired to Ampthill on 14 August. *'Hope you completely disengaged.'*

The Times Correspondent and the Acting Viceroy had been at Oxford together and were old friends;* but from the words which I have italicised it is clear that Landon regarded himself as bound on a confidential mission of some import, and this impression is borne out by his subsequent conduct. Ampthill replied, a shade huffily, on 20 August: 'Am never disengaged. Work fourteen hours a day, but you will be most welcome here whenever you can arrive.' Landon deferentially lowered his sights: 'Alas! I know your unending work and prayed only against abnormal preoccupations.'

He was by then already past Phari. He covered the four hundred miles between Lhasa and the nearest railway-station in twelve days, and reached Simla in fifteen, London in thirty-five. His ride to the railway was a creditable feat, but its speed was due solely to the fact that he had the pick of the

* Landon also knew Curzon, but he seems to have taken an over-sanguine view of the sort of claims he could make on friends who had attained viceregal status. From Gyantse he wrote to Curzon in London soliciting his interest in the Tibetan rug-trade, for which he (Landon) contemplated setting up a profitable agency. 'If,' he suggested to the Viceroy, 'you think that a beginning could be made with rugs and can arrange with Hampton, or Treloar, or any of the larger firms for a considerable order, I shall be glad to act for them so far as I can.' The vision of Lord Curzon touting Tibetan rugs round even the largest London emporiums is so excessively far-fetched that one cannot help wondering whether Landon's acquaintance with him was as close as he imagined it to be.

ponies with which the Mounted Infantry ran the mail-service to India from one staging-post to the next. As a civilian he had no right to use these facilities; and it is clear that his journey was facilitated, if not inspired, by Younghusband, but that Younghusband was anxious to play down his role as its sponsor.

This emerges plainly enough in a letter from Younghusband to Ampthill on 26 September. A fortnight earlier, after *The Times* Correspondent's brief sojourn in Viceregal Lodge, Ampthill had written to Younghusband:

> Perceval Landon seems to me to have been a fool to have left Lhasa before the end of the show. . . . He tried to justify himself by saying that he was going on some mysterious mission from you to Lord Curzon which he did not explain, but as he has no official status and Lord Curzon is not Viceroy at present or in any way officially concerned with negotiations between myself and the Home Government I could hardly believe that this was his real reason for going home. Perhaps you can tell me what was up? Landon has always been somewhat vague and mysterious in his ways and his sojourn in the land of mystery seems to have made him more so than ever.

'The mystery,' Younghusband hastened to assure Ampthill, 'is easily explained. He wanted to get home and get his book out first. From *The Times* point of view I think he was very unwise to leave Lhasa when he did. . . . From the Government point of view it was distinctly advantageous that he should get to Simla and London and give you and the India Office and Lord Curzon the benefit of personal discussion with an intelligent man who had come straight from Lhasa. When therefore he asked me if he could "carry despatches" from me as an excuse for getting transport facilities on the way down, I humoured him and gave him in a sealed cover copies of letters I was sending to the Foreign Office by the ordinary *dak* [mail]. One copy was addressed to Foreign Office, Simla, one to Political Secretary, India Office.'

247

The impression here conveyed that Younghusband's conscience was not entirely clear is strengthened by the rest of the
letter, which goes on: 'What surprised me was that a man of his
sense should have taken himself so seriously.' Landon had
(Younghusband claimed) said that, if he was delayed and was
unable to make the detour to Simla before catching his boat at
Bombay, 'no doubt Your Excellency and Lord Kitchener would
come down to Calcutta to meet him! He also thought that a
Cabinet Council would be held immediately on his arrival in
England!'

Why, after this, Younghusband should have been 'surprised'
by *further* evidence that Landon took himself seriously it is
difficult to see; this is the only one of his letters which has a
flavour of guile, if not of duplicity. To his father, however, he
made only a passing reference to Landon's departure for
England; if it had been his own idea, if he had engineered it in a
deliberate attempt to impress his views on Simla and London
through a staunch adherent who had the *entrée* everywhere, he
would almost certainly have made his father privy to the plot.
The chances are that Landon, for his own ends, wished to get
home quickly; that Younghusband, realising that *The Times*
Correspondent would advantage his cause in influential circles,
gave him a fair wind; and that Landon, partly from a natural
self-importance and partly from a slight feeling of guilt at
leaving Lhasa prematurely, overplayed his largely self-allotted
role as a confidential emissary. It is not uncommon for men,
when they have an excuse for doing something that they ought
not to do, to make too much of it.

Although Landon personally was not taken very seriously
('rather vague and discursive,' Ampthill found him, 'and misled
by strange delusions') and although allowance was made for
his partisanship ('he will reveal himself,' Curzon was warned
in the same letter, 'as a hero-worshipper of Younghusband and
a bitter despiser of Macdonald') his revelations about the state
of affairs at Lhasa had a marked and immediate effect.

'Am I,' Younghusband had wired in desperation on

25 August, 'to receive orders from the military authorities as to the date of my return?' On 2 September, two days after this telegram reached them and a day or so after Landon left Simla, the Government of India replied: 'You are the head of the Mission, and you can only take orders from the Government of India.' They saw 'no reason whatever' why the Mission should not stay at Lhasa until the middle of October if necessary, but set the 15th of that month as the latest permissible date for departure. A message to the same effect, but more brusquely worded, was simultaneously sent to Macdonald. Both communications were drafted by Ampthill and approved in Council.

Hardly had they been despatched when Younghusband's clear-the-line telegram of 31 August, describing the Mission's efforts to procure warm clothing for the troops, arrived. It had a sting in its tail. Macdonald had told Younghusband that, unless he received orders to the contrary, the Escort would leave Lhasa on 15 September. 'If,' Younghusband threatened, 'my negotiations are not completed by then, I shall in the event of his leaving put myself under Chinese protection.'

This prospect filled the Viceroy with an alarm which would have been even more acute if he had seen with his own eyes the lamentable halberdiers who formed the Amban's bodyguard. 'We cannot,' he wrote to Brodrick on 5 September, 'leave our Envoy to shift for himself in such a way, or humiliate ourselves by letting him beg for the protection of the Chinese. We must support and protect Colonel Younghusband in every way.' And he proceeded to unfold his plan for doing so by the demotion of the Escort Commander—'but to arrange that I have got to persuade Lord Kitchener to my view, which is no easy matter.'

There is, as we have seen, no evidence that Macdonald was originally Kitchener's nominee in the sense that Younghusband was Curzon's; but—partly no doubt because Younghusband *was* so closely identified with his arch-enemy—the Commander-in-Chief lost no opportunity of championing his fellow-Sapper, in whom he repeatedly expressed his entire confidence. A fortnight earlier Ampthill had written to Curzon that the slightest criticism of Macdonald in the Council Chamber 'is enough to make Lord Kitchener and Sir Edmund Elles rise up in arms and deliver a violent counterattack on Younghusband. I have had to protect Younghusband from their fury on at least a score of occasions and to resist their schemes for "breaking" him.'

Kitchener, fortunately for Ampthill, was on tour. On the 4th he wrote, and secured Elles's acceptance of, a memorandum in which, after recapitulating Macdonald's failings and the strain they were imposing on Younghusband, he suggested that Macdonald should be recalled 'at any rate to the base in Chumbi' and that Brander should succeed him in command of the Mission's Escort at Lhasa. Macdonald had, after all, 'thought it proper to supervise' most of the advance from Chumbi; his recall thither would be a logical step and 'a way of letting him down easy.' Kitchener, returning unexpectedly on the following day, even more unexpectedly approved these proposals and embodied them in a telegram to Macdonald.

Macdonald's reply to the Commander in Chief's suggestion —it was not a direct order—has not survived; but it was probably of small interest, for by the time Kitchener's telegram reached Lhasa the Tibetans had accepted Younghusband's terms. Nothing remained to do but to see the treaty signed. The force would be well on its way back to India by the end of the month; its commander doubtless felt reluctant to quit the centre of the stage on the eve of an historic occasion, and at such a moment his superiors could hardly insist on his ill-played part being handed over to an understudy.

CHAPTER TWENTY

The Treaty Signed

'IN spite,' a Foreign Office official wrote plaintively when all was over, 'of the struggles of the Treaty Department, I find that this Agreement has been signed as a *Convention*, our warnings having reached the Government of India too late.' His point was that, technically, international negotiations can culminate in a Convention only when they are carried on between heads of states; treaties made between one Government and another are, or should be, styled Agreements.

It was not, however, the inappropriate title but the un-authorised content of Younghusband's treaty with the Tibetans that led to trouble. In the following summary of the terms of the Convention, as signed by the Tibetans, I have italicised the two items in respect of which Younghusband exceeded his instructions:

Article i. The Tibetan Government undertook to respect the Anglo-Chinese Convention of 1890 and to recognise the frontier of Sikkim as therein defined.

Article ii. Additional trade-marts were to be opened at Gyantse and Gartok.

Article iii. The amendment of the Trade Regulations of 1893 was to receive active consideration.

Article iv. No dues were to be levied on trade from India other than those provided for in a tariff to be agreed upon later.

Article v. Roads leading to the new marts were to be kept open by the Tibetans, and Agents stationed at them to co-operate with the British Agents.

Article vi. Tibet was to pay an indemnity of 750,000 Rupees (£50,000) in seventy-five annual instalments.

Article vii. As security for this indemnity and for the proper operation of the trade-marts, *the British were to occupy the Chumbi Valley until the indemnity had been paid (i.e. for seventy-five years).*

Article viii. All fortifications between Lhasa and the Indian frontier were to be razed.

Article ix. Tibet was to have no dealings of any kind with any Foreign Power without Britain's consent.

A Separate Agreement, outside the Convention but appended to it, *gave the British Agent at Gyantse the right to visit Lhasa* 'to consult with high Chinese and Tibetan officials on such commercial matters of importance as he has found impossible to settle at Gyantse.'

This last item, together with Article vii, was to have serious consequences for Younghusband, and its origins, which are complex, need to be briefly reviewed.

Younghusband had always believed, with Curzon, that the placing of an Agent at Lhasa should be a main aim of British policy in Tibet, where no permanent results would be achieved until this aim had been accomplished. Ten years earlier, as Political Agent in Chitral, he had been stationed, not at the capital, but at Mastuj, sixty-five miles away; had vainly protested at an arrangement which seemed to him dangerously unsound; and in due course had seen his forebodings confirmed by a violent flare-up which British influence was powerless to avert *in absentia.* 'I have always been of the opinion,' he wrote to Curzon at the end of 1903, 'that if I had been kept at Chitral in 1893, instead of being withdrawn to Mastuj, the Chitral campaign need never have been undertaken.' All his experiences in Tibet reinforced his pristine conviction that a Political Agent must be stationed at the centre of affairs.

Such being the main article of his faith, it was inevitable that the embargo placed by the Home Government on the idea of a Lhasa Agent went against the grain, and that Young-husband was ready to snatch at anything that looked like a pretext for disregarding or circumventing his instructions in the matter. The actual sequence of the negotiations provided him, in the end, with some excuse for acting as he did; it is not a complete excuse, but it deserves a fairer hearing than his critics gave it at the time and, indeed, a closer analysis than he himself subjected it to in print.

The terms proposed by the Government of India for a treaty reached Younghusband on 26 June at Gyantse. He was warned clearly that these terms had not been approved by His Majesty's Government; he was to confine himself to 'ascertaining how the Tibetan Government is likely to regard them.' The first of seven conditions envisaged the stationing of an Agent either at Lhasa, or at Gyantse with the right of access to Lhasa.

His Majesty's Government, after indicating in two cautionary telegrams that they were not entirely happy about the Government of India's proposals, produced on 6 July their own formula; it began by stipulating that 'neither at Lhasa nor elsewhere is Resident* to be demanded.' But it ended by stating that the terms would be 'subject to alteration' if an advance to Lhasa became necessary. This advance, it will be remembered, began a week later. In the interim several telegrams exchanged between Gyantse and Simla, and Simla and London, indicated that some modification of the London terms was under consideration; and on 26 July a revised version of them was telegraphed to India. His Majesty's Government still set their face against any demand for an Agent in Tibet; the principal difference between their first thoughts and their second was that a place had been found in the latter for the two Lachung men. This telegram did not reach Younghusband until just before he got to Lhasa on 2 August.

Some time, however, before he received this authorised version, Younghusband had transmitted to Lhasa, through the

* 'Resident' here meant a Political Agent. Trade Agents at the marts to be established were, as will appear, provided for in the London terms.

Tongsa Penlop, a set of terms based on the earlier telegrams about the treaty which had come in; the National Assembly acknowledged the receipt of 'the letter which contains the nine terms of the Convention' in the communication which they sent him on 24 July. These terms, which may for convenience be called the Tongsa Penlop terms, included one item taken from the original Government of India terms—the demand for the Agent at Gyantse to have the right of access to Lhasa. 'I am asking,' Younghusband wrote to his sister Emmie on 22 August, 'what Government of India *proposed*, not what Secretary of State *sanctioned*.' He ought not to have done this.

But the circumstances in which he found himself went far to condone his action. He was working against time. The minds of the Tibetans moved so slowly, especially when digesting unwelcome facts, that it was essential to get the outlines of a treaty into Lhasa as early as possible; and when the Tongsa Penlop terms were dispatched, some time about the middle of July, Younghusband had no means of foretelling what form the final version of the London terms would take. He was gambling on an outside chance that the Home Government would at the last moment see the light and sanction an Agent with access to Lhasa. If this gamble came off it would be difficult, if not impossible, to insert at a late hour an entirely new clause in proposals which the Tibetans had been studying for several weeks; by the time Younghusband knew for certain that his gamble had failed he had seen that the Tibetans were perfectly content to accept the access-to-Lhasa clause, and—his views in the matter being what they were—he could not bring himself to withdraw it.

He knew perfectly well that he was acting *ultra vires*. Two days after the Convention was signed he thus described to his father the background of the 'sealed agreement outside the Treaty' which kept the gates of Lhasa ajar: 'Do not mention a word about this for the S. of S. absolutely forbade my asking for it. I had proposed it at Gyantse. The Government of India had forwarded my proposal to the Secretary of State, and so when on the way here I sent in our terms to the Tibetans

I entered this, for it would have been hard to enter afterwards if the S. of S. *did* sanction it, while if he did *not* it would be [a] useful thing to give way on if I had to make concessions. However as I was able to ram the whole treaty down their throats I left it in—only not letting it appear in the treaty itself but in a separate agreement which may or may not be published or accepted by Government as they like.'

In the matter of the indemnity Younghusband had a clear—or anyhow a much clearer—conscience and deserves from history far more tolerance than he got from his superiors in England. Every version of the instructions which he received on this point is identically worded: 'The occupation of the Chumbi Valley will be the security for the indemnity, and for the fulfilment of the conditions in regard to the trade marts to be opened. The occupation will continue till the payment of the indemnity shall have been completed, or the marts opened effectively for the space of three years, whichever is the latest.' Nobody in London, or indeed in Simla, knew anything about Tibet's capacity to pay a large indemnity. 'Our ignorance of the resources of the country,' Brodrick wrote to Ampthill on 5 August, 'makes it impossible to speak with any certainty;' the whole matter, he went on, must be left to Younghusband's discretion. On 18 August he was relying on a 'substantial' indemnity to save the Government's face, and on 26 August, perking up at the improved news from Tibet, he discerned 'at least a good chance of a treaty, and as Younghusband has a free hand on the indemnity he can decide what will tell most.'

The last four monosyllables echo the war-cry of the reparationists. But it was very far from being Younghusband's purpose to exact from the Tibetans an indemnity which, by virtue either of its size or the manner of its payment, would inflict the maximum hardship on them; his overriding concern was to secure Tibetan adherence to the Convention as a whole, and he was prepared—and had indeed been authorised—to treat the question of the indemnity with a certain amount of flexibility.

The total amount which the Tibetans would have to pay was arrived at by fining them 50,000 Rupees for every day between the date of the attack on the Mission at Chang Lo and the signing of the treaty; the longer this event was delayed, the greater would be their liability. Throughout the negotiations the Tibetans (who made up for their deficiencies as diplomats by their aptitude for commercial bargaining) protested that so large an indemnity was more than they could afford; and by the last days of August an *impasse* had been reached. The Tibetans had agreed to everything else—'to what,' as Younghusband pointed out, 'cost them nothing and was, indeed, to their advantage. . . . The only thing that really cost them anything they were consistently refusing.' The indemnity was a stumbling-block which not only appeared irremovable but (and this did nothing to abate Tibetan stubbornness) grew daily larger to the tune of 50,000 Rupees.

The Secretary of State had laid down that 'the sum demanded should not exceed an amount which, it is believed, will be within the power of the Tibetans to pay, by instalments if necessary, spread over three years. Colonel Younghusband will be guided by circumstances in this matter.' Younghusband used this margin of latitude, first, by offering to extend the period to five years; the Regent replied that the sum would still be beyond their means. Younghusband then indicated that he would consider proposals for payments over an even longer period, or indeed any other reasonable formula which the Tibetans cared to put forward; and on 4 September the Regent came, at the head of a deputation including the Tongsa Penlop and the Nepalese representative, and offered to accept the clause dealing with the indemnity (by now running at 750,000 Rupees) if it could be paid in seventy-five annual instalments.

O'Connor kept them in play while Younghusband pondered the implications of this proposal, which were far-reaching; for they gave Britain the right to occupy for three-quarters of a century a large slice of Tibetan territory which Younghusband himself described as 'the key to Tibet . . . the only strategical

The Potala

The Amban Yu-t'ai

point of value in the whole north-eastern frontier from Kashmir to Burma.' Such an outcome would, he realised, be difficult to reconcile with the pledges which Britain had given, on more than one occasion, to Russia. At last he turned to the Tibetans, made certain that they fully understood the arrangement to which they were committing their country, and accepted their offer. After a short discussion of inessentials the Regent affixed his private seal to the draft Convention.

'I knew that I was not acting within my instructions,' Younghusband wrote afterwards. When the storm of White-hall's indignation broke over his head, Ampthill and the Government of India upheld his conduct: 'we consider,' they wrote to the Secretary of State, 'that Colonel Younghusband used his discretion in very difficult circumstances with great perspicacity and a fearlessness of responsibility which it would be a grave mistake to discourage in any of our Agents.'

What alternatives were open to him? He could not, without jeopardising his prospects of a treaty, go on presenting the Tibetans with a daily lengthening bill which they had refused to meet even when it was much smaller. At any moment the Regent might fade, disgruntled or apprehensive, from the scene; the National Assembly might be attacked by recalcitrance; the Amban might receive orders from Peking to thwart the British aims. Younghusband had a chance of averting all these dangers and securing his main object. Ought he to have refused it? On this point history will find it hard to take the side of his critics.

It can be argued—since the Tibetans had made it plain by about 25 August that they were not prepared to swallow the indemnity in its existing form—that Younghusband should have referred the matter to India and asked for authority to reduce the sum demanded, or to extend the time allowed for paying it, or both. But it took (as the Government of India pointed out in the despatch quoted above) twelve days at the speediest for the telegraph to work between Lhasa and India and back to Lhasa; and in this matter His Majesty's Government would have had to be consulted. How many days Mr

Balfour's Cabinet (few if any of whose members were in London at the end of August) would have taken to reply is imponderable; and it must be remembered that at this juncture Younghusband had strong reasons to fear that Macdonald and the Escort would leave Lhasa on 15 September. It would have taken the best part of three weeks, and probably longer, to get his instructions modified, and he had not got the best part of three weeks to play with. Nor was there any certainty, or even much probability, that they would be modified in such a way as to further his dealings with the Tibetans on a particularly difficult point.

Younghusband had to choose between two courses. He could on his own initiative conclude a treaty, upon two clauses in which he knew that his superiors would look askance; or he could stick to the letter of his instructions, report a dead-lock over the indemnity and ask what he was to do now. If he had followed the second course it is highly improbable that an Anglo-Tibetan Convention would have been signed.

The terms of the treaty having been agreed, Younghusband insisted that it should be signed in the Potala. Throughout Asia, he shrewdly observed, 'few would know what was in the Treaty, but the fact that the British had concluded it in the Potala would be an unmistakable sign that the Tibetans had been compelled to come to terms.' He overruled the objections of the Regent and his colleagues, who argued strongly in favour of a less ostentatious ceremony at the Amban's residence. The date was fixed for 7 September, a day which Tibetan sooth-sayers discovered to be propitious.

Various attempts had been made by the Regent and the Amban to persuade the Dalai Lama to return to his capital; these had failed, and he was now well on his way to Outer Mongolia, in company (it was believed) with Dorjieff. The ever-helpful Amban had recommended to Peking, in a telegram transmitted through British channels, that the Emperor should denounce the Dalai Lama, and this step, for which a precedent

existed,* was taken by the Chinese authorities with a speed
for which no precedent existed; by the end of August the
thirteenth Incarnation, ambling on a shaggy pony across the
north-eastern marches of his domain, had been reduced, at any
rate in Chinese eyes, to the ranks of the priesthood. In Lhasa
the proclamations announcing his degradation were torn down
or, where this was not possible, defiled.

But the Regent would sign the treaty with the Dalai Lama's
seal, and other signatories for Tibet included the Shapés and
representatives of the three great monasteries and of the
National Assembly. A severe critic of the whole expedition
argued afterwards that their signatures had 'no more binding
effect than if the Archbishop of Canterbury and the Chairman
of the London County Council were to sign a new treaty with
France.'† But in Lhasa no doubts as to the constitutional
propriety of the transaction were entertained at the time, or
raised later.

On the morning of 7 September troops lined the route from
the British camp to the Potala; a battery of ten-pounders, with
some blank but more live ammunition in its limbers, took up a
position from which it could with equal convenience fire a salute
or bombard the sacred edifice, for it was feared in military
circles that the outraged lamas might at the last moment
attempt some desperate *coup*. Early in the afternoon Younghusband and Macdonald rode side by side, followed by their
staffs and escorted by the Mounted Infantry, to the main
entrance. They dismounted, and prepared to enter what
certainly was then, and perhaps is still, the most extraordinary
building in the world.

The men and women of their generation regarded the East
as mysterious. They saw Asia as possessing—they almost
willed it to possess—some inner, hidden quality which Europe
lacked. Of what this quality consisted they were not sure.
Wisdom? Spirituality? Ripeness? They could not say; they

* The sixth Dalai Lama was deposed for licentious living.
† A. MacCallum Scott: *The Truth about Tibet*.

knew only that there was *something* there, something of which the proudest among them was prepared to stand in awe.

Lord Curzon was by no means the humblest among them, and he knew a great deal about Asia. Some idea of the spell, strong but nebulous, which that continent exerted may be gained from a speech which he made after an Old Etonian banquet, shortly before leaving for India as Viceroy.

'The East,' he intoned, 'is a University in which the scholar never takes his degree. It is a temple where the suppliant adores but never catches sight of the object of his devotion. It is a journey the goal of which is always in sight but is never attained. There are always learners, always worshippers, always pilgrims. . . .'

The pilgrims who entered the Potala on 7 September 1904 had come a long way. Their goal was the most unattainable in Asia. Here, surely, if anywhere, was to be found the heart of the mystery, or at least an important clue to it. Here, if (and the point is admittedly debatable) Lord Curzon's words meant anything at all, Asia would vouchsafe a flash of self-revelation, would place upon some less esoteric footing her claim to inspire awe. Here, on a solemn occasion, her secret would be disclosed. Alas, nothing of the sort transpired.

The ascent to the great Audience Hall in which the Convention was to be signed was long and steep. The stones which paved it, worn smooth as glass by the bare-foot traffic of the centuries, offered no purchase to the intruders' boots. Skidding, clawing, stumbling, lurching, the British officers and their hob-nailed bodyguard clambered crabwise upwards like men negotiating some device in a fun-fair. Only Macdonald, who always wore a pair of red rubber gumboots, retained his equilibrium and his dignity and was seen for the first time leading an advance.

At last the stone ramp levelled out. They plunged into a network of dark and very dirty corridors, dimly illumined by what are best described as nightlights made of rancid butter. Over the shoulders of the Fusiliers on guard-duty monks peered at them from the shadows. They emerged into the pillared Audience Hall of the Dalai Lama.

It was crowded. On the right were the Tibetans, the Shapés in yellow silk robes and many others richly attired; with them was the Tongsa Penlop in full regalia, attended by myrmidons scarcely less ornate, and matched by Jit Bahadur and his gaudy Nepalese. Opposite, with their cameras to the fore, were drably ranked the khaki-clad British spectators. In the centre a row of tables had been arranged; they had to be large tables to accommodate five copies of the Convention, each consisting of one huge sheet of paper on which the terms were set out in English, Tibetan and Chinese. The place of honour was reserved for Younghusband's own camp-table, covered by a Union Jack which had flown for more than a year outside his tent and is still preserved in Windsor Castle. The wall behind the British Commissioner's chair was garnished with a huge silk curtain, magnificently embroidered.

It was perhaps appropriate that the representative of the Suzerain Power should occupy a seat between the representatives of Britain and Tibet, and thus appear to preside over the ceremony; it was certainly characteristic of Yu-t'ai that he had arranged this nicety. But the proceedings began, and continued, in an atmosphere of amity which was imperilled only when a British officer ignited a flashlight to further the interests of photography; this gravely disconcerted the Tibetans for a moment.

Tea and dried fruits were served. The terms of the Convention were read out in Tibetan, then the process of signing began. There were five Tibetan seals besides the Dalai Lama's to be affixed to each of the five copies—one for Simla, one for Calcutta (where the Government of India wintered), one for London, one for the Chinese Government and one for the British Legation in Peking; the separate agreement covering the British Agent's right of access to Lhasa also had to be signed, and the formalities took a considerable time. Throughout them the Tibetans showed the utmost good humour, giggling and chaffing each other. As for the British spectators, one of them recorded that 'we were rather a rowdy lot and made a beastly noise.'* The atmosphere in the heart of the Dalai Lama's barbaric, holy fastness was nearer to that in the changing-room after a football match between two schools than devotees of the mysterious East would have believed possible.

When the last seal had been affixed Younghusband addressed the assemblage, his words being translated, sentence by sentence, first into Tibetan and then into Chinese. Britain and Tibet, he said, were now at peace. The misunderstandings of the past were over, the foundations of future friendship had been laid. The British had no intention of interfering in Tibet, but the Tibetans must abide by the treaty; the British would observe it rigidly but they would, at need, enforce it no less rigidly. He hoped that peace between the two countries would last for ever, and as a token of goodwill he was asking General Macdonald to release all prisoners of war.

This brought the proceedings to an end; they had lasted an hour and a half. The Tibetans, beaming, crowded round to shake the hands of the British officers. The Amban expressed his pleasure at a reference to Chinese suzerainty which Younghusband had made in his speech. Mr Mitter, Younghusband's Bengali clerk, carefully rolled up the three copies of the Convention which the Mission would take to India. The British were escorted back through insalubrious corridors and out into the sunlight.

The long stone ramp was even harder to negotiate from above than from below; 'it was the funniest sight imaginable to see officers hanging on to the walls, on to the Tommies, on to anything they could catch hold of.'* The monks, watching this exodus from the terraces of the Potala, grinned with unfeigned delight as their strange visitors, cursing and laughing, slithered helter-skelter down the face of the great sanctuary. Out on the edge of the plain the gunners put their shrapnel back in the limbers.

* Officer's diary.

CHAPTER TWENTY-ONE

A Question of Honour

YOUNGHUSBAND reported the signing of the Convention direct to the Secretary of State. His short telegram was amplified two days later by the Acting Viceroy, who summarised the modifications in the authorised terms. Ampthill explained that the arrangements regarding the indemnity had been made at the special request of the Regent. 'Younghusband, after considerable demur, was obliged to give way on this point, having regard to the necessity for obtaining early signature of treaty and to the Tibetans' anxiety to conclude settlement. In the circumstances, he begs for confirmation of his action. Agreement should, in my opinion, be accepted as it stands.' This telegram made no reference to the Separate Agreement dealing with access to Lhasa, for the good reason that the Government of India as yet knew nothing about it; Younghusband reported his action in this matter only in a written despatch, sent off on 9 September. This slightly furtive procedure was almost certainly a mistake.

London's first reactions were enthusiastic. On the 13th Brodrick asked that his 'hearty congratulations' should be conveyed to Younghusband, whose 'action will be generally supported.'* He indicated, however, that His Majesty's Government had reservations about the indemnity clause.

Felicitations poured in. All down the ages it has been the lot of soldiers on active service to feel neglected by the nation for whom they are fighting. Until the Second World War, when

* 'Generally' was an afterthought, inserted in the original text by a later telegram.

improved communications made it much easier than it had ever been before for a sense of grievance at the front to generate a sense of guilt at home, this feeling of being forgotten was accepted as an occupational hazard; the troops no more expected to receive regular evidence that their deeds were appreciated than sailors expected never to lose sight of land. But the more stoically they put up with being forgotten, the more true pleasure they got from finding that they were, after all, remembered; and a laudatory telegram to the whole expedition from King Edward VII—despatched, although he was taking the waters at Marienbad, with no less promptitude than the Secretary of State's from London—gave keen satisfaction.

For Younghusband the ceremony in the Potala was followed by an interlude of relatively carefree relaxation. On the evening after the treaty was signed Macdonald and his staff entertained the Mission to dinner; the Escort Commander, Younghusband told his father, 'made a very nice speech in which he said everybody admired boldness and no one could say I was not bold.' Next day the British released their prisoners of war, giving each a gratuity of five rupees. The Tibetans produced from their oubliettes four spectral figures, two of whom had been incarcerated for befriending the Japanese traveller Kawaguchi and two for helping Sarat Chandra Das, the Bengali spy employed by the Government of India; these last had been kept in chains for nineteen years. 'All,' Younghusband wrote, 'were in abject fear of the Tibetans, bowing double before them. Their cheeks were sunken, their eyes glazed and staring, their expression unchangeably fixed in horror, and their skin as white and dry as paper.' The warm-hearted Candler commented: 'We who looked on these sad relics of humanity felt that their restitution to liberty was in itself sufficient to justify our advance to Lhasa.'

The only fly in the diplomatic ointment was a telegram from the Chinese Government to the Amban forbidding him to sign the Adhesion Agreement, a supplementary instrument designed to secure China's formal recognition of the Anglo-Tibetan

Convention which her representative had done so much to bring about; Peking felt that it 'robbed China of her suzerainty.'

This was a shrewd move—shrewder, probably, than the Chinese Government realised. The last six weeks had seen a marked improvement in the Suzerain Power's position at Lhasa. Yu-t'ai, by jumping on the British bandwagon, had become a key figure in the negotiations; while actively furthering Younghusband's aims, he borrowed some of Younghusband's authority to increase his own and, toadying to the British, was able to browbeat the Tibetans. Younghusband, who as Resident in an Indian Native State had occupied a position comparable to Yu-t'ai's in Tibet, was much struck by his highhandedness. When they visited him the Tibetan leaders, including even the Regent, 'all had to sit on cushions on the ground, while the Amban and his Chinese staff sat on chairs. . . . He did not rise from his chair to receive them, as any British Resident would rise to welcome Indian gentlemen or high officials; he merely acknowledged their salutation on entrance with a barely noticeable inclination of his head. And, in dismissing them, he simply said over his shoulder to his interpreter, "Tell them to go." '

The Emperor's denunciation of the Dalai Lama, engineered by Yu-t'ai, was another feather in his cap. A proclamation which he caused to be posted in the streets three days after the signing of the treaty announced that: 'In future, Tibet being a feudatory of China, the Dalai Lama will be responsible for the yellow-cap faith and monks, and will only be concerned slightly in official matters, while the Amban will conduct all Tibetan affairs with the Tibetan officials; important matters will be referred to the Emperor. . . . You must all understand this and act accordingly, so that no punishment may befall you. You must not transgress my orders.' The fluid and confused situation created by the arrival of the British and the flight of the Dalai Lama was greatly to China's advantage. From her point of view, the longer that situation lasted, and the more fluid and confused it became, the better; and one sure way to prolong and bedevil it was to withhold recognition of the Anglo-Tibetan treaty, thus obliging the British to depart with an agreement which—as with the Sino-British Convention of 1890—only two of the three parties affected by its provisions accepted as valid.

News of the unhelpful Chinese *démarche* did not reach India until 18 September, and a few days later the *Peking Gazette* announced that one T'ang Shao-yi had been deputed to proceed to Tibet 'to investigate and conduct affairs.' Shortly afterwards the British Minister in Peking was informed that T'ang would travel via Calcutta, where the matter of the Adhesion Agreement could be negotiated with the Indian authorities. Younghusband was thus not seriously concerned with a question which clearly could not be resolved in Lhasa. The last news that anyone in India had of Yu-t'ai came from his former subordinate Ho Kuang-hsi who, passing through Darjeeling at the end of October, reported that trouble had arisen in Lhasa over a Tibetan prostitute whom the Amban was keeping; in the resultant disturbances five Chinese and fifteen Tibetans had been killed. This story may not have been even partly true; but it cannot be dismissed as implausible.

The expedition was seven weeks at Lhasa. The numerous records of its sojourn there, private and official, contain much that is of interest; but to anyone who has studied the origins and the development of the Tibetan enterprise nothing is more interesting than what they all omit. There is no mention of the Power whose supposed influence, malign and crescent, in the Forbidden City was the ultimate cause of British soldiers playing breathless football-matches in the shadow of the Potala.

Prominent among the bugbears conjured up by Russophobia was the arsenal at Lhasa, to which, during the advance, references recurred in intelligence reports. 'Younghusband reminds us,' Brodrick was told by Ampthill in May 1904, 'that the arsenal at Lhasa is in charge of the Russian Buryat Dorjieff.' On 30 June Ampthill made a slightly more sophisticated but equally unfounded report to King Edward VII: 'This man Dorjieff is now said to be devoting the whole of his attention to the minting of silver coins at the Lhasa arsenal instead of to the casting of cannons and jingals, and it may be inferred from this circumstance that he meditates flight from Lhasa before the arrival of the Mission.'*

There was an arsenal at Lhasa, and there was a mint. Ottley, who inspected the latter, found that it had been newly built but was equipped with no machinery of any kind. White and Wilton visited the arsenal. It was, Younghusband reported, 'a very small affair, and scarcely, in their opinion, worth destroying;' it contained some English-made lathes, but all the machinery was hand-worked and the fly-wheel was made of wood.

Younghusband, it is true, was shown an undated document purporting to be the draft of a treaty between Russia and China; both parties agreed to protect Tibet, and Russia undertook to provide instructors for the Tibetan army. Scraps of evidence which came to light later from Chinese sources suggest that this document had been drawn up more than ten years earlier, soon after the conclusion of the Convention of 1890. No documentary evidence of more recent Russian activities was found, and Russia was virtually never mentioned by anyone during the long, wide-ranging discussions which preceded the signing of the treaty.

Russian rifles were considerably scarcer than Huntley & Palmer biscuits. In May a translation of Kawaguchi's narrative, describing his three years' wanderings in Tibet, had reached the War Office, who circulated a summary, drawing attention to the passages dealing with 'Russian intrigues.' One such passage told of the arrival at a place fifty miles north of Lhasa of a caravan of two hundred camels coming from the north-east and laden with chests containing 'small fire-arms, bullets and other interesting objects.' During the advance to Lhasa the British war-booty had included only very few weapons of Russian manufacture, and at one stage Younghusband was accounting for their paucity with a theory that the main Tibetan armoury was being held in reserve for the defence of the capital.

* Royal Archives.

The armoury was a fable, the arsenal a false alarm. No trace was discovered of the 'skilled mechanicians' or the military advisers from Asiatic Russia who had been so often postulated in the Mission's reports. The British, having found a mare's nest, conveniently forgot what it was that they had been looking for. Not a drum was heard, not a funeral note, as the Russian bogey was interred.

Brodrick's telegram of congratulations had hardly been despatched when misgivings began to assail him and his colleagues. A further telegram on the same day (13 September) asked Ampthill whether—'without prejudice to the signed agreement'—the amount of the indemnity could be reduced; and on 15 September Brodrick, who three weeks earlier had been hoping for a 'substantial' indemnity, referred in scandalised tones to the sum demanded by Younghusband as 'prodigious'. The real trouble was not the size of the indemnity but the method of its payment; the occupation of the Chumbi Valley for seventy-five years was very far from according either with British policy as defined in the telegram of 6 November 1903 or with the assurances given, in the light of that telegram, to Russia.

'Things got really bad at the Foreign Office,' Brodrick explained to Ampthill in a letter, 'as Lansdowne felt his honour involved.' The Foreign Secretary's minutes echo perturbation and disapproval; 'we are sure to be told that the payments have been spread over this long term in order to give us an excuse for holding on to the Chumbi Valley.' He considered, too, that 'as a *punitive* measure, an indemnity, a great part of which will fall upon the shoulders of an unborn generation, is quite inappropriate.' In a flurried exchange of telegrams between London and India the decision was taken to reduce the indemnity by two-thirds in return for certain concessions, of which the most important was the opening of an additional trade-mart in Eastern Tibet, and to make part of it payable, under a new set of Trade Regulations, by revenue derived from Customs dues; the Chumbi Valley was not to be occupied for more than three years and only a token payment—'say 50,000 Rupees'—was to be exacted before its evacuation.

Meanwhile the Government's perplexities were increased by *The Times*, whose very able Correspondent in Peking, Dr Morrison, got hold of a substantially accurate version of the Convention from the Chinese; this was published in London on 17 September. Oddly enough, the only point on which Morrison was seriously misinformed was the length of time for which the Chumbi Valley was to be occupied; he put it at three years. But even this relatively innocuous version of the true facts brought the Russian Chargé d'Affaires round to the Foreign Office. On being told that *The Times* report was in some respects inaccurate, he reserved his Government's right to protest when the official text was published, and went away. 'It is clear that we shall have a serious controversy,' groaned Lansdowne.

The Germans also raised objections, on the grounds that Article ix gave Britain the status of Most Favoured Nation in a part of the Chinese Empire; America, France and Italy made the same point through their Legations in Peking. On 3 October the harassed India Office was constrained to issue a communiqué, stating 'we are informed that the Convention still awaits ratification by the Viceroy of India, and the terms are not yet finally settled.' Only a few weeks earlier the prospect that the Mission would be forced to leave Lhasa without a treaty had been accepted by His Majesty's Government with fatalistic despondency; the unlooked-for success of the negotiations was now causing them a far keener distress.

Younghusband was unaware of these developments. 'The greatest success of my life has been accomplished and I do not suppose I shall ever have the chance of doing anything bigger,' he wrote to his father on 9 September. A jolly, end-of-term atmosphere pervaded the British camp. On the 14th a convoy arrived with badly needed supplies of whisky, and the different regiments took it in turn to give farewell dinner-parties. The leading citizens of Lhasa attended race-meetings. A Tibetan play was staged in the headquarters of the Mission. It began at half-past six in the morning and unexpectedly proved to be, as one officer recorded, 'quite proper from beginning to end.' But the end was a long time coming; it was not until six o'clock in the evening that the same diarist was able to write 'The play is over, the drum is silent, the cymbals are quiet, and all I can say is THANK GOODNESS.'

On 12 September Ampthill had reported to London that Younghusband hoped to leave Lhasa on the 20th, and on the same day Macdonald was ordered by GHQ to 'roll up' the troops on the line of communications. But in the days that followed there emerged from the frantic interchange of telegrams between London and Simla an impromptu plan for Younghusband to remain in Lhasa with an escort of up to five hundred men after the departure of the main body (now definitely fixed for 23 September), so that he could negotiate the alterations in the treaty upon which London was insisting. A telegram authorising, but not ordering, Younghusband to carry out this plan was despatched from Simla on 16 September, and a further telegram to the same effect three days later. The wording of the second message, in particular, seemed to imply that its originators suspected they were asking the impossible. 'The Government of India,' this telegram ended, 'trust that you will endeavour to meet their wishes on this point.'

It reached Younghusband on the evening of 22 September, a few hours before he was due to quit the city in which he had once pleaded so hard and unavailingly for permission to prolong his stay. This was now the last thing he wished to do. It had taken him more than a year to get a treaty out of the Tibetans; it had been signed with pomp and finality in the Potala and the Tibetans were perfectly satisfied with it. His farewells had been made, gifts exchanged, prayers said for him in the monasteries. To abandon at the eleventh hour the favourable position thus dearly won; to dismantle the treaty and reopen negotiations; to explain to the Tibetans that there had been a mistake, that in the solemn, lasting compact which they had signed some clauses now needed to be changed and other fresh ones inserted

—to attempt this was folly, to accomplish it in three weeks impossible. Such at least were Younghusband's views, and it is difficult to refute them.

For once he had a staunch ally in Macdonald. Five hundred men, or for that matter fifty men, could not be left in Lhasa unless the four-hundred-mile line of communication continued to be manned. For the past ten days the elaborate organisation of posts and depots and the shuttle-services between them had been thinning out; to countermand this process would cause havoc. After discussion with his Escort Commander, Younghusband put the Government of India's telegram in his pocket and rode out of Lhasa on the morning of 23 September. Next day he sent a telegram to India briefly justifying his action on political grounds; he had already outlined the military objections to delaying his departure in an earlier message, despatched on 20 September.

In London—or rather in Ministerial circles, for neither the press nor the public was disposed to undervalue his achievements—feeling against Younghusband hardened with a rapidity for which it is hard to account. In a stuffy telegram on 3 October Brodrick drew Ampthill's attention—for the second time—to the fact that 'Colonel Younghusband . . . has contravened our instructions in a most important respect.' The opportunity to repair matters by reducing the indemnity 'has now unfortunately been lost owing to Colonel Younghusband's departure from Lhasa.' The Convention would have to be amended before it was ratified; 'in the meanwhile we cannot accept the situation created for us by our representative's disobedience to orders.'

The intention to make Younghusband a scapegoat emerges starkly from the correspondence that passed behind the scenes. 'When I consulted my colleagues,' Brodrick wrote to Ampthill on 6 October, 'I found it was held, as I held at first sight, that we must reduce the indemnity and the term [of seventy-five years], but beyond this, we must make it clear that Younghusband had "sold" us.' Two days earlier Brodrick had written to Curzon, Younghusband's patron and supporter: 'It seems impossible to avoid throwing over Younghusband to some extent, and the great point to avoid is the appearance of doing so under pressure from Russia. . . . Arthur Balfour considers the honour of the country is involved in repudiating Younghusband.'

Honour has several meanings, and many unbecoming things have been done in its name. Writing to Younghusband on 10 August, Lionel Cust described an interview with the Prime Minister—'one of the most intimate of personal friends that I have got'—in the course of which he had pressed Younghusband's views about Tibet. Cust, explaining why his advocacy had failed, wrote that Balfour 'has got this unhappy knack of making promises without any necessity, and not only is he unwilling to break them as a man of honour but also the very breaking of them weakens his position as a statesman.'

Balfour's standpoint is made clear in a letter which he wrote from his house in Scotland on 6 October. 'Younghusband, by disobeying our explicit orders, has placed us in a very false position.' The letter went on to rehearse the old arguments against a forward policy in Tibet, particularly in view of the pledges given to Russia, as a direct result of which Britain stood to gain important advantages in Egypt. 'Both in policy and honour,' the Prime Minister wrote, 'we are committed to a non-interventionist policy. . . . It is melancholy to think that, whatever we do now, Colonel Younghusband's indiscretion makes it impossible for us fully to clear ourselves from the very unjust imputation of copying the least creditable methods of Russian diplomacy. The only chance of any permanent arrangement with that Power in Central Asia depends on the mutual confidence that engagements will be adhered to; and if, as I fear, Colonel Younghusband, in acting as he has done, wished to force the hands of the Government (whose policy, doubtless, he disagrees with) he has inflicted upon us an injury compared with which any loss to the material interests affected by our Tibetan policy is absolutely insignificant.'

Mounted Infantry Mess at Lhasa

OTTLEY   WALLACE-DUNLOP   CANDLER
RYBOT   BAILEY

Lhasa Races: Younghusband in the Judge's Box

The Thirteenth Dalai Lama entering Indian territory in 1910

Chinese troops leaving Tibet for repatriation via India in 1913

Throughout a long letter, of which this extract conveys the gist, the Prime Minister's reasoning was lucid and high-minded; he stated with precision the case against Young-husband in terms of the nation's interest. But the significant thing about the letter was that it was addressed to the King's Private Secretary, Lord Knollys, and that it was inspired by Brodrick, 'with regard to whose affairs I am making the present communication.'*

Brodrick had written to Knollys on the previous day (5 October). His letter began: 'As regards Younghusband I am sorry to say that things have taken a very unfavourable turn since Balfour left Balmoral.' On the 4th, Brodrick said, he had heard from Lansdowne that 'a position of very grave embarrassment would be caused with Russia' if the Government did not at once declare their intention of reducing the Tibetan indemnity. Brodrick, who was at Longniddry, not far from Balfour's house at Whittinghame, immediately telegraphed to the Prime Minister, 'who came here and considers that the honour of the country, as well as public policy, is involved; and that we must throw over Younghusband and make it clear that he acted in direct disobedience to orders.' Balfour, he added, would very shortly be writing to Knollys on the subject.

There begins here to emerge an atmosphere of conspiracy; for two days later Brodrick was writing darkly to Ampthill 'Younghusband has got hold of someone near the King, and it will do him no good in this crisis.' Balfour's letter to Knollys, which was purely informative and contained no suggestions or requests, can only (seeing that Brodrick was its instigator) have been written to counteract the influence of that 'someone near the King' through whom, it was feared, Younghusband might plead his cause when the blow fell. Brodrick was taking no chances. He was out for Younghusband's blood. He wished to forestall any possibility of a reprieve for the scapegoat.

The object of his arbitrary but (as it proved) implacable

* Royal Archives.

malevolence was meanwhile riding briskly through the first snowstorms of a Tibetan winter towards the ambush which his superiors in England were preparing for him. Younghusband was still filled with a proud sense of achievement. Six years later he described how, when camp was pitched at the end of their first homeward march, he climbed a hill and looked back towards Lhasa, the scene of his triumph. 'I was insensibly suffused with an almost intoxicating sense of elation and good-will. This exhilaration of the moment grew and grew until it thrilled through me with overpowering intensity. Never again could I think evil, or ever again be at enmity with any man. All nature and all humanity were bathed in a rosy glowing radiancy; and life for the future seemed naught but buoyancy and light.' *

A fortnight later the little cavalcade—the Mission and its escort of Mounted Infantry were travelling ahead of the main body, and at twice its pace—dropped down over the snow-bound Natu La into the warm, lush Tista Valley. 'A scientific gentleman once asked,' Younghusband wrote, 'what was the chief effect of being a long time at high altitudes, and I told him the principal effect was a desire to get back to a lower altitude as soon as possible.' His sense of well-being increased as the strain imposed by the cold and the thin air left him. Sikkim in October seemed like Paradise. A tea-planter played 'See the Conquering Hero Comes' on his gramophone as the column of bearded men on fine-drawn ponies trotted past his bungalow. Younghusband rejoiced in the thought that his wife and child, whom he had not seen for a year, were waiting for him at Darjeeling.

He was only one day's ride away from them when, on the last evening of his long journey, an official envelope was delivered to him. It enclosed Brodrick's telegram of 3 October, forwarded by the Government of India and containing the merciless strictures on the British Commissioner's conduct which have been summarised above. In the matter of the indemnity Younghusband had acted 'in defiance of ex-

* *India and Tibet.*

press instructions.' He had been guilty of further insubordination in leaving Lhasa without attempting to amend the
Convention. The Government which he had served so tire-
lessly found itself unable to accept the situation created by his
disobedience.

For Younghusband the bright day was done.

CHAPTER TWENTY-TWO

The Scapegoat

ON the morning of the next day, 11 October, Younghusband
replied to this communication in a telegram to the Government
of India which showed how bitterly he had been hurt:

> When I reach Simla I hope I shall be able to show that
> I have disobeyed no orders of His Majesty's Government
> which it was practicable for me to carry out and that the
> severe censure now passed by the Secretary of State on
> action which only a week before I left Lhasa he said he
> would support is wholly undeserved. My return to India
> is now marked by a sense of deep regret that I ever con-
> sented to be an agent in carrying out in a time too limited
> to admit of proper reference to London a policy decided
> on in detail by His Majesty's Government before they were
> aware what the political situation in Lhasa was or in what
> circumstances their agent would find himself placed. I
> hope the earliest opportunity will be given me to return to
> England to personally represent the position to the Prime
> Minister and His Majesty the King.

Younghusband's reunion with his wife, and the flattering
welcome given him in Darjeeling, could not dull the pain and
anger that now possessed him. He set off for Simla in a
dangerous mood. At their first encounter Ampthill found him,
as he told Brodrick on 20 October, 'sullen and resentful to a
most unpleasant degree. . . . Those two hours' conversation
with Colonel Younghusband took more out of me than six
hours' routine work.' Mrs Younghusband was 'suffering from

swelled head' and 'in a highly hysterical state.' But the
Ampthills, using tact and sympathy, managed to soothe their
guests, and the Government of India, which had always supported Younghusband as far as Kitchener would allow it to, set
about preparing a despatch which, while admitting that the
British Commissioner had been guilty of a serious error of
judgment in the matter of the indemnity, argued that mitigat-
ing circumstances 'afford sufficient reason for generous con-
donation.'

The Foreign Department produced a first draft which
Ampthill considered 'wretched.' He sat up late rewriting it and
sent it off on 27 October with a private letter to Godley at the
India Office; 'I only want to tell you that it was written by me
in the midst of a fearful liver-attack and headache so that if you
do not like it I hope you will make allowances.'

It was in fact an able document, couched in deferential yet
judicious terms. The same cannot be said of Younghusband's
own memorandum vindicating his conduct, which was forwarded with the despatch. The whole tone of this memorandum was ill-judged. Younghusband stated his case lucidly
enough, but he stated it without a semblance of contrition. To
write, for instance, in such a context that to limit the occupation
of the Chumbi Valley to three years 'is a very serious sacrifice
of the interests of the Government of India,' and to continue with a passage revealing his hope that His Majesty's
Government might still see the light in this matter, was
a cardinal error which he should have had the gumption to
avoid.

Younghusband sought to prove that the censure passed upon
him was undeserved; in this he had the almost unqualified
support of the Government of India, and his arguments were
backed by much telling evidence. He spoilt his case by his
refusal to eat humble pie, his inability to conceal his conviction
that he had been right all along. It would indeed have been
difficult to mollify the vengeful mind of Brodrick; but Younghusband harmed his cause by giving the Secretary of State
an excuse for writing to Ampthill: 'His explanation is not very

convincing . . . his whole tone is impenitent . . . his "apology" is not couched in the least in a tone of regret but of vindication.'

The question of what decoration Younghusband should receive in recognition of his Tibetan services had been under consideration for some time. As early as June the King, who took a close interest in the expedition, had canvassed the question of conferring an honour on Younghusband in the field, but the idea was dropped after his Private Secretary, Knollys, had consulted Brodrick, who in his turn consulted Curzon. Both thought it premature, since the Mission had not reached its destination and Younghusband had as yet had no opportunity of opening negotiations.*

But now that the whole thing was over, the problem of how, if at all, the Sovereign should reward an officer whom his Ministers had reprimanded for an act of disobedience, which they regarded as detrimental to the national interest, had to be solved. Brodrick took an almost morbid interest in it. 'I still hope,' he wrote to Ampthill on 6 October, 'to get an accommodation without too open an *esclandre* but how all this will affect *honours* I know not.' Three weeks later he returned to the subject. 'The question of his receiving *any* decoration must remain undecided until we see how he tumbled into a course of action which is at present inexplicable;' and on 11 November he foresaw that, if Younghusband got anything, it would probably be 'the minimum reward.'

Honours and decorations conferred on members of the Mission and the Escort were to be gazetted in a Special Honours List in December; recommendations from India had therefore to be put in the mails in the preceding month. Ampthill forwarded his to the Secretary of State on 4 November; he recommended Younghusband for a KCB (i.e. a knighthood in the Order of the Bath). Younghusband was already a Companion of the Order of the Indian Empire; merely to promote him one grade in that order to KCIE 'would,' Ampthill

* Royal Archives.

felt, 'be considered shabby and inadequate.' To make him
KCSI (the Order of the Star of India) would give him a higher
distinction, but it would be wrong to reward him less amply
than Macdonald, who had been made a Companion of the
Bath for his services in Africa, and 'who will assuredly receive
the KCB.' Since Younghusband's work in Tibet had been
'Imperial in its character,' he was eligible for this honour; it
had more lustre than the KCIE or the KCSI, which were conferred on deserving officials for purely Indian services. In
those days, within the small society which ran a huge
Empire, these totemistic niceties were of considerable importance.

. Brodrick, for not easily fathomable motives, had embarked
on a vendetta against Younghusband. In demi-official correspondence he took his stand on a point of principle. 'I can see
from your letters,' he wrote to Ampthill on 18 November, 'that
you think we have been a little unreasonably angry about
Younghusband;' but in his view Younghusband had acted not
only wrongly in Tibet but indiscreetly in defending his action
in private letters which criticised the Government's policy as
'unwise and pusillanimous.' Brodrick assured Ampthill that
'when I get your list of Honours, I will try and do what I can to
prevent there being more public discussion than is necessary.
But the feeling that the Indian Civil Service ought to have a
lesson as to behaving as Younghusband has done is very strong
here at present.'

This *pour-encourager-les-autres* feeling (for the existence of
which no other evidence survives) was far from strong in the
breast of the Permanent Under-Secretary of State at the India
Office. Sir Arthur Godley had seen every move in the game
since the Tibetan enterprise was first mooted; he had no axe
to grind, and his were by far the most fair-minded of all the
comments made upon the affair by men in high places. In a
letter to Ampthill on 20 October he hoped that 'the Government will treat Younghusband with as much consideration as
possible in the future. They have snubbed him quite enough—
but he certainly did a foolish thing.' A week later he speculated,

in the same correspondence, on the verdict which the Cabinet
would require the Secretary of State to pass in his final despatch, to be composed after Younghusband's self-defence had
been received.

'I hope,' he wrote to Ampthill, 'that we may be allowed to
make it as appreciative of Younghusband's really important
achievement, and as little harsh towards his errors, as is consistent with a full and fair statement of the case. Four or five
months ago, as I reminded Mr Brodrick, His Majesty's Government were very much inclined to believe that they, in the
person of their envoy, would have to come back from Lhasa
with their tails between their legs, without a treaty, and with
the whole thing to do again next year. The actual situation is a
very different one from this, and I think they ought to show
some gratitude to the man to whom their escape from a very
awkward position is largely due.'

Then Younghusband's defiant apologia arrived, and Godley
received his orders as to the form in which judgment was to be
passed on him. They stuck in his throat. 'Granted,' he wrote
on 11 November, 'that Younghusband did wrong, it seems to
me that there is no sufficient reason for censuring him *in the
despatch*, which is, whether we like it or not, a manifesto *urbi et
orbi*, and which ought to deal with the diplomatic history of
the Tibet expedition . . . and not with our dirty linen. I am
afraid, however, that whatever we draft, the Cabinet will
insist on giving a public wigging to Younghusband, instead
of being content with noting the fact of his having been
thrown over on two points, and with giving him an inferior
decoration.'

Godley, the permanent head of the Department over which
Brodrick presided, knew already that Younghusband was to
receive no higher honour than the 'shabby and inadequate'
KCIE. What he almost certainly did not know was that Brodrick
was intriguing to get a more signal distinction for Brigadier-
General Macdonald. Kitchener had recommended the Escort
Commander for a KCB; and on 28 November Brodrick wrote to
Arnold Forster, who had succeeded him at the War Office, 'As

Macdonald is already CB and we have no *official* knowledge of his being anything but an unqualified success I hardly see how we can avoid a KCB for him.' *

Brodrick's method of championing Macdonald's cause was highly disingenuous. To maintain that he had 'no official knowledge' of Macdonald's shortcomings was the hollowest of pretences. He was allowing, as he revealed to Ampthill, third-hand reports about Younghusband's 'indiscreet' private correspondence after he had left Tibet to influence his ungenerous treatment of Younghusband; yet in seconding Macdonald's claims to recognition he was prepared to suppress the knowledge, derived from the Acting Viceroy's letters to him, that (for instance) at Lhasa the Escort Commander, who had 'undoubtedly gone to pieces,' had been 'a real obstacle to the success of the Mission.' Brodrick's conduct in this matter is curiously unattractive.

For some reason (far the most likely being that the SS *Mongolia*, with Younghusband on board, was due to dock at Tilbury on 3 December) he felt a need for urgency. On 2 December a minute by the Military Secretary on the War Office file recorded that 'Mr Brodrick particularly wanted these honours submitted to the King, if possible—he said—tomorrow;' but honours, the Military Secretary pointed out, could not be gazetted in advance of the despatches describing the services for which they were given. These awaited Curzon's approval. The Viceroy was on his way back to India, and would telegraph from Port Said or Suez; there would have to be a few days' delay. It looked, nevertheless, as if Brodrick was going to get his way; the announcement of Macdonald's promotion to Knight Commander of the Bath went to the printer and appeared in the proofs of the *London Gazette* in which the Tibet honours were due to be published on 16 December.*

Brodrick meanwhile was fighting with great tenacity a rearguard action against the Palace. The King had accepted the advice of Brodrick, supported by Curzon, that it would be premature to give Younghusband a decoration while the

* War Office Archives.

Mission was still at Gyantse; but something about Young-husband's exploits had fired his imagination and he was determined that they should not go unrewarded. Letters from Brodrick to Knollys on 24 September, 5 October and 10 October show that the former was well aware of this ('The King has repeatedly pressed me to submit Younghusband for a decoration'), and the last of these letters suggests that the King had made some concession in the matter to his Secretary of State for India; most probably, he had agreed to await the arrival of Younghusband's explanation of his conduct before reopening the question.*

The King's attitude dashed the hopes, which Brodrick had undoubtedly entertained at an earlier stage, of denying Young-husband any form of recognition. He was however resolved that his scapegoat should get nothing more than the 'minimum reward.' 'I am prepared,' he wrote to Knollys on 3 December (the day after he had supported Macdonald's candidature for a KCB), 'to submit the KCIE, but if a higher decoration is proposed the position in Parliament will be very difficult.' He harked back to the precedent of Sir Redvers Buller, who in 1901, when the first honours for the Boer War were gazetted, had on the King's suggestion been made GCMG. Later in that year Buller, who had returned from South Africa to the Aldershot Command, attempted a public and inept defence of his conduct in Natal, where, carefully though the Spion Kop and Ladysmith despatches had been edited, everyone knew that he had bungled affairs to an almost ludicrous extent. A storm blew up in Parliament, where the Opposition made great play with the Government's inconsistency in giving Buller a Grand Cross of the Order of St Michael and St George for services which, as their own official despatches revealed, had brought disaster after disaster on the troops under his command. As Secretary of State for War Brodrick had borne the brunt of these embarrassing disputations; he was anxious to avoid finding himself in a similar dilemma over Younghusband.

A note on the letter to Knollys in which he made this point

* Royal Archives.

reads: '*Rec'd 6 Dec. Ans'd 6 Dec. King agrees to a* KCIE.'* But although his mind can hardly be described as subtle, King Edward VII was no fool. He knew a good deal, officially and unofficially, about the Tibet expedition. In the Foreign Office archives the original copies of all the more important telegrams are marked for distribution to the King and the Prince of Wales; and in late October 1904 he was being shown by his Assistant Private Secretary, Sir Frederick Ponsonby, certain correspondence from Younghusband in Tibet.

This consisted of letters written by Younghusband to his brother-in-law, Colonel Vesey Dawson; Dawson forwarded them to Ponsonby, who was a friend of his, and Ponsonby showed extracts from them to the King. From the dates, and from the fact that Ponsonby, on the internal evidence of his replies to Dawson, suppressed any passages which seemed to him tendentious, it looks very much as if Younghusband's brother-in-law was the channel through which, after the signing of the Convention, the British Commissioner hoped to place his views on Tibet (not his personal grievance; the letters were written before he knew that he had been censured) before his Sovereign. This tenuous link with royal circles, possibly duplicated by a similar link through Cust, was almost certainly the basis for Brodrick's assertion that 'Younghusband has got hold of someone near the King.'

A letter written by Ponsonby to Dawson on the last day of October indicates that the King felt more than a polite curiosity about the Tibetan venture.

> The King was very much interested in the extract you sent from Younghusband's letter. . . . As the Mission to Tibet has been a subject of the greatest interest to HM, I think he was disappointed at not seeing all the letter but I hinted that all the rest was probably purely private and family business! When the King was in Austria [at Marienbad] he had all the telegrams in full sent in cypher

* Royal Archives.

to him. . . . This I know to my cost as I had to decypher pages every day.

Younghusband was received in audience by the King on 19 December, a fortnight after his return to England. 'I saw him quite alone,' he wrote in *India and Tibet*. 'He placed me in a chair by his desk and then in some indefinable way made it possible for me to speak to him as I would have to my own father. He was himself most outspoken. . . . He was well aware of the deeds, and even character, of individual officers, and he spoke most feelingly of the loss of Major Bretherton.' It is difficult to believe that no allusion was made to Macdonald during this interview, or that Younghusband's opinion of his Escort Commander, however reticently expressed, aroused any doubts in the King's mind as to the wisdom of the unusual action which he had taken a few days earlier. On 15 December, the day before the honours awarded to the Tibet Mission Escort were due to appear in the *London Gazette*, the War Office was notified by the India Office that Macdonald's KCB had been cancelled; the King had decided to confer on him, instead, the KCIE. One at least of Brodrick's cards had been trumped.

War Office,
December, 1904.

The KING has been graciously pleased to give orders for the following promotion in and appointments to the Most Honourable Order of the Bath, in recognition of the services of the undermentioned Officers with the Tibet Mission Escort :—

To be an Ordinary Member of the Military Division of the Second Class, or Knights Commanders, of the said Most Honourable Order, viz. :—

Major and Brevet Colonel (Brigadier-General) James Ronald Leslie Macdonald, C.B., Royal Engineers.

To be Ordinary Members of the Military Division of the Third Class, or Companions, of the said Most Honourable Order, viz. :—

[handwritten annotation in margin: 16 Dec 04 infd. by India Office that he is to receive KCIE]

CHAPTER TWENTY-THREE

A Secret Pamphlet

THE India Office despatch, to the composition of which Godley
looked forward with so little relish, had been completed. It was
printed as a secret document (No. 58), addressed to His Excellency the Right Honourable the Governor General of India in
Council, signed by Brodrick, and dated 2 December 1904. On
the envelope containing his copy of it Younghusband wrote
'*Handed to me in person by Mr Brodrick.*'

To those who have followed my narrative thus far the despatch is of small interest. It gives grudging credit to Younghusband for his achievements, and then recapitulates the strictures already passed on his conduct in official correspondence.
Its closing paragraph seems to be aimed as much at Curzon
as at his Agent. Questions, wrote Brodrick, of Indian frontier
policy could no longer be regarded from an exclusively Indian
point of view, and the course to be pursued in such cases must
be laid down by His Majesty's Government alone. 'It is
essential that this should be borne in mind by those who find
themselves entrusted with the conduct of affairs in which the
external relations of India are involved, and that they should
not allow themselves, under the pressure of the problems which
confront them on the spot, to forget the necessity of conforming
to the instructions which they have received from His Majesty's
Government, who have more immediately before them the
interests of the British Empire as a whole.'

The official effect of the despatch was to register a black
mark against Younghusband's name in the records of the
Government of India, whose servant he was; since, however,

285

virtually all those who read it knew already the main facts of the case, such damage as the despatch was capable of inflicting on Younghusband's career had been done before it was written. Of greater concern to Younghusband, and to his friends, was the Blue Book now being prepared in Whitehall for presentation to Parliament; this collection of documents, the third of a series, covered events in or relating to Tibet from February 1904 until the return of the expedition to India in October. It was in the light of the evidence provided by the Blue Book that Parliament, the public and the press would judge the conduct of the British Commissioner.

Cd. 2370, as this publication was numbered, was edited in a reasonably fair way. All save the most indirect clues to the differences between Younghusband and Macdonald were suppressed by omitting the telegrams in which they occurred; and a similar discretion was observed in regard to the various messages in which Younghusband tendered his resignation. But the Blue Book ended with the condemnatory India Office despatch of 2 December, and included the various antecedent expressions of censure summarised therein, as well as the attempts made by Younghusband and the Government of India to defend his actions. No mention was made of the Cabinet's decision, taken in mid-August, to sack Lhasa and come away with a handful of hostages but without a treaty.*

Brodrick was still pursuing, by dubious methods, his strange campaign against Younghusband. On 28 January 1905 the latter received a confidential letter from H. A. Gwynne, then editor of the *Standard* (and later of the *Morning Post*); the two men were not acquainted, but Gwynne had, a short time previously, sent Younghusband a warning through a mutual friend that the Government meant publicly to call his conduct in question.

Gwynne now reported that he, and doubtless other editors,

---

* This does not imply that available evidence was suppressed. The proceedings of the Cabinet (of which in any case no written record was kept in those days) have never been open to scrutiny by Parliament.

had received a letter from the Secretary of State for India. In it Brodrick announced that the Blue Book was about to be released to the press and went on to provide what would nowadays be called a 'hand-out.' He drew attention to four 'important and governing despatches' (all from his own Department) and summarised the Government's Tibetan policy as revealed in them. The Government's views, 'though repeatedly pressed on the Government of India from the beginning of 1903 . . . did not prevent our representative from pursuing a somewhat more adventurous policy.' He ended by claiming that 'trustworthy evidence' (the archives suggest that he can only have been referring to one inconsequential report from Nepal) indicated that the two clauses in the Convention which the Government had modified 'were the most strongly resented by the Tibetans, and would have certainly led to trouble.'

Gwynne, apart from being an admirer of Younghusband's achievements, was indignant that a Minister of the Crown 'should have used these means to induce newspapers to write in a given sense instead of leaving the verdict to the impartial investigation of the staff.' He was not the only editor to react in this way. Brodrick's shabby stratagem was soon common knowledge in London. A Member of Parliament, Ian Malcolm, obtained Younghusband's consent to ask a question about it in the House; but Younghusband's well-wishers saw more clearly than he did that it would do him no good to be made a 'party shuttlecock,' and the project was abandoned.

The Blue Book, meanwhile, was having a bad press. Lord Roberts wrote to Younghusband: 'I felt sure when I read extracts from it that public opinion would be in your favour, and would deprecate the action taken by the Secretary of State for India.' This was what happened. 'It will,' *The Times* considered, 'be an evil day for the Empire when Ministers at home shall set about to discourage by churlish strictures the readiness of public servants abroad to assume responsibility in cases of extreme difficulty and urgency.' The *Edinburgh Review* spoke for the press as a whole when it wrote: 'What is obvious to everyone who reads the account of the expedition is that if it reflects credit on any one man more than another . . . it is creditable in the highest degree to Colonel Younghusband. It was upon his shoulders that the whole responsibility really lay; it was upon his knowledge and judgment that all really depended; it was owing to his coolness and courage and knowledge of character that the Mission accomplished even so much as it did.'

From India the *Pioneer* made a point which was adumbrated in many editorial comments elsewhere: 'The general trend of public opinion will concur in regretting the unseemliness of the language employed. . . . Assuming it was imperative to negative the action of the Younghusband Mission, it need not have been effected in such a public fashion, nor ought it to have found expression in terms which a headmaster would hesitate to use to his sixth form. . . . Sir Francis Younghusband has been disowned by the Secretary of State; but it is Mr Brodrick himself who stands discredited.'

The central mystery of the whole Tibetan affair is Brodrick's attitude to Younghusband, a man whom he had never met until he handed him, without comment, the despatch which blighted his official career. One has the impression that Brodrick, impelled by some strong but almost certainly subconscious impulse, was striking at Curzon through Younghusband; that the expedition to Tibet and its leader became, and for ever remained, associated in his mind with the bitter animosity which in the short space of two years replaced in both men's hearts their deep-rooted friendship. This impression is strengthened by events belonging to a later period.

Curzon resigned the Viceroyalty, amid a storm of controversy and ill-feeling, in 1905. He died in 1925. His biography by Lord Ronaldshay, in three lucid and judicious volumes, appeared in 1928. It can only have been to this work that Brodrick (by now the Earl of Midleton) referred in a speech which he made at Guildford on 19 November 1930, of which the ostensible purpose was to return thanks for a presentation made to him to commemorate the fiftieth anniversary of his entry into politics.

A SECRET PAMPHLET

'Dissatisfied with the account given in a recent biography,' he said, 'Lord Balfour, not long before his death [in March 1930], laid it on me to make clear at some appropriate moment that it was on no merely personal grounds that his Government had had to terminate Lord Curzon's career as Viceroy of India.' Since the matter had not been debated in Parliament, no full explanation of the facts had ever been given; 'all that was known was that a serious disagreement on a point of military policy had arisen between Lord Curzon and Lord Kitchener.' This, however, was not the crux of the matter; the real trouble was that Curzon 'claimed to direct the foreign policy of India . . . without sufficient regard to its effect on British policy throughout the world.' There followed a reference to Curzon's 'most unfortunate' advice regarding operations in Tibet and Afghanistan.*

This speech, which attracted no attention, contained the first, and for some time the last, faint clue to the existence of a secret pamphlet entitled *Relations of Lord Curzon as Viceroy of India with the British Government, 1902–05*. It is dated May 1926, signed by Brodrick,† and franked 'Seen and approved by the Earl of Balfour, June 1926.' Its main purpose is to prove, or rather to assert, that Curzon's adventurism in Tibet and Afghanistan, combined with his high-handed attitude towards Whitehall, were 'the key to the trouble' which came to a head over Kitchener. The Viceroy is depicted as being 'almost at the end of his tether' as early as 1902, and his conduct as so headstrong and intolerant of control that, even before the storm over Kitchener blew up, he had forfeited the confidence of the Cabinet.

The secondary purpose of this pamphlet is to vindicate at every turn the actions taken by the author as Secretary of State for India. It is full of minor inaccuracies, placing (for instance) Khamba Jong on 'our side of the frontier' and dating the expedition's arrival at Lhasa in July. There is nothing to show for whose eyes it was intended or, indeed, if anyone ever

---

* *The Times*, 20 November 1930.

† To avoid confusion I shall continue to refer to Lord Midleton by the name under which he is already familiar to the reader.

read it at all. It is no longer to be found in the India Office archives.

Brodrick's testimony about events in which he and Curzon were concerned was flawed by more serious defects than an inevitable lack of impartiality. One instance will suffice. In his memoirs he thus described his own reaction, as Secretary of State for War, to Kitchener's appointment as Commander-in-Chief in India: 'The appointment lay with the War Office, and although Curzon did not know it, I had, on strong public grounds, done all in my power to prevent Kitchener going till Curzon had left India.'

Kitchener's appointment, for which Curzon had been pressing, was decided on in principle by the Cabinet in March 1901. Writing shortly afterwards from London, the first Lady Curzon gave her husband this account of Brodrick's attitude in the matter: 'St John did nothing but talk of the huge sacrifice he was making in giving you Kitchener—only friendship and love for you had induced the sacrifice. If he hadn't been where he was [at the War Office] you would never have got him. Only you might have written your case to urge this appointment to *him* and not to George Hamilton [Secretary of State for India].'*

It is clear that Brodrick was deceiving either Lady Curzon in 1901, or his readers in 1939, on a point of some importance. A man who gives two diametrically opposite accounts of his own conduct, the first to the wife of his oldest friend and the second, forty years later, to the world at large, can hardly be accepted as a witness of truth at any intermediate stage in his career; and there is a disingenuous flavour about Brodrick's references to the secret pamphlet in which the termination of Curzon's Vice-royalty was reappraised after the lapse of nearly a quarter of a century.

In April 1939 a series of extracts from Brodrick's memoirs was published in *The Times*. Younghusband (whose example was followed by O'Connor and by Curzon's brother) wrote a letter

* Ravensdale-Metcalfe MSS.

to the Editor challenging, in good-humoured terms, Brodrick's version of the Tibetan affair and its effect on his relations with Curzon. Brodrick replied that 'Sir Francis Younghusband has obscured the facts by reducing them to a personal difference between Lord Curzon and myself,' and claimed that what he had written was based on 'an official record drawn up and printed, at Lord Balfour's instance, after careful review of the correspondence by Indian officials, in case at any time doubt should arise as to the action of his Cabinet.'

This gives an impression of the pamphlet's status which is not only misleading but at variance with Brodrick's own account of it in his memoirs, where he admitted to writing it himself but said that it had been 'reviewed by the then head of the India Office, and accepted in every respect by Balfour himself.' The text, as the reader will have gathered, shows no sign of having been based on a 'careful review of the correspondence;' it makes only a shallow pretence of impartiality, and contains matter which can scarcely have been the fruits of intradepartmental research, such as a slighting reference to the first Lady Curzon who, 'though possessing many brilliant qualities, had not been brought up in England and had none of the traditional knowledge that many Englishwomen possess of the "give and take" of public life.'

The reader is by now a long way from Tibet, and from the year 1904. But to me it seems that the hounding of Younghusband can only be explained as a by-product of Brodrick's breach with Curzon; and on this breach some indirect light is thrown by the secret pamphlet of 1926, which ends with an expression of its author's sorrow at 'having been forced to play the leading part in a struggle which warred with all his private sympathies and personal inclination.'

Whether Balfour ever 'laid it upon' Brodrick to make public the matter contained in the pamphlet 'at an appropriate moment,' and why Brodrick regarded the celebration of his fiftieth year in politics as constituting such a moment, are matters for speculation. What seems probable is that, four years earlier, Brodrick took the initiative in promoting the compilation of the pamphlet. What is certain is that he compiled it. Why? Curzon was dead. Kitchener was dead. Whence came the impulse to place in a new and spurious perspective the events of more than twenty years ago?

The most likely explanation is that in May 1926 Brodrick had reason to fear the publication, in the legal rather than the commercial sense of that word, of some of Curzon's private papers dealing with his Viceroyalty. On its termination there had been a grave danger that Curzon, transfused with *saeva indignatio*, would make known the inner and far from savoury history of his combat with Kitchener; in such a record Brodrick, 'the man who brought about my downfall,' would have been roughly handled. This danger was averted, in September 1905, by the intervention of the King.*

But Brodrick, according to his memoirs, knew of the existence of 'a document of 400 pages prepared for publication, justifying his [Curzon's] action *vis à vis* Kitchener.' There was clearly a risk that this bombshell might burst after Curzon's death. Brodrick would have been the chief of the surviving targets for Curzon's posthumous wrath, but Balfour would not have come off unscathed. Balfour, left to himself, would have awaited the explosion with equanimity; but he would have been unlikely to deny the more vulnerable Brodrick an opportunity for creating among the archives some semblance of a blast-proof shelter.

The part which Brodrick played in the Kitchener controversy had, at the time, struck even Curzon's critics as unbecoming. Many of them agreed with *The Times* in finding the tone of a key despatch from the India Office 'unnecessarily harsh;' and by an ex-Viceroy, Lord Ripon, it was described to the House of Lords as being 'framed in language in which no Viceroy of India ought to be addressed.'† If the spotlight of public interest was going to be focused again on Curzon's Viceroyalty, Brodrick had strong motives for deflecting it from the fatal wrangle

* Ronaldshay, Vol. II.
† *Ibid.*

with Kitchener on to the earlier disagreements—more Imperial, more impersonal—over Tibet and Afghanistan.

This, at any rate, is what his pamphlet attempted to do. Whether it was a feeling of guilt, or inadequacy, or personal loss that Brodrick hoped to sublimate by recording that Curzon was 'almost at the end of his tether,' and implying that his Viceroyalty was already doomed, before he himself took over the India Office, there are no means of telling. But that is what he did record and imply. This curious pamphlet bears out the impression that Brodrick was obsessed by the mutilation of his friendship with Curzon, and that Younghusband was not far from a simplified version of the truth when he wrote to the Editor of *The Times* on 17 April 1939 that 'the mutual indignation of these two great men spilt over on to my poor head.'

Epilogue

A CHRONICLER with a romantic turn of mind might be tempted to suggest that Tibet placed some kind of curse on her invaders. They came, they conquered, they saw what only a handful of white men had seen before; but those who led them or who sent them to Lhasa did not prosper. Curzon suffered downfall and bereavement. Balfour's Government foundered. Brodrick was haunted by his part in the affair. Macdonald ended his career in command of the puny garrison of Mauritius. Younghusband's services were soon lost to the Empire in which he passionately believed. Did, perhaps, the violated arcana of Asia exact their revenge?

Although in the transactions of the human race almost nothing can be dismissed as impossible, this seems most unlikely. Curzon's rule in India had, from the first, almost as little chance of ending happily as Coriolanus's rule in Rome. As for Mr Balfour and his colleagues, it can scarcely be held that in December 1905 some mystic effluence from the Potala swayed the sympathies of the British electorate towards the Liberal Party. Brodrick's muddled malice was not implanted in him by demoniac agents of the lamaist pantheon. Younghusband, who dedicated the rest of his life to loftier ideals than those of Empire, cut a far from hag-ridden figure as, serene and unembittered, he set out to explore the uplands of his own and other men's religions. Anyone who feels that history can usefully be interpreted in the light of mumbo-jumbo will find it easier to follow a converse line of thought, and to argue that it was the British who laid a curse upon Tibet.

In 1906 Younghusband was back in India. His long career on the Frontier ended mellowly in Kashmir. The Residency was a plum; 'it must surely be,' he wrote, 'the most delightful appointment in the whole world.' For four years he presided sagaciously over the pleasant valleys to which, on his earlier expeditions across the mountains beyond them, he had so often looked with yearning. When his tour of duty finished he resigned from the Government of India's service, in which he had spent twenty-eight years. He was forty-seven.

It may be that he discerned few prospects for advancement in a hierarchy for whose highest posts the administrator-bureaucrat was considered to be better qualified than the frontier officer; but his main motives were the reverse of worldly. Since early manhood Younghusband had felt strongly drawn to a spiritual life; in Chitral in 1894 he wrote 'I began to make religion the first interest of my life,' and thereafter he was intermittently but keenly aware of 'the feeling that I was born for some great thing. . . . It wants an exploring spirit to go on in front and show men the way across the unknown. . . . The feeling of being tied to Government service makes me long to leave it and be free and unfettered.'

It was not the contemplative existence that he craved. The mystic was still a thruster. He believed that destiny had selected him for the leadership of a crusade which would break down the barriers between the established religions and enable all mankind, by reaching out to a Divine Spirit animating the whole universe, to attain to higher things. Younghusband was a seer rather than a thinker, a vessel for mystical experience rather than a philosopher. 'The man,' wrote one of his obituarists, 'was greater than his message.' To decypher that message, which though always luminous is often obscure, is beyond the scope of my narrative; but its bearer became, in 1933, the founder of the World Congress of Faiths, an organisation through which some of the leaders of most of the world's religions strove, and still strive, to establish the ideals of love and unity so vividly apprehended by Younghusband.

Fate was less than generous to him after his retirement. In 1911 a serious motor accident in Switzerland almost ended his life; the slow and painful recovery took two years to complete.

In 1914 he made a tour of America, meeting among others Theodore Roosevelt ('he would have made a great explorer if he had not thrown himself away in politics'). In the First World War the India Office could find no active employment for him, but he obtained a staff appointment dealing with what would nowadays be called public relations and for his services was promoted to KCSI.

After the War he became President of the Royal Geographical Society, and in that capacity fathered all the early Everest expeditions. It was a task for which he was exceptionally well qualified. Mountaineers and ex-mountaineers are not always at their best in committee; Younghusband's leadership overcame countless obstacles to the launching of the expeditions and remained an inspiration to the climbers in adversity. It is perhaps needless to say that the perfectionist strongly deprecated the use of oxygen.

In his later years the spiritual crusade increasingly absorbed his energies. He worked for reconciliation between Christians and Hindus, Buddhists and Muslims: between man and whatever force it was that made him. He never became a crank; he remained what he had always been—an idealist, clear-eyed, clear-headed and in some ways childlike. Many saw him as a kind of saint; and because of what he was, and the way he did things, the new, worthy, nebulous causes he espoused acquired a standing—and perhaps also a sort of glow—which without him they might have lacked. He never led his second mission to its Lhasa; but he got a lot of people as far as Khamba Jong.

He was in London in 1940, undismayed by the German bombs and seeking, as at Tuna, solace in daybreak walks round a different kind of desolation. 'The sunrises are not so clear and delicate as the Himalayan sunrises, but still they are very beautiful, and it is lovely to see London in this state of tranquillity right in the midst of this great battle for civilization.' He did not spare himself, and in July 1942, after opening, in the teeth of war-time difficulties, a meeting of the World Congress of Faiths in Birmingham, he had a severe stroke.

He was taken to a friend's house at Lytchett Minster in

Dorset and died there p...
seventy-nine. He was buri...
a gravestone bearing a bas-re...
'Blessed are the pure in heart, fo...
coffin was placed an image of Buddh...
had given him on the morning he left...
that 'he treasured that little image more...
possessions.' One of his closest colleagues re...
'the happiest person I have ever come across.'

However high a value is placed on the extraneous...
which the British Government derived from emascu...
Younghusband's treaty, it cannot be denied that their act...
led to a steady deterioration, a sort of crumbling, in Britain's
new, hard-won and scrupulously restricted position in Tibet.
'The main result, diplomatically, of the Younghusband Mission, which was designed to bring Tibet and the Indian Government closer together, was to make it even more difficult than it
had been before for the British to make their influence felt at
Lhasa.'* This began to appear while the rearguards of the
Escort, obstructed by blizzards and tortured (for most of them
had long ago lost their goggles) by snow-blindness, were still
struggling over the passes into Sikkim.

From Gyantse, where he was left as Trade Agent, O'Connor
reported a minor shooting affray to the Foreign Department;
he said that he attached little importance to it but would hold
the Lhasa officials responsible. The Government of India's
prompt reply showed how strictly it was fettered by the
amended Convention. O'Connor was told that there was no
objection to his mentioning the incident to Lhasa—'but remember that you are not a Political Officer, but only a Trade Agent,
and cannot insist on the Tibetan Government taking any
particular action, or even urge them to do so, without sanction
of the Government of India, whose orders you must always
obtain.' These were derisory spoils to bring back from a long
campaign.

* Lamb.

eacefully a week later, at the age of
d in the little churchyard, under
lief of Lhasa and the epitaph
they shall see God.' On his
a which the Ti Rimpoche
Lhasa. A friend wrote
than all his earthly
nembered him as

benefits
lating
ion

t avert-
a myth,
g which
t is true,
d up' to
ted with
d other
country
ood, the
ly under-
genuine
een laid.
returned
in north-
er 1904:
y by the
ith them.
he people
s; all this

gradually changed until during the latter half of our journey
we have been welcomed everywhere and given the best of
everything.'

But the immediate beneficiary of the enterprise which Curzon
sponsored was the Power whose Tibetan pretensions he had
derided as a 'constitutional fiction.' The British, by expelling
the thirteenth Dalai Lama, had recreated those conditions of
leaderless disunity which best suited Chinese policy and which,
thanks to the early deaths of the ninth, tenth, eleventh and
twelfth Incarnations,* had obtained for almost a century; they
had moreover expelled him, via Mongolia, towards Peking,
where he could be taught a lesson. And they had abrogated the
right, procured for them by Younghusband, to keep an eye on
affairs at Lhasa. 'Hence,' writes Lamb, 'the most apparent
result of the Younghusband Mission . . . was to lay Tibet open
to a reassertion of Chinese authority.'

* At the ages of eleven, twenty-three, seventeen and twenty. Poisoning
was suspected in each case.

EPILOGUE

Inside Tibet China's methods were clumsy and brutal, but outside it she played her hand with considerable skill. The strongest card in it was Britain's need for her signature to the Adhesion Agreement. This, after being promoted to a Convention, was eventually signed in Peking in April 1906. The effect of its six articles was to modify in China's favour the terms of Younghusband's treaty, already modified in Tibet's. Tibet was not a party to the new Convention, no Tibetan representative was present during the negotiations, and it is doubtful whether more than half a dozen men out of a population of three million knew what it meant or could be made to imply.

But Lhasa was once more a Forbidden City, and the manner in which the Chinese exploited their minor diplomatic success is well summarised by a close student of the period. 'Great Britain having intentionally denied herself the right of keeping in close touch with the Tibetan Government by stationing a British representative at Lhasa, the Chinese were able to carry out their plans without any opposition. The Tibetans were gradually led to believe that, though the Peking Government had not had time to send an army to expel the British from Tibet at the time of the 1904 expedition, yet it was fear of Chinese displeasure which led the British to withdraw their troops immediately after signing the Treaty; and that China had since compelled Great Britain to sign another Agreement cancelling the Lhasa Convention, acknowledging the right of the Chinese to control Tibet, and prohibiting all intercourse between British and Tibetans except through the medium of the Chinese authorities.' *

China further strengthened her position as the sole patron of Tibetan interests by insisting that she, and not her vassal, was responsible for paying the indemnity about which there had been such a fuss in 1904. In this matter the British were out-manoeuvred. The cheques were indeed handed over (the last of them in 1908) by a Tibetan official, but—as when a child presents its nanny with a Christmas gift bought for the occasion

* Teichman: *Travels of a Consular Officer in Eastern Tibet.*

by its mother—the illusion thus created was perfunctory. The Amban saw to it that nobody in Lhasa was taken in.

Meanwhile yet another nail was being driven into the coffin of Curzon's trans-Himalayan aspirations. The Anglo-Russian Convention, signed in St Petersburg in 1907, had as its object the removal of causes of friction in Central Asia between the two countries. It effect was to delimit Afghanistan, Persia and Tibet as spheres of, so to speak, mutual disinterest; it brought the Great Game to an end by declaring the playing-fields out of bounds. It was in many ways an admirable agreement, to which both parties loyally adhered. Britain's gains were substantial, for not only was the threat of aggression against India's frontiers neutralised but Russia was thereby deprived of a diplomatic blunt instrument which she had wielded to good effect for the best part of a century.*

For Tibet the consequences of the Anglo-Russian Convention were less happy, since its signatories undertook to negotiate on Tibetan matters only through the Suzerain Power, and the agreement thus reaffirmed and in a sense sanctified China's already dominant position. Peking, moreover, not having been consulted about a Convention which dealt with part of the Chinese Empire, had lost face and expressed resentment by invigorating the campaign of pin-pricks which she was now in a position to wage against the tiny British bridgeheads in Western Tibet. These were sharply contracted in 1908 when, the last instalment of the indemnity having been paid, British forces were withdrawn from the Chumbi Valley; they comprised only four companies of infantry and a dozen policemen.

In the same year a fresh set of Trade Regulations was drawn up; 'their general effect,' wrote Sir Charles Bell, 'was still further to push British and Indians out of Tibet.'† Even pilgrims could now go no further than Gyantse, where Tibetan officials were soon being ordered to seek Chinese permission before accepting social invitations from the British Trade Agent,

* For an analysis of the Convention's wider, European implications see Sir Harold Nicolson: *Sir Arthur Nicolson, Bart., First Lord Carnock*, Chapter IX.
† *Tibet Past and Present.*

who for his part was obliged to buy all his local supplies through
Chinese middlemen. Little remained of Younghusband's treaty
save the telegraph-line which had bedevilled its negotiation.

The main Chinese reaction to the success of the Younghusband Mission was however not diplomatic but military, and it
took place not in Western but Eastern Tibet. In this always
turbulent territory a revolt broke out in the spring of 1905 and
spread southward to the Yunnan border in the months that
followed. Chinese officials were killed, several French missionaries and one English botanist were massacred, small Chinese
punitive forces were defeated in detail. Peking despatched
Chao Erh-feng, a ruthless but an able commander, to restore
order in the area.

In this he was successful. After three years of battle, bribery
and betrayal the dissident monasteries were subdued; the important centres of Batang, Derge, Chamdo and Traya were in
Chinese hands; and most of the large slice of Tibetan territory
now known as the Chinese province of Sikang had been in-
corporated into the Empire. The occupied districts were ruled
with great severity and a complete disregard for the feelings of
their traditionally-minded and deeply religious population.
Lamaseries were razed, monks butchered or degraded. Hereditary princedoms were extinguished. The Tibetans were
ordered to shave their heads and grow pigtails as a symbol of
their allegiance to the Emperor, and both sexes were enjoined
to wear trousers 'in the interests of morality.' A swingeing
land-tax was levied. Tibetan officials were made to learn
Chinese. Large-scale Chinese immigration was planned.

By the end of 1909 it was apparent that the Peking Government had designs on Lhasa. The Government of India received, and refused, a request for transit-facilities for Chinese
troops destined for Tibet. The Amban gave notice to the
Tibetan authorities that not more than a thousand of Chao
Erh-feng's soldiers were being brought to the capital to provide
garrisons for Gyantse, Phari and other places in Western Tibet.
In February 1910 a force of twice that size, advancing almost

unopposed from Chamdo, entered Lhasa. The Dalai Lama, who had returned from his long exile less than six weeks earlier, once more took flight. This time he fled not from the British but to them.

Since July 1904 the Dalai Lama's wanderings had been extensive and aimless. His stay in Urga (now known as Ulan Bator), the seat of another and only slightly less exalted Incarnation, imposed upon the faithful in Mongolia a strain roughly comparable to that which the Church in the north of England would have undergone if a mediaeval Archbishop of Canterbury had sought political asylum in York; his sojourn in Outer Mongolia, the British Legation in Peking reported in April 1905, was 'ruining the local Incarnate Buddha or Bogdo Lama both in revenues and reputation.'

Early in 1906 he removed to Kumbum, a great monastery not far from the Kokonor in North East Tibet; thence, after two years in retreat, he gravitated to Peking. Only one of his predecessors (or rather, to speak correctly, of his earlier embodiments) had visited the Chinese capital. For the fifth Dalai Lama—'the Great Fifth,' as he is still known in Tibet—a special ramp had been built on which his palanquin was carried over the city-walls, since it would have been unfitting for him to pass underneath gate-towers which were frequented by ordinary mortals; the Emperor descended from his throne and advanced eighteen paces to meet him. The thirteenth Incarnation, who arrived by train, was received with less ample ceremony. He was obliged to kneel to the Emperor (after eight days' argument they excused him from kowtowing) and to his honorific titles was added one meaning 'Loyally Submissive.' He had, under Chinese supervision, a number of inconclusive contacts with the diplomatic representatives of the Powers; the British Minister, to whom he gave a pound of jujubes intended to promote longevity, found him in a conciliatory mood. On 21 December 1908 he left Peking. By the time he reached Lhasa a year later his country was in turmoil and his capital threatened; a series of messages appealing to foreign Governments for help, mostly transmitted through the British Agent at Gyantse, brought no response. Early in February 1910 the thirteenth Incarnation slipped out of Lhasa with Chinese troops at his heels; fifty years later history was to repeat itself, save that the pursuers of the fourteenth Incarnation were not Imperialists but Communists.

The Dalai Lama's bodyguard fought a successful rearguard action at the Chaksam ferry, in which they claimed to have killed seventy Chinese for the loss of two of their own number; the latter figure may well have been accurate. The fugitives made swift progress to Sikkim, and a week after leaving the capital rode, late at night, into Gnatong. Here there was a telegraph-station manned by two British sergeants called Luff and Humphreys. Aroused from sleep by their servants with surprising news, they emerged from their hut to find a bedraggled posse of fur-clad horsemen awaiting them in the uncertain light of a hurricane-lantern. It was in its way an historic moment, this nocturnal encounter between the fleeing God-King and the army which, six years earlier, had expelled him from his domains. Sergeant Luff rose to the occasion. 'Which of you blighters,' he demanded, 'is the Dalai Lama?'*

The two sergeants made their august visitor as comfortable as they could, and next morning, with bayonets fixed and buttons gleaming, escorted him three miles along the road to Kalimpong. He reached Darjeeling on 24 February 1910 and on the following day was, for the second time, deposed by the Chinese Government in an edict which sweepingly described him as 'proud, extravagant, lewd, slothful, vicious and perverse.'

In India the Dalai Lama found asylum for himself but no support for his cause. The Government of India provided him with a house at Darjeeling and attached to him as mentor Sir Charles Bell, a gentle, wise official who had seen much service on the Tibetan frontier and spoke the language well. But the Home Government refused to sponsor even the mildest diplomatic counteraction to China's forward policy in Tibet, although this placed in still further jeopardy what was left of

* Bell: *Portrait of the Dalai Lama.*

British interests there; and Bell had the invidious task of informing the Dalai Lama that Britain recognised the puppet administration set up in Lhasa as the *de facto* Government of his realm. 'The Tibetans,' Bell commented, 'were abandoned to Chinese aggression, an aggression for which the British Military Expedition to Lhasa and subsequent retreat were primarily responsible.' For a year the Chinese grip on Tibet was tighter than it had ever been before, and they were taking a keen and equivocal interest in the affairs of Nepal and Bhutan.

In 1911, however, the Manchu Dynasty was overthrown, and China was plunged into chaos from which she emerged as a precarious Republic. The Lhasa garrison mutinied and a situation of the utmost confusion developed. The Chinese fought fitfully among themselves, both sides being aided, from motives of expediency, by various Tibetan factions, some of whose forces were led by Chinese officers. In June 1912 the Dalai Lama (to whom the Chinese almost immediately restored his titles) returned to Tibet, and the fighting, which had by now taken on a more clear-cut, international character, gradually petered out. In January 1913 the last Chinese troops marched out of Lhasa, destined for internment in India pending repatriation. The sequence of events which Curzon had set in motion ten years earlier was at an end.

It is beyond the scope of this work to follow subsequent developments in Tibet, but a brief outline of them may be of service to the reader. The collapse of Chinese authority at Lhasa was followed by three and a half decades of Tibetan independence. Although not without its alarms and disturbances, the period was on the whole a happy one for Tibet, and throughout it Britain acted as a kind of *concierge*, discouraging unwelcome visitors, passing on news from the outside world and keeping herself informed of what went on upstairs. Cartographers ceased to show Tibet as a part of China. It began to look as if the country, with its strange blend of barbarism and spirituality, of mystery and jolly squalor, was going to become a sort of Asiatic Switzerland, neutral, uncommitted, free.

EPILOGUE

At the moment when she lost control of Tibet, China was bent on up-grading her status there; as an Empire she had never claimed more than suzerainty, as a Republic (in whose National Assembly seats were allotted to Tibetan delegates) she enlarged this claim to one of sovereignty. The gesture was ill-timed. At the Simla Conference, promoted by Britain in 1914 and designed to reimpose upon the altered state of Tibetan affairs a recognisable and accepted pattern, Tibet's representative was a plenipotentiary, co-equal with his Chinese and British colleagues. The resultant Convention distinguished between 'Outer Tibet'—the region, including Lhasa, nearest to India—which was to be autonomous, and to the east of it 'Inner Tibet,' where China could exercise her suzerain rights with greater latitude.

All three plenipotentiaries initialled the Convention after six months of discussion, but the Chinese delegate was promptly forbidden by Peking to append his full signature. Thereupon Britain and Tibet announced that they regarded themselves as bound by the Convention, but that China would be debarred from enjoying the rights and privileges which it conferred on her until she signed it. Its terms are now of little more than academic interest: except, perhaps, to readers of this narrative, for one article secured for the British Agent at Gyantse the right of access to Lhasa. The wording used is almost identical with that of Younghusband's Separate Agreement, so hotly disavowed by the British Government ten years earlier.

Interest in Tibet languished during the First World War. The country's eastern marches were still under military pressure from China, but the Dalai Lama, mindful of the kindness he had been shown in India, offered a thousand soldiers to fight on the British side against Germany. The offer was declined, but throughout the war special services to invoke divine aid for Britain's cause were held in the main monasteries of Tibet. This was not a perfunctory gesture. These services were a charge, and not a light one, on public funds, and the Tibetans believed firmly in their efficacy and importance—so much so, indeed, that the Dalai Lama privately transferred to,

as it were, the British account a number of services ostensibly
held on behalf of the Tibetan Government; this was done, he
told Bell, to avoid causing 'needless alarm,' presumably by
creating the impression that the British must be on their last
legs if they needed praying for so often.

When Japan invaded China in 1937 Tibet's response to her
former Suzerain's pressing need for help was less open-handed
and perhaps less spontaneous; she sent 50,000 sheepskins to
China but made no offer of troops.

Between the two World Wars China strove, with scant success, to re-establish her hold over Tibet. In the twenties the
new Republic was weak and disunited, in the thirties its energies
were increasingly absorbed by Japanese aggression. In so far
as Tibet was subject to any foreign influence, she was subject to
Britain's. Tibetan youths went to school in India—four even
went to England; the Tibetan army was trained and equipped
on British lines, and was soon able to hold its own against the
Chinese in the fighting which flickered on in Eastern Tibet.

But British policy towards Tibet continued to be charac-
terised by a caution which seems to have been based as much
on instinct as on reason. It was not until 1920 that Bell, who
had spent several years as Agent at Gyantse, was allowed to
accept one of the pressing invitations to visit Lhasa which he
received at regular intervals from his old friend the Dalai
Lama. The Government of India gravely prejudiced Tibet's
security by refusing for a long time to sell her munitions, and
was slow in acceding to her requests that the telegraph should
be extended from Gyantse to Lhasa. It was not until 1936 that
a British Agent for the first time took up residence in Lhasa;
his post, though described as 'temporary,' came to be tacitly
accepted as a permanent one. The Dalai Lama had died two
years earlier; the fourteenth Incarnation was installed in 1940.

Although Japan made an attempt, through a lama living in
Peking, to induce Tibet to join the 'Great East Asia Co-Pros-
perity Sphere,' as she styled the vast but short-lived empire
created by her conquests, the country was not directly affected

by the Second World War. Nor did the end of British rule in India in 1947 produce any immediate consequences; the Indian Government, which inherited Britain's loosely defined responsibilities and privileges together with the various treaties on which they were based, wisely retained the services of H. E. Richardson, the last British Agent in Lhasa.

Two years later the Chinese Communists ousted the Nationalists from the mainland to Formosa, and the Tibetans took the opportunity to extrude the latter's representatives from Lhasa. But the victors in China were already making known their intention to liberate Tibet from her Imperialist bonds. The international horizon was darkened by the war in Korea. The Tibetan Government tried, tardily and without success, to send a delegation to Peking in the hope of salvaging some of its threatened independence.

But the Red Army was already on the march. Western Tibet was invaded from Sinkiang by way (this fact escaped notice at the time) of Indian territory in Ladakh; two other forces, advancing from Chinghai and Szechwan, joined hands at Chamdo, where they halted for the winter. India protested weakly and unavailingly; 'Tibet,' claimed Peking, 'is an integral part of China and the Tibetan issue is an entirely domestic problem.' At the United Nations a Tibetan appeal for intercession was put on the agenda by the small Central American Republic of El Salvador. Although Britain and, still more, India had a clear moral responsibility, nobody took any practical interest in the matter, and the Chinese Nationalist delegate, while deploring the Communists' aggression, supported their contention that Tibet belonged to China. Her armies, no longer opposed, entered Lhasa in September 1951.

Thus a chapter in the history of Asia ended in a manner which would have surprised Lord Curzon and saddened Sir Francis Younghusband. The liberties of a small nation were extinguished, their prized religion set in disarray, their ruler driven—eight years later—into exile. The buffer-state, whose existence as such had for so long been regarded as indispensable to the security of India's North East Frontier, disappeared almost overnight. For India the strategic problem thus created may be compared with that which suddenly faced Soviet Russia when in 1931 the Japanese Army seized Manchuria and converted the tilt-yard of decrepit war-lords into a modern military base threatening the whole Russian position east of Lake Baikal.

China's reconquest of Tibet gave her advantages over India similar to those which, sixty or seventy years ago, Russia enjoyed over Britain by virtue of her Central Asian campaigns. In hyperbole Russia's position could have been described as a dagger pointed at the heart of India; in fact it more closely resembled the bulge of a pistol in the pocket of a well-cut suit, something to be patted discreetly when matters not necessarily relevant to Afghanistan or Persia were under discussion. In 1951 China acquired a weapon of the same sort—a pistol which scarcely needs to be cocked, let alone fired, to produce an influence upon India.

The ultimate motive of the Younghusband Mission was the fear that Russian intrigue would, from a base at Lhasa, disaffect Nepal, Bhutan and Sikkim, which like a barbed-wire entanglement insulated India's manned defences from the no man's land of Tibet. This fear, which though misplaced was not unreasonably entertained, assumed on Russia's part no motive more compelling than the desire to make mischief, to score points in the Great Game. China's interest in the border-states goes much deeper than this; it goes, indeed, almost as deep as her interest in Tibet itself and is based on precisely similar historical claims. How far her present or her future rulers will be minded to press these claims, and whether they will be tempted to revive parallel claims—some of them easier to authenticate—to such dependencies of the old Empire as Burma and Outer Mongolia, it is impossible to predict. What is certain is that the conception underlying British policy towards Tibet was wise as well as humane—that an independent Tibet made for stability in the heartlands of Asia, and that it may not be only the Tibetans who will rue the demolition of their ramshackle autonomy.

On the impulses which drove China to demolish it the Manchus had a more formative influence than Marx. It would be idle to assume that the subjugation of Tibet represents the limit of China's territorial ambitions. Ancestral piety and pride of race give her a vested interest in the wide boundaries of her vanished Empire. Expediency alone will determine how, when and where that interest will be reasserted. It was to further aims beyond the Tibetan frontier that Britain sent her Lee Metfords to Lhasa; those aims were defensive. China, too, had ulterior motives, but they were of a different kind. No threat, real or imagined, to her western borders set the Red Armies on the march. It was not a bastion but a sally-port that China gained in Tibet.

FINIS

BIBLIOGRAPHY

[A note on unpublished sources will be found on pp. 15–17.]

BAILEY, Lt.-Col. F. M.: *China, Tibet, Assam* (London, 1945)
BELL, Sir Charles: *Tibet: Past and Present* (Oxford, 1924)
    Portrait of the Dalai Lama (London, 1946)
BRANDER, Lt.-Col. H. R.: *Regimental History of the 32nd Sikh Pioneers* (Privately, 1905)
BUCK, E. J.: *Simla Past and Present* (Bombay, 1925)
CANDLER, Edmund: *The Unveiling of Lhasa* (London, 1905)
O'CONNOR, Sir Frederick: *On the Frontier and Beyond* (London, 1931)
    Things Mortal (London, 1940)
CURZON, George N.: *Russia in Central Asia* (London, 1889)
    Frontiers (Romanes Lecture, 1907)
DALLIN, J.: *The Rise of Russia in Asia* (London, 1950)
DAS, Sarat Chandra: *Journey to Lhasa and Central Tibet* (London, 1902)
DAVIS, H. W. C.: *The Great Game in Asia, 1800–1844* (Raleigh Lecture on History, 1926)
DUGDALE, Mrs Blanche E. C.: *Arthur James Balfour.* 2 Vols. (London, 1936)
FLEMING, Peter: *News from Tartary* (London, 1936)
GREAVES, Rose Louise: *Persia and the Defence of India, 1884–1892* (London, 1959)
HARRER, Heinrich: *Seven Years in Tibet* (London, 1953)
HEDIN, Sven: *Central Asia and Tibet.* 2 Vols. (London, 1903)
HOLDICH, Sir Thomas: *Tibet the Mysterious* (London, 1906)
HUXFORD, Lt.-Col. H. J.: *The 8th Gurkha Rifles, 1824–1949* (Aldershot, 1952)
KAWAGUCHI, Ekai: *Three Years in Tibet* (Madras, 1909)
LAMB, Alastair: *Britain and Chinese Central Asia.* Vol. I (London, 1960)
    'Some Notes on Russian Intrigue in Tibet', JRCAS, 1959
LANDON, Perceval: *Lhasa.* 2 Vols. (London, 1905)
LATTIMORE, Owen: *Inner Asian Frontiers of China* (London, 1940)
LI, Tieh-Tseng: *The Historical Status of Tibet* (Columbia University, 1956)
LOBANOV-ROSTOVSKY, Prince A.: *Russia in Asia* (New York, 1933)
MACDONALD, David: *Twenty Years in Tibet* (London, 1932)
MACLEAN, Sir Fitzroy: *A Person from England* (London, 1959)

BIBLIOGRAPHY

MacMunn. Lt.-Gen. Sir George: *The History of the Sikh Pioneers* (London, undated)

Magnus, Sir Philip: *Kitchener* (London, 1958)

Manning, Thomas, see Markham

Markham, Sir Clements: *Narratives of the Mission of George Bogle to Tibet and of the Journey of Thomas Manning to Lhasa* (London, 1876)

Mehra, L. P.: 'Tibet and Russian Intrigue', JRCAS, 1958.

Midleton, Earl of: *Records and Reactions, 1856–1939* (London, 1939)

'Millington, Powell': *To Lhasa at Last* (London, 1905)

Morison, J. L.: *From Alexander Burns to Frederick Roberts* (Raleigh Lecture on History, 1936)

Newton, Lord: *The Life of Lord Lansdowne* (London, 1929)

Nicolson, Sir Harold: *Curzon: The Last Phase* (London, 1934) *Sir Arthur Nicholson, Bart., First Lord Carnock* (London, 1930)

Ottley, Major W. J.: *With Mounted Infantry in Tibet* (London, 1906)

Pelliot, Paul (ed.): *Travels in Tartary, Tibet and China, by Huc and Gabet.* 2 Vols. (London, 1928)

Perham, Margery: *Lugard: The Years of Adventure* (London, 1956) *The Diaries of Lord Lugard* (Oxford, 1959)

Roberts, Field-Marshal Lord: *Forty-One Years in India* (London, 1898)

Ronaldshay, The Earl of: *The Life of Lord Curzon.* 3 Vols. (London, 1928)

Sandberg, Graham: *The Exploration of Tibet* (London, 1904)

Scott, A. MacCallum: *The Truth about Tibet* (London, 1905)

Seaver, George: *Sir Francis Younghusband* (London, 1952)

Seton-Watson, Hugh: *The Decline of Imperial Russia, 1855–1914* (London, 1952)

Spring Rice, Sir Cecil: *Letters and Friendships.* Edited by Stephen Gwynn. 2 Vols. (London, 1929)

Teichman, Eric: *Travels of a Consular Officer in Eastern Tibet* (Cambridge, 1922)

Waddell, L. A.: *Lhasa and its Mysteries* (London, 1905)

Waters, Major R. S.: *History of the 5th Battalion (Pathans) 14th Punjab Regiment, formerly 40th Pathans* (London, 1936)

Woodruff, Philip: *The Guardians* (London, 1954)

Younghusband, Sir Francis: *The Relief of Chitral* (London, 1895) *The Heart of a Continent* (London, 1896) *India and Tibet* (London, 1910) *But In Our Lives* (London, 1926)

Index

313

INDEX

INDEX

INDEX

Lhasa, lack of knowledge concerning, 36–8; early contacts with, 49–50, 52, 53; Russian intentions and, 55–56, 266–8; Curzon plans a mission to, 56, 57–65; Nepal and, 88; emissaries from, 132–5, 147–52, 202, 211, 221–2; question of an Agent at, 211–15, 252, 306–7; description of, 232–3; the Tibetan Treaty and, 252, 254, 263, 299; entered by the Chinese, 301–4, 307

'Lhasa General,' 132, 133, 146–52

Li, Tieh-Tseng, *The Historical Status of Tibet*, 60 and n, 230 and n

Lo Tun-jui, 230 n

London Gazette, 281, 284

Luff, Sergeant, 303

Lugard, Captain Frederick, and Macdonald, 107–9, 141–3

Ma, General, 160, 162, 173

Macartney, Sir George, 29

Macdonald, Brigadier-General J. R. L., 294; and the Tibetan Mission Escort, 106, 110–12, 116–17, 122–3, 125–8, 139, 142, 144–7, 157, 158–9, 161, 182, 187, 195, 200, 201, 203, 204–7, 242 ff, 270, 271; and Lugard in Africa, 107–9; and Younghusband, 117–19, 142–3, 180, 189, 226–7, 242–5, 264; Brander and, 165–6, 168; his ill-health, 205–6, 226, 228; and the advance to Lhasa, 218–19, 222–3, 226–7, 228; demoted, 249–50; his decoration, 279, 280–1, 284

Mackworth-Young, Robin, 15

Magniac, Helen Augusta, 70

Magniac, Vernon, 189

Magnus, Sir Philip, *Kitchener*, 72 n

Malcolm, Ian, 287

Manning, Thomas, 51–2, 119, 221, 224 n, 232, 233

Maxim-gun detachment, 90, 105, 128, 140, 145, 151–2, 159, 161, 175, 185

Maywood, J. S., 17

Meerut, 67

Merv, 23, 47

Metcalfe, Lady Alexandra, 15, 92 n, 93 n, 290 n

"Millington, Powell," *To Lhasa at Last*, 157 and n

Mitter, Mr (Parsee clerk), 189, 262

Morrison, Dr G. E., 269

Mountain Battery, 104, 145, 159, 186, 241

Mounted Infantry, 117, 130, 145, 146, 148, 151, 157–9, 161, 175, 177, 185–6, 192, 195, 200, 219, 222, 223–5, 232

Mules, 103

Mule Corps, 134, 162, 219

Murray, Major, 168, 192 and n

Nagartse, 221–2

Nain Sing, 53

Naini, 201

Nansen, Fridtjof, 23

Natu La, 141, 244

Nepal, 26, 27, 28, 37–8, 56, 308; and Tibet, 51, 61, 88, 94, 141–2, 200, 220, 235, 256

New Chumbi, 116, 117, 123, 128, 137, 161

Newbolt, Sir Henry, 67

Newman, Henry, Reuter's correspondent, 182

Nicholas II, 21 n, 39, 40, 42, 43 and n, 47

Nicolson, Sir Harold, 24, 35–6; *Curzon: The Last Phase*, 33 and n; *Sir Arthur Nicolson, Bart*, 300 n

Norfolk Regiment, *see* Maxim-gun detachment

Norzanoff, 82, 83

Nyang Chu, 158, 160

O'Connor, Major Frederick, and the Tibet Frontier Commission, 72, 73, 74–5, 84, 130, 131–2, 134, 147, 148, 186–7, 202, 204, 221, 256, 290; as Trade Agent, 297

Ottley, W. J., 151, 177 and n, 220, 223, 224, 228, 267; *With Mounted Infantry in Tibet*, 117 and n, 151, 186

Owen, Major Roddy, 70

Palla, 186–7

Panchen Lama, 50 n

Parr, Capt. Randall, 58, 114–15, 116, 162, 187

Pathans, 207, 219

Pearson, Capt., 194

Pehte Jong, 223

Peking Convention, 60

Peking Gazette, 266

Penjdeh Incident, 23, 68

INDEX

INDEX

OXFORD

BAYONETS TO LHASA
PETER FLEMING

China has recently opened Tibet to foreign visitors,
creating renewed interest in a land that was, for much of
its history, isolated and inaccessible. In modern times, that
isolation first came to an end (albeit temporarily) with the
Younghusband Mission to Lhasa of 1903–4, one of the
stranger episodes in British imperial history. Conceived by
Curzon as a move in the Great Game which Russia and
England had been playing for years in Central Asia,
reluctantly sanctioned by A.J. Balfour's government, and
carried out in the face of immense physical obstacles, the
British incursion into Tibet was a shot in the dark. It was
led by Colonel Francis Younghusband, soldier, explorer
and mystic; and thanks to his patience, his force of
character and his flair, a treaty was signed and the
foundations of Anglo-Tibetan friendship laid.

But the expedition had throughout been bedevilled
by remote control from Whitehall and the commander of
the force escorting Younghusband's Mission jeopardized
its success by his egotism and overcaution. So the story
of a singular and creditable achievement was not in all
respects a happy one, and in the end Younghusband
was publicly censured.

This edition is reprinted with the addition of an Introduction
by Brian Shaw, Lecturer in Asian Politics at the University
of Hong Kong.

ISBN 0 19 583832

Main cover illustration: Lhasa, Tibet.
Inset illustration: Captain (later Colonel) Francis Younghusband.
(Both photographs are reproduced courtesy of the BBC Hulton
Picture Library.)

Oxford Paperbacks
Oxford University Press

9 780195 8386